12

Health Care Comes Home

The Human Factors

D1328424

Committee on the Role of Human Factors in Home Health Care

Board on Human-Systems Integration

Division of Behavioral and Social Sciences and Education

NATIONAL RESEARCH COUNCIL
OF THE NATIONAL ACADEMIES

THE NATIONAL ACADEMIES PRESS
Washington, D.C.
www.nap.edu

THE NATIONAL ACADEMIES PRESS   500 Fifth Street, N.W.   Washington, DC 20001

NOTICE: The project that is the subject of this report was approved by the Governing Board of the National Research Council, whose members are drawn from the councils of the National Academy of Sciences, the National Academy of Engineering, and the Institute of Medicine. The members of the committee responsible for the report were chosen for their special competences and with regard for appropriate balance.

This study was supported by Contract No. HHSP23320042509XI, task order HHSP233200800004T, between the National Academy of Sciences and the U.S. Department of Health and Human Services. Any opinions, findings, conclusions, or recommendations expressed in this publication are those of the author(s) and do not necessarily reflect the views of the organizations or agencies that provided support for the project.

Library of Congress Cataloging-in-Publication Data

National Research Council (U.S.). Committee on the Role of Human Factors in Home Health Care.
  Health care comes home : the human factors / Committee on the Role of Human Factors in Home Health Care, Board on Human-Systems Integration, Division of Behavioral and Social Sciences and Education, National Research Council of the National Academies.
      p. ; cm.
  Includes bibliographical references.
  ISBN 978-0-309-21236-6 (pbk.) — ISBN 978-0-309-21237-3 (pdf) 1. Home care services--United States. 2. Human engineering--United States. 3. Home nursing--United States. I. Title.
  [DNLM: 1. Home Care Services—United States. 2. Human Engineering—United States. 3. Equipment and Supplies—standards—United States. 4. Health Policy—United States. 5. Home Nursing—United States. WY 115 AA1]
  RA645.35.N38 2011
  362.14—dc22
                                2011017463

Additional copies of this report are available from the National Academies Press, 500 Fifth Street, N.W., Lockbox 285, Washington, DC 20055; (800) 624-6242 or (202) 334-3313 (in the Washington metropolitan area); Internet, http://www.nap.edu.

Printed in the United States of America

Suggested citation: National Research Council. (2011). *Health Care Comes Home: The Human Factors.* Committee on the Role of Human Factors in Home Health Care, Board on Human-Systems Integration, Division of Behavioral and Social Sciences and Education. Washington, DC: The National Academies Press.

THE NATIONAL ACADEMIES
Advisers to the Nation on Science, Engineering, and Medicine

The **National Academy of Sciences** is a private, nonprofit, self-perpetuating society of distinguished scholars engaged in scientific and engineering research, dedicated to the furtherance of science and technology and to their use for the general welfare. Upon the authority of the charter granted to it by the Congress in 1863, the Academy has a mandate that requires it to advise the federal government on scientific and technical matters. Dr. Ralph J. Cicerone is president of the National Academy of Sciences.

The **National Academy of Engineering** was established in 1964, under the charter of the National Academy of Sciences, as a parallel organization of outstanding engineers. It is autonomous in its administration and in the selection of its members, sharing with the National Academy of Sciences the responsibility for advising the federal government. The National Academy of Engineering also sponsors engineering programs aimed at meeting national needs, encourages education and research, and recognizes the superior achievements of engineers. Dr. Charles M. Vest is president of the National Academy of Engineering.

The **Institute of Medicine** was established in 1970 by the National Academy of Sciences to secure the services of eminent members of appropriate professions in the examination of policy matters pertaining to the health of the public. The Institute acts under the responsibility given to the National Academy of Sciences by its congressional charter to be an adviser to the federal government and, upon its own initiative, to identify issues of medical care, research, and education. Dr. Harvey V. Fineberg is president of the Institute of Medicine.

The **National Research Council** was organized by the National Academy of Sciences in 1916 to associate the broad community of science and technology with the Academy's purposes of furthering knowledge and advising the federal government. Functioning in accordance with general policies determined by the Academy, the Council has become the principal operating agency of both the National Academy of Sciences and the National Academy of Engineering in providing services to the government, the public, and the scientific and engineering communities. The Council is administered jointly by both Academies and the Institute of Medicine. Dr. Ralph J. Cicerone and Dr. Charles M. Vest are chair and vice chair, respectively, of the National Research Council.

www.national-academies.org

COMMITTEE ON THE ROLE OF HUMAN
FACTORS IN HOME HEALTH CARE

David H. Wegman (*Chair*), Department of Work Environment, University
of Massachusetts, Lowell (*Emeritus*)
Sara J. Czaja, Department of Psychiatry and Behavioral Sciences, Center
on Aging, University of Miami Miller School of Medicine
K. Eric DeJonge, Washington Hospital Center, Washington, DC
Daryle Jean Gardner-Bonneau, Bonneau & Associates, Portage, Michigan
Michael Christopher Gibbons, Johns Hopkins Urban Health Institute,
Johns Hopkins University Center for Community Health
Laura N. Gitlin, Johns Hopkins School of Nursing
Judith Tabolt Matthews, Department of Health and Community Systems,
University of Pittsburgh School of Nursing
Misha Pavel, Division of Biomedical Engineering, Department of Science
and Engineering, Oregon Health and Science University
P. Hunter Peckham,[1] Donnell Institute of Biomedical Engineering and
Orthopaedics, Case Western Reserve University
Jon Pynoos, Ethel Percy Andrus Gerontology Center, Davis School of
Gerontology, University of Southern California
Robert M. Schumacher, User Centric, Inc., Oakbrook Terrace, Illinois
Mary D. Weick-Brady,[2] Food and Drug Administration, Rockville,
Maryland
Jennifer L. Wolff, School of Public Health and School of Medicine, Johns
Hopkins University

Mary Ellen O'Connell, *Study Director* (from September 2010)
Molly Follette Story, *Study Director* (from April 2010 through September
2010)
Susan B. Van Hemel, *Study Director* (through March 2010)
Julie Schuck, *Research Associate* (from September 2010)
Kristina Krasnov, *Program Officer* (from April 2010 through December
2010)
Renée L. Wilson Gaines, *Senior Program Assistant*

DISCARD

---

[1]Resigned from the committee in March 2010.
[2]Resigned from the committee in April 2010.

---
[1]Resigned from the committee in April 2010.

Preface

In the United States, health care devices, technologies, and care practices are rapidly moving into the home. This transition, which is likely to accelerate in the future, has raised a host of issues that have received insufficient attention in the past. Care recipients and caregivers have particular capabilities and limitations that can shape home health care processes and procedures. Very few homes have been designed for the delivery of health care, yet the aging of the population and changes in medical practice and health care reimbursement are leading to greater reliance on care at home. Medical equipment and technologies that are designed for hospitals and clinics can be ill suited for use in the home. The community environment can support or detract from home health care.

The rapid growth of home health care has and will have consequences that are far too broad for any one group to analyze in their entirety. Yet a major influence on the safety, quality, and effectiveness of home health care will be the set of issues encompassed by the field of human factors research—the discipline of applying what is known about human capabilities and limitations to the design of products, processes, systems, and work environments. For that reason, the Agency for Healthcare Research and Quality (AHRQ) asked the then-Committee on Human-Systems Integration of the National Research Council (NRC) to conduct a wide-ranging investigation of the role of human factors in home health care. In response, the multidisciplinary Committee on the Role of Human Factors in Home Health Care was formed to examine a diverse range of behavioral and human factors issues resulting from the increasing migration of medical devices, technologies, and care practices into the home. Its goal is to lay the groundwork for a thorough integration of human factors research with the design and implementation of home health care devices, technologies, and practices. The planning and conceptual efforts of the committee were greatly assisted by the interest and support of Kerm Henriksen, AHRQ human factors advisor for patient safety, and Teresa Zayas-Caban, senior manager, Health IT at AHRQ.

As part of its work, the committee conducted a workshop on the role of human factors in home health care on October 1-2, 2009, in Washington, DC. The committee would like to thank the many people who contributed to the workshop, in particular the many experts who provided presentations or wrote papers: Neil Charness of Florida State University, Richard Schulz of the University of Pittsburgh, independent consultant Carolyn Humphrey, Colin Drury of the State University of New York at Buffalo, Molly Follette Story of Human Spectrum Design, George Demiris of the University of Washington, Jon Sanford of the Georgia Institute of Technology, Steven Albert of the University of Pittsburgh, and Peter Boling of the Medical College of Virginia Hospital. The workshop included discussions led by Margaret Quinn of the University of Massachusetts at Lowell, R. Paul Crawford of Intel Corporation, and Carol Raphael of the Visiting Nurse Service of New York. Their contributions are greatly appreciated, as are the insightful comments of the many workshop attendees.

Lastly, the committee is greatly indebted to the NRC staff. Throughout its work the committee depended heavily on the high quality intellectual and administrative skills of the staff under the direction, first of Susan Van Hemel and then Molly Follette Story. Committee work was further enhanced through the process of review and final revision by the experience, wisdom, and careful attention to detail provided by Mary Ellen O'Connell assisted by Julie Schuck.

The workshop and its report, *The Role of Human Factors in Home Health Care: Workshop Summary,* represented the culmination of the first phase of the study, and this report, which contains the committee's conclusions and recommendations concerning the best use of human factors in home health care, is the product of the second phase. In addition, the committee oversaw preparation of a designers' guide for the use of health information technologies in home-based health care.

The landmark report, *To Err Is Human: Building a Safer Health System*, published in 2000 by the Institute of Medicine, found that illness, injuries, and other adverse health consequences often result from poor interactions between care recipients and the health care delivery system. By highlighting the importance of human factors in the inpatient hospital setting, that report led to a broad array of reforms aimed at improving the quality of health care delivery.

The committee's hope is that the preceding workshop report and this report will motivate similar reforms for home health care, even as the terrain of the health care delivery system is undergoing dramatic changes. In the future, individuals will play a greater role in managing their own health care needs and those of their family members at home and in the community. The extent to which human factors research is incorporated into home-based devices, technologies, and practices will have a big influence on whether greater reliance on home health care proves to have beneficial or detrimental effects on people's lives.

This report has been reviewed in draft form by individuals chosen for their diverse perspectives and technical expertise, in accordance with procedures approved by the Report Review Committee of the NRC. The purpose of this independent review is to provide candid and critical comments that will assist the institution in making its published report as sound as possible and to ensure that the report meets institutional standards for objectivity, evidence, and responsiveness to the study charge. The review comments and draft manuscript remain confidential to protect the integrity of the deliberative process. We wish to thank the following individuals for their review of this report: Ruzena Bajcsy, College of Engineering, Electrical Engineering and Computer Sciences, University of California, Berkeley; David W. Bates, General Medicine Division, Brigham and Women's Hospital, Boston, Massachusetts; Mary A. Blegen, Center for Patient Safety School of Nursing, University of California, San Francisco; Victor Paquet, Department of Industrial and Systems Engineering, University at Buffalo, State University of New York; Marcia J. Scherer, Institute for Matching Person & Technology, Webster, New York; Howard D. Wactlar, School of Computer Science, Carnegie Mellon University, and Directorate for Computer & Information Science & Engineering, Division of Information and Intelligent Systems), National Science Foundation; Marlyn S. Woo, School of Nursing, University of California, Los Angeles; and David D. Woods, Institute for Ergonomics, Ohio State University.

Although the reviewers listed above have provided many constructive comments and suggestions, they were not asked to endorse the conclusions or recommendations nor did they see the final draft of the report before its release. The review of this report was overseen by Matthew Rizzo, Division of Neuroergonomics/Department of Neurology, Industrial Engineering, and Public Policy, University of Iowa. Appointed by the NRC, he was responsible for making certain that an independent examination of this report was carried out in accordance with institutional procedures and that all review comments were carefully considered. Responsibility for the final content of this report rests entirely with the authoring committee and the institution.

Contents

Summary

As attention is increasingly devoted to U.S. society's needs for access to health care and health care delivery, one change that requires immediate attention concerns the many aspects of care that are migrating out of formal medical facilities and into the home. Although the costs of care are one driver of this change, there is also recognition that health care delivered at home is valued by patients and, when managed well, can promote healthy living and well-being. These changes in the location of care are involving more people, both professional and lay, who are sometimes performing difficult tasks, with unfamiliar equipment, in environments not designed to support these activities. All of these factors need to be addressed, and among the most critical are the human-systems interactions, also known as human factors. If the demands of providing or self-administering health care exceed a person's capabilities, then the safety, efficacy, and efficiency of that care will suffer.

The Agency for Healthcare Research and Quality asked the National Research Council (NRC) to explore home health care issues through the lens of human factors and make recommendations for improving the situation when health care is provided in the home environment. In this report, the NRC Committee on the Role of Human Factors in Home Health Care examined the wide range of people, tasks, technologies, and environments involved in health care in the home to provide an understanding of the most prevalent and serious threats to safety, the quality of care experienced, and care recipient and provider well-being associated with this care. The committee sought to enhance the viability and quality of home-based health care through recommendations that promote systems that successfully accommodate the diversity, strengths, and limitations of humans, both as care recipients and caregivers, and facilitate necessary improvements to the physical environments of homes.

The recommendations are organized into four areas: (1) health care technologies, including medical devices and health information technologies involved in health care in the home; (2) caregivers and care recipients; (3) residential environments for health care; and (4) research and development needs. The committee chose not to prioritize the recommendations, as they focus on various aspects of health care in the home and are of comparable importance to the different constituencies affected.

HEALTH CARE TECHNOLOGIES

Health care technologies include medical devices that are used in the home as well as information technologies related to home-based health care. The four recommendations in this area concern (1) regulating technologies for health care consumers, (2) developing guidance on the structure and usability of health information technologies, (3) developing guidance and standards for medical device labeling, and (4) improving adverse event reporting systems for medical devices. The adoption of these recommendations would improve the usability and effectiveness of technology systems and devices, support users in understanding and learning to use them, and improve feedback to government and industry that could be used to further improve technology for home care.

Regulation

U.S. government regulations that apply to devices and systems used in home health care have the potential to ensure that sound human factors principles are followed in the design and implementation of these technologies and thus to support the development of usable and accessible devices and systems.

Recommendation 1. **The U.S. Food and Drug Administration and the Office of the National Coordinator for Health Information Technology should collaborate to regulate, certify, and monitor health care applications and systems that integrate medical devices and health information technologies. As part of the certification process, the agencies should require evidence that manufacturers have followed existing accessibility and usability guidelines and have applied user-centered design and validation methods during development of the product.**

Guidance and Standards

Developers of information technologies related to home-based health care, as yet, have inadequate or incomplete guidance regarding product content, structure, accessibility, and usability to inform innovation or evolution of personal health records or of patient access to information in electronic health records. The lack of guidance in this area, particularly related to the requirements in the home care setting, makes it difficult for developers of personal health records and patient portals to design systems that fully address the needs of consumers.

Recommendation 2. The Office of the National Coordinator for Health Information Technology, in collaboration with the National Institute of Standards and Technology and the Agency for Healthcare Research and Quality, should establish design guidelines and standards, based on existing accessibility and usability guidelines, for content, accessibility, functionality, and usability of consumer health information technologies related to home-based health care.

The committee found a serious lack of adequate standards and guidance for the labeling of medical devices operated by lay users. Furthermore, we found that the approval processes of the U.S. Food and Drug Administration (FDA) for changing these materials are burdensome and inflexible.

Recommendation 3. The U.S. Food and Drug Administration (FDA) should promote development (by standards development organizations, such as the International Electrotechnical Commission, the International Organization for Standardization, the American National Standards Institute, and the Association for the Advancement of Medical Instrumentation) of new standards based on the most recent human factors research for the labeling of and ensuing instructional materials for medical devices designed for home use by lay users. The FDA should also tailor and streamline its approval processes to facilitate and encourage regular improvements of these materials by manufacturers.

Adverse Event Reporting Systems

The committee notes that the FDA's adverse event reporting systems, used to report problems with medical devices, are not user-friendly, especially for lay users, who generally are not aware of the systems, unaware that they can use them to report problems, and uneducated about how to do so. Improving these systems would increase the FDA's knowledge of user problems with existing and future devices, supporting its regulation, guidance, and approval processes.

> *Recommendation 4.* The U.S. Food and Drug Administration should improve its adverse event reporting systems to be easier to use, to collect data that are more useful for identifying the root causes of events related to interactions with the device operator, and to develop and promote a more convenient way for lay users as well as professionals to report problems with medical devices.

CAREGIVERS IN THE HOME

Health care is provided in the home by formal caregivers (health care professionals), informal caregivers (family and friends), and individuals who self-administer care; each type of care provider faces unique issues. Properly preparing individuals to provide care at home depends on targeting efforts appropriately to the background, experience, and knowledge of the caregivers. To date, however, home health care services suffer from being organized primarily around regulations and payments designed for inpatient or outpatient acute care settings. Little attention has been given to how different the roles are for formal caregivers when delivering services in the home or to the specific types of training necessary for appropriate, high-quality practice in this environment.

> *Recommendation 5.* Relevant professional practice and advocacy groups should develop appropriate certification, credentialing, and/or training standards that will prepare formal caregivers to provide care in the home, develop appropriate informational and training materials for informal caregivers, and provide guidance for all caregivers to work effectively with other people involved.

RESIDENTIAL ENVIRONMENTS FOR HEALTH CARE

Health care is administered in a variety of nonclinical environments, but the most common one, particularly for individuals outside health care institutions who need the greatest level and intensity of health care services, is the home. The two recommendations in this area encourage (a) modifications to existing housing and (b) accessible and universal design of new housing. The implementation of these recommendations should provide critical infrastructural changes needed to advance the safety and ease of practicing health care in the home. It could improve the health and safety of many care recipients and their caregivers and facilitate adherence to good health maintenance and treatment practices. Ideally, improvements to housing design would take place in the context of communities that provide transportation, social networking and exercise opportunities, and access to health care and other services.

Safety and Modification of Existing Housing

The committee found poor appreciation of the importance of modifying homes to remove health hazards and barriers to self-management and health care practice and, furthermore, that financial support through federal assistance agencies for home modifications is very limited. The characteristics of the home can present significant barriers to autonomy or in-home care management and present risk factors for poor health, injury, compromised well-being, and greater dependence on others. Conversely, supportive physical characteristics of homes, such as grab bars, increased lighting, and communication services, enhance safety and the ability to perform daily health care tasks and to utilize effectively health care technologies that are designed to enhance health and well-being.

Recommendation 6. **Federal agencies, including the U.S. Department of Health and Human Services and the Centers for Medicare & Medicaid Services, along with the U.S. Department of Housing and Urban Development and the U.S. Department of Energy, should collaborate to facilitate adequate and appropriate access to health- and safety-related home modifications, especially for those who cannot afford them. The goal should be to enable persons whose homes contain obstacles, hazards, or features that pose a home safety concern, limit self-care management, or hinder the delivery of needed services to obtain home assessments, home modifications, and training in their use.**

Accessibility and Universal Design of New Housing

Almost all existing housing in the United States presents problems for conducting health-related activities because physical features limit independent functioning, impede caregiving, and contribute to such accidents as falls. In spite of the fact that a large and growing number of persons, including children, adults, veterans, and older adults, have disabilities and chronic conditions that can and should be managed at home, new housing continues to be built that does not account for their needs (current or future). Although existing homes can be modified to some extent to address some of the limitations, a proactive, preventive, and effective approach would address potential problems in the design phase of new and renovated housing, before construction.

Recommendation 7. Federal agencies, such as the U.S. Department of Housing and Urban Development, the U.S. Department of Veterans Affairs, and the Federal Housing Administration, should take a lead role, along with states and local municipalities, to develop strategies that promote and facilitate increased housing visitability, accessibility, and universal design in all segments of the market. This might include tax and other financial incentives, local zoning ordinances, model building codes, new products and designs, and related policies that are developed as appropriate with standards-setting organizations (e.g., the International Code Council, the International Electrotechnical Commission, the International Organization for Standardization, and the American National Standards Institute).

RESEARCH AND DEVELOPMENT

In our review of the research literature, the committee learned that there is ample foundational knowledge to apply a human factors lens to home health care, particularly as improvements are considered to make health care safe and effective in the home. However, much of what is known is not being translated effectively into practice, either in the design of equipment and information technology or in the effective targeting and provision of services to those in need. Consequently, the four recommendations in this area support research and development to address knowledge and communication gaps: (1) research to enhance coordination among all the people who play a role in health care in the home, (2) development of a database of medical devices in order to facilitate device prescription, (3) improved surveys of the people involved in health care in the home and their residential environments, and (4) development of tools for assessing the tasks associated with home-based health care.

Health Care Teamwork and Coordination

Home-based health care often involves a large number of elements, including multiple caregivers, support services, agencies, and complex and dynamic benefit regulations, which are rarely coordinated. However, research has shown that coordinating those elements has a positive effect on patient outcomes and costs of care. When successful, care coordination improves communication among caregivers and care recipients and ensures that care recipients obtain appropriate services and resources.

Barriers to coordination include insufficient resources available to (a) help people who need health care at home identify and establish connections to appropriate sources of care, (b) facilitate communication and coordination among caregivers involved in home-based health care, and (c) facilitate communication among the care recipients and caregivers.

Recommendation 8. The Agency for Healthcare Research and Quality should support human factors–based research on the identified barriers to coordination of health care services delivered in the home and support user-centered development and evaluation of programs that may overcome these barriers.

Medical Device Database

It is the responsibility of physicians to prescribe medical devices, but unlike the situation for prescription drugs, typically little information is readily available to guide them in determining the best match between the devices available and a particular care recipient's needs. In the area of assistive and rehabilitation technologies, annotated databases (such as AbleData) are available to assist physicians in determining the most appropriate one of several candidate devices for a given patient. Such a database for home health care devices could alleviate prescription questions, but it does not exist at this time.

Recommendation 9. The U.S. Food and Drug Administration, in collaboration with device manufacturers, should establish a medical device database for physicians and other providers, including pharmacists, to use when selecting appropriate devices to prescribe or recommend for people receiving or self-administering health care in the home. Using task analysis and other human factors approaches to populate the medical device database will ensure that it contains information on characteristics of the devices and implications for appropriate care recipient and device operator populations.

Characterizing Caregivers, Care Recipients, and Home Environments

As delivery of health care in the home becomes more common, more coherent strategies and effective policies are needed to support the workforce of individuals who provide this care. Developing these will require comprehensive understanding of the number and attributes of individuals engaged in providing health care in the home as well as better information about the environment in which care is delivered. Data and data analysis are lacking to accomplish these objectives, although some existing surveys could provide the needed data if they were better designed. Better coordination across government agencies that sponsor surveys and more attention to information about health care that occurs in the home could greatly improve the utility of survey findings for understanding the prevalence and nature of health care delivery in the home.

Recommendation 10. Federal health agencies should coordinate data collection efforts to capture comprehensive information on elements relevant to health care in the home, either in a single survey or through effective use of common elements across surveys. The surveys should collect data on the sociodemographic and health characteristics of individuals receiving care in the home, the sociodemographic attributes of formal and informal caregivers and the nature of the caregiving they provide, and the attributes of the residential settings in which the care recipients live.

Tools for Assessing Home Health Care Tasks and Operators

Persons caring for themselves at home as well as informal and formal caregivers vary considerably in their skills, abilities, attitudes, experience, and other characteristics, such as age, culture/ethnicity, and health literacy. At this time, health care providers lack the tools needed to assess whether particular individuals would be able to perform specific health care tasks at home, and medical device and system designers lack information on the demands associated with health-related tasks performed at home as well as the human capabilities needed to perform them successfully.

Recommendation 11. The Agency for Healthcare Research and Quality should collaborate, as necessary, with the National Institute for Disability and Rehabilitation Research, the National Institutes of Health, the U.S. Department of Veterans Affairs, the National Science Foundation, the U.S. Department of Defense, and the Centers for Medicare & Medicaid Services to support development of assessment tools customized for home-based health care, designed to analyze the demands of tasks associated with home-based health care, the operator capabilities required to carry them out, and the relevant capabilities of specific individuals.

Improvements to health care in the home hold the promise of providing healthy living, comfort, and effective treatment to care recipients and of contributing to a growing and vital part of health care delivery in the United States. The recommendations presented here call for federal leadership and improved data collection and analysis in an effort to provide home-based care appropriate to each care recipient and to make the work of caregivers less burdensome. We have also identified many opportunities for researchers and developers to study and use human factors to support positive change and maximize the promise of successful health care at home. We sincerely think that this promise is well within reach.

1

Introduction

Health care is coming home. For a number of reasons, health care is increasingly occurring in residential settings rather than in professional medical settings. This change in the locus of care needs to be seen in context. In this first decade of the 21st century, great attention is being devoted to U.S. society's needs for access to health care and health care delivery. To date, however, there has been too little focus on the transition of care into the home. A wide range of procedures and therapies are now performed far from any medical facility, often with no health care professional on site, with highly variable results. Although each situation is unique, all are dependent on the people involved—the human factors.

Given converging trends of an aging population, an increasing human life span, medical technology migrating into the home, and design features of the home in contrast to health care institutions, it is important to gain an understanding of the most prevalent and serious threats to safety, the quality of care experienced, and the well-being of care recipients and caregivers. Developing a human factors approach to health care in the home that can accommodate the diversity, strengths, and limitations of humans, both as care recipients and caregivers, is critical to addressing these threats effectively.

Human factors focuses on the interactions between people and the other elements of a system, generally with the goal of optimizing safety and performance. Elements of the system may include tasks, technologies, and environments, as well as other people. The success of these interactions is dependent on the degree to which the physical, sensory, cognitive, and emotional capabilities of the people match the corresponding demands imposed

9

by elements of the system. If the individual is not sufficiently capable or the system's demands are too high, then the tasks cannot be performed. In these situations, there are usually several solutions, the most appropriate of which will depend on the results of an analysis of the individual, the tasks, the technologies, and the environmental context. In some cases, tasks can be modified to reduce the demands on the individual; in others, the technology itself can be modified to augment the individual's capabilities or simplify task execution. In still others, training to augment an individual's skills is the most appropriate solution.

Members of the then-standing Committee on Human-Systems Integration[1] at the National Research Council (NRC), a division of the National Academies, became interested in the topic of human factors and its role in improving health care in the home. The Agency for Healthcare Research and Quality at the U.S. Department of Health and Human Services agreed that the issues were worth exploring and agreed to fund this study.

To conduct the study, the NRC appointed the Committee on the Role of Human Factors in Home Health Care. This committee of 11 experts included physicians and nurses with knowledge of home health care and experts from various technological, social, and behavioral science disciplines. Members of the committee were selected following standard NRC procedures for committee formation that ensure individual member qualification and independence, as well as freedom from conflicts of interest and overall committee balance and diversity. Brief biographical sketches of the committee members are contained in the Appendix.

The charge to the committee is shown in Box 1-1. The committee's overall objective was to gain a deeper understanding of (1) the role human factors can play in developing systems that address the relevant sensory, behavioral, and cognitive capabilities of care recipients and caregivers; (2) the nature of the care processes, procedures, and therapies increasingly occurring in the home; (3) the steady migration and use of medical equipment and technologies in the home environment; (4) the design of the physical home environment to facilitate the delivery of care; and (5) the impact of cultural, social, and community factors on home health care and healthy lifestyles.

This report, prepared by members of the committee, documents the current state of health care in the home and identifies existing problems and opportunities for the improvement of care through applying human factors knowledge and methods. Throughout our work, the committee was constantly reminded that delivery of health care in the home occurs in the larger context of the health care system and policies that impact that

---

[1]In December 2010, the Committee on Human-Systems Integration was reconstituted as the Board on Human-Systems Integration.

BOX 1-1
Charge to the Committee

An ad hoc study committee will examine the impact of human factors issues relevant to the safety and quality of home health care. The study will synthesize and analyze the research literature to gain an understanding of the human factors challenges relevant to sensory, behavioral, and cognitive capabilities of care recipients and caregivers and the increasing use of medical devices, equipment, and technologies in the home environment. The committee will develop a conceptual and methodological framework to guide the study; conduct a review of the existing research literature and sources of evidence; and describe its findings, conclusions, and recommendations regarding strategies, methodologies, and best practices of successful home care practices.

In addition to providing an overarching review and synthesis of the findings and consensus regarding the research evidence, the committee will

- identify and describe strategies, methodologies, best practices, and guidelines that can be used by designers, equipment manufacturers, home care providers and patients when preparing and configuring spaces, equipment, and tasks for home health care;
- identify existing and potential barriers and obstacles to successful implementation, including potential remedies;
- identify gaps in our current understanding, as well as suggest research efforts to remedy these gaps;
- provide an integrative framework for the various disciplines and stakeholders that need to collaborate for improved understanding; and
- provide recommendations or roadmap for a more programmatic approach to subsequent research, practice, and policy.

system. Decisions about reimbursable services, populations eligible for publicly funded health care, and providers qualified for reimbursement have a significant impact on the availability of this care. However, while the committee recognized the importance of these issues, thorough consideration of them was viewed as beyond the charge, which focused on a human factors perspective on health care in the home.

THE RISE OF HOME HEALTH CARE

A number of factors are driving the migration of health care practice from professional facilities to the home and, as a result, significantly increasing the numbers of people who must provide health care in the home:

- The costs of providing health care at formal medical facilities are increasing. Advanced medical technologies and procedures, as well as the training of medical professionals to employ them, can be very expensive.
- Hospitals are discharging patients, including premature infants, sooner into home care, sometimes with complex care regimens.
- The U.S. population is aging (see Figure 1-1), and consequently the demand is growing for various health services (particularly related to conditions associated with aging). At the same time, people are focusing increasingly on overall wellness and quality of life, even into advanced age.

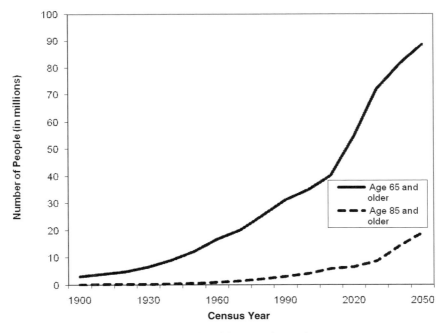

FIGURE 1-1 Projected increase in the older population by 2050.
SOURCE: Administration on Aging (2009).

- The prevalence of chronic conditions across the entire age spectrum is growing (particularly conditions related to obesity, such as diabetes), and growing along with it is the demand for health care. More people are living longer with increasingly complex medical and social needs.
- Larger numbers of veterans are surviving military conflicts and returning home to live with disabilities.
- People who may have had a rapidly fatal illness years ago, such as a heart attack or AIDS, are instead now living with longer chronic illnesses, such as congestive heart failure or HIV.
- Some types of health care professionals are in short supply, which shifts the burden of some types of care onto lay caregivers to fill the gap.
- Consumers want to be independent in their health management and are seeking more home-based services.
- Innovations in information technology, along with consumer demands for more health care quality and personal independence, are shifting the focus from health care providers, procedures, and prescriptions onto consumers and how they can manage care at home (Yogesan et al., 2009). Health care tasks managed at home range from health maintenance and disease prevention activities (regular exercise, good nutrition, healthy behaviors, wellness through ongoing monitoring) and self-care (adherence to medication and other therapeutic regimens) to the use of complex medical devices (e.g., home dialysis, ventilators) and end-of-life care.

Bringing health care to people in their homes can have significant benefits—reduced costs, added convenience (particularly for frail, elderly people who have difficulty getting to a doctor's office), and improved well-being, to name a few. For example, the Washington Hospital Center in Washington, DC, has been providing house calls for more than a decade and now serves approximately 600 care recipients. Their staff has found that the program returns significant financial savings. The codirector of the program, George Taler, in acknowledgment of a recent survey of home-based primary care sites (Edes et al., 2010), reported that similar house call programs have reduced expected hospitalizations among this group by almost two-thirds. Jim Pyles, a lawyer and member of the board of directors of the American Academy of Home Care Physicians, commented, "We found that you could afford to treat a patient for a whole year at home by avoiding just one hospitalization" (Andrews, 2010).

The rise of home health care, as well as the services and technologies to provide such care, show promise to make health and medical care more effective and efficient, allowing people to heal or age "in place," live more independently, and avoid more expensive institutional care. However, the range of home settings and health and medical needs leaves much to be considered.

THE DIVERSITY OF HOME HEALTH CARE

Overall, health care that occurs at home is a complex experience, involving various types of individuals, tasks, technologies, and environments.

- The *people* involved in health care in the home include people receiving care, who may care for themselves, and those providing care, who may be professional or lay caregivers, family or friends, or some combination. These individuals have a wide range of personal and health literacy skills, social needs, and economic and social resources. People have different perceptions of the power differential between care recipient and the health care system, different cultural views about health and illness, and different language capabilities and preferences. All of these can affect the form and quality of health care received. The majority of people providing care in the home (care recipients themselves, families, and direct-care workers) vary widely in their training and generally have very limited formal training or credentialing; direct-care workers may be employed by families outside the formal health care system and be involved in reimbursement without oversight.
- The *tasks* involved in home-based health care include activities for maintaining health, activities associated with episodic care (e.g., in response to illness or injury) or chronic care, or activities to support the end of life. The medical conditions involved may be simple and involve little time and no medical equipment, or they may be very complex and consume many hours every day and require the use of complicated devices.
- The *devices and technologies* for health care in the home cover a vast range, from simple first aid tools to respiratory equipment, and from meters and monitors to computer equipment and software associated with interconnected electronic systems. Some of this equipment was designed only for professional use but is finding its way into the home nevertheless. A particular concern for health care that occurs outside medical facilities is the use of "legacy" (outdated) equipment, which may not have technical support available or even come with instructions; if instructions are available, they generally were not written for lay users.
- The *environments* of health care delivered in the home, with few exceptions, are not designed for this use and often contain numerous

barriers, such as stairs that block a wheelchair user, low lighting that makes device controls difficult to see, or insufficient electrical supply for power-hungry medical equipment. If the home does not have Internet access, the occupants lack connectivity to enable any type of telehealth activity (e.g., data transfer, remote monitoring, information seeking). Each physical home environment resides within its respective social environment of family, friends, or colleagues, which is affected by the community environments of neighborhood and town and by the health policy environment defined by the presiding health and social service organizations and governmental bodies.

Although each situation is unique, all of these factors—the people, tasks, technologies, and environments—affect the safety and quality of the health care that occurs in the home.

The factors involved in health care outside formal medical facilities are dynamic and often uncontrolled and unpredictable. The health status of the care recipient may improve or decline; the identity, technical qualifications, and personal capabilities of the caregivers or professional medical providers may change. The tasks required, or the particular medical issue involved, or the device being used, or the environment(s) in which the task is performed may be modified in response to any kind of stimulus, including changes in the care recipient's health condition. The physical, social, community, and health policy environments may shift in any number of ways.

The reorientation of the culture of health care to the home setting, as well as the range of individuals, tasks, technologies, and environments involved in home health care, heightens the importance of human factors. Care recipients and other caregivers, now expected to perform procedures previously executed only by trained professionals, bring a range of knowledge, capabilities, environments, and subsequent interactions to health care. Numerous issues arise in home settings that are not often considered in institutional-based practice. This report aims to shed light on those issues and the opportunities to improve care through application of human factors.

THE REPORT

In conducting our work, the committee determined it appropriate to restrict our focus to health care that occurs in residential environments. Although health care is also conducted in many other community settings, such as schools, workplaces, senior centers, day care centers, and while traveling, the committee decided that investigating those locations was beyond the scope of what we could accomplish. Similarly, we decided that investigating the circumstances of people who are homeless or are undocumented was also beyond the study scope.

We found it useful to subdivide caregivers into two groups: "informal" caregivers, who include unpaid laypersons (often family or friends), and "formal" caregivers, who include paid and trained professionals. These types of caregivers are described further in Chapter 2. We are using these terms to contrast informal, unpaid caregiving with formal, paid caregiving, as was done in the workshop report prepared for Phase I of this study (National Research Council, 2010).

Chapter 2 also describes the growing population of people who receive care. This chapter details the diversity of both care recipients and caregivers. The range of abilities and characteristics as well as cultural experiences presented demonstrates the importance of a human factors focus to the design of safe and effective health care in the home. In this chapter, as well as in Chapters 4, 5, and 6, we include family vignettes, drawn from the clinical or research experience of committee members, to illustrate and personalize the important points in the chapter for the readers.

Chapter 3 defines human factors by providing an overview of human factors tools and methods and their potential application. Chapter 4 considers the wide range of tasks and their demands relevant to health care in the home. It also introduces methods of analyzing home health tasks.

Chapter 5 takes a look at the technologies increasingly entering the home. We found it useful to subdivide technologies into two categories: (1) standalone devices and equipment and (2) information technologies, while recognizing the expanding interconnections between these categories. Some technologies were designed for medical purposes, and other technologies on the market or in development for different uses are being adapted for health care applications.

Chapter 6 examines the factors in multiple environments (physical, social/cultural, community, and policy) that impact home health care. This chapter aims to raise awareness of attributes of different environments as well as the challenges and benefits of bringing health care into the home.

Chapter 7 summarizes the committee's findings regarding the status of the various components of health care in the home and presents our recommendations for addressing the most evident needs through application of human factors knowledge and methods.

REFERENCES

Administration on Aging. (2009). *Projected future growth of the older population.* Available: http://www.aoa.gov/AoARoot/Aging_Statistics/future_growth/future_growth.aspx [March 29, 2011].

Andrews, M. (2010, July 13, 2010). House calls: An old idea that may make a comeback. *The Washington Post,* p. E2.

Edes, T., Kinosian, B., Davis, D., and Hossain, M. (2010, May). *Financial savings of home-based primary care for frail veterans with chronic disabling disease.* Presentation at American Geriatrics Society Annual Scientific Meeting (Orlando, FL).

National Research Council. (2010). *The role of human factors in home health care: Workshop summary.* S. Olson, Rapporteur. Committee on the Role of Human Factors in Home Health Care. Committee on Human-Systems Integration, Division of Behavioral and Social Sciences and Education. Washington, DC: The National Academies Press.

Yogesan, K., Bos, L., Brett, P., and Gibbons, M.C. (2009). *Handbook of digital homecare.* Series in Biomedical Engineering. Berlin: Springer.

2

People Involved in
Health Care in the Home

The health care delivery system is rapidly changing, and individuals are assuming an increasing role in management of their own health. In this environment, individuals and their families are expected to perform a range of health care tasks and interact with a vast array of medical devices and technologies in residential settings. However, the population of people who receive and provide care is very diverse and possesses variable skills, resources, knowledge, and experiences. They also differ on a number of other characteristics, such as age, cultural and ethnic backgrounds, education, and living arrangements.

Management of health care at home presents numerous challenges, especially since the characteristics of individuals who engage in health care tasks and interact with health care systems and technologies vary so greatly. Ensuring that health care in the home is safe, efficient, effective, and responsive to individual needs requires identifying potential user groups who will be interacting with home health systems; understanding the capabilities/limitations, needs, and preferences of these populations; and matching these capabilities, needs, and preferences to the demands generated by health care and health management tasks, technologies, and the environments in which these tasks occur.

This chapter provides an overview of users—the people who receive and the people who provide health care in the home. We define the broad populations of interest and describe abilities and characteristics of each group relevant to the tasks that they are expected to perform.

We begin by broadly defining and briefly describing three groups of

TABLE 2-1 Types of People Involved in Health Care in the Home

Category	Examples
Care Recipients	Infants
	Children
	Adults
	Elders
Informal Caregivers	Care recipients themselves
	Immediate family members
	Extended family members
	Friends
	Neighbors
	Colleagues
	Other acquaintances
Formal Caregivers	Home health aides, personal care attendants, social service aides
	Nurses
	Physicians
	Pharmacists
	Social workers
	Physical, occupational, vocational, respiratory, speech-language therapists
	Dieticians

individuals who engage in health care in the home: people who receive care (recipients), people who are informal providers of care (informal caregivers), and people who are formal providers of care (formal caregivers) (see Table 2-1). One distinction between informal and formal caregivers is that informal caregivers are typically not paid for the care provided. In addition, formal caregivers are more likely to have health care training, although it is not always specific to the provision of care in the home. We describe abilities and characteristics of people relevant to the performance of health care tasks that are common across all three groups. We also describe circumstances (e.g., living arrangements) and qualifications (e.g., type of certification) that are unique to each group and how they may influence the performance of health care tasks in the home. The overarching goal is to demonstrate how an understanding of the characteristics and abilities of these people is critical to the design of safe and effective systems of health care in the home.

RECIPIENTS OF HEALTH CARE IN THE HOME

People involved in health care in the home range from young to old and include people who are well and those with a variety of medical conditions, disabilities, and impairments. People who receive care vary in as many characteristics as the population at large, including culture/ethnicity, education, and socioeconomic status, as well as in physical abilities, such as strength and stamina, manual dexterity, visual acuity, cognition, health and technology literacy, and level of skill.

Almost everyone is involved in some type of health care activity at home. These activities include disease prevention and health maintenance activities (e.g., regular exercise, health information seeking) and management of acute ailments (e.g., colds, minor infections, injuries) and chronic diseases (e.g., diabetes, multiple sclerosis) and disabilities (e.g., vision, hearing, mobility or cognitive impairment). Everyone has the potential to become a recipient or provider of health care, and these roles can change over time.

One large population of people who receive care at home are those with chronic conditions, such as hypertension, asthma, diabetes, cancer, HIV/AIDS, chronic respiratory disease, neuromuscular disease, dementia, or emotional disorders. Currently, about 60 percent of the adult civilian noninstitutionalized population of the United States has at least one chronic condition, and people with chronic conditions incur approximately 75 percent of the nation's health care expenditures (Centers for Disease Control and Prevention, 2009a). The Centers for Disease Control and Prevention (2009a) defines chronic diseases as "noncommunicable illnesses that are prolonged in duration, do not resolve spontaneously, and are rarely cured completely." The five most costly chronic conditions in 2006 were heart conditions, cancer, trauma-related disorders, mental disorders, and asthma (Soni, 2009).

Although chronic conditions may be acquired at any point in the life course (e.g., those resulting from trauma-related injuries), some are more prevalent in various age groups. Examples are children on ventilators; children with diabetes or asthma who require insulin or inhaler treatments; adults with sleep apnea who use positive airway pressure equipment; people with renal failure who use home dialysis while waiting for or avoiding costly kidney transplantations; and middle-aged or older people with diabetes, arthritis, cardiovascular conditions, dementia, or AIDS who follow complex medication regimens.

The population of people involved in health care in the home also includes persons with physical, sensory/perceptual, cognitive, and emotional disabilities. According to the U.S. Census Bureau (Brault, 2008), approximately 49 million people in the United States over 15 years of age have some form of disability. This includes people who have long-lasting conditions that make it difficult to do routine activities, such as seeing, hearing, learning, remembering, walking, climbing stairs, dressing, bathing, leaving the home, or working at a job. The likelihood of having a disability and the likelihood the individual will need assistance increase with age, particularly after age 65 (Brault, 2008). Figure 2-1 illustrates how the percentage of people with disabilities increases with age, rising from 10 percent of 15-24-year-olds to 70 percent of those over age 80. As the population ages in coming decades, the number of people with disabilities may increase, although there is some evidence that disability rates may be declining (Freedman et al., 2007). Individuals with disabilities represent a significant population of people who engage in or receive care at home.

The population of people with disabilities includes large numbers of veterans who have served in U.S. military forces during conflicts including and since World War II. Approximately 2.6 million veterans were receiving disability compensation benefits in September 2007 (Economic Systems Inc., 2008). The types of disability observed in veteran populations tend to differ from those in the civilian population. Veterans' disabilities are often musculoskeletal disorders (45 percent) and mental disorders that include posttraumatic stress disorder (15 percent). A high percentage of veterans have multiple disabilities (Economic Systems Inc., 2008), such as co-occurring musculoskeletal and hearing problems.

These prevalent types of disability have implications for home health care system design. Health care device manufacturers must design for ease

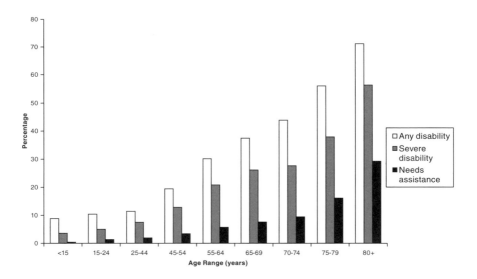

FIGURE 2-1 Percentage of disability prevalence and needs for assistance by age, 2005.
SOURCE: Brault (2008).

of manipulation (e.g., they must permit one-handed operation of devices similar to requirements for keyboard use in Section 508 of the Rehabilitation Act) and delivery of instruction through text rather than (or in addition to) voice (Charness, 2010). Similarly, for veteran populations, vision rather than hearing should often be the preferred channel for providing information about system states and warnings. The large numbers of veterans who experience cognitive problems due to head trauma or to multiple traumas, such as limb amputation coupled with head trauma, must also be recognized. These individuals may find it particularly difficult to interact with a variety of technologies and devices. They are also likely to need assistance with routine activities as well as emotional support for many years, given that many acquired these disabilities as young adults.

It is important to recognize that disability is associated with health care disparities. Data from the 2006 National Health Interview Survey show that disability and disability coupled with gender were predictive of lack of access to health care. Specifically, people with disabilities were two to three times less likely than those without disabilities to have access to health care. In addition, women with disabilities had less access to health care than either women without disabilities or men with disabilities (Smith, 2008).

CAREGIVERS

People who provide care to ill or disabled individuals in the home can be broadly categorized as either informal (e.g., family) or formal (e.g., professional) caregivers. Informal caregivers include individuals providing their own care as well as people who provide health-related assistance to individuals to whom they are related or otherwise associated. Informal caregivers typically do not receive financial compensation for the care they provide and are predominantly relatives, but they may include individuals' friends, neighbors, or members of volunteer organizations. Informal caregivers are also referred to as family caregivers, lay caregivers, or simply family and friends who provide assistance by virtue of kinship, friendship, or altruism.[1]

In contrast, formal caregivers (sometimes referred to as professional caregivers[2]) have often had formal health care training and have some level of service delivery skill and education. However, some formal caregivers who provide care in the home have no formal health care training. Formal caregivers include physicians and physician assistants, nurses, nurse

---

[1]In places where research cited is specifically referring to family members who provide care, the term family caregiver is used.

[2]The committee decided to use the term *formal caregivers* in recognition of the fact that some family members or other informal providers of care are also professionals.

practitioners, social workers, physical, occupational and speech therapists, pharmacists, and home health aides.

Both informal and formal caregivers are also quite heterogeneous, varying widely in their skills, abilities, and attitudes.

CHARACTERISTICS AND ABILITIES

The person component of the home-based health care equation is complex, and understanding people's abilities and characteristics is critical to the design and selection of safe, efficient, and effective care devices (Scherer et al., 2007) as well as the overall care system for the home. Performance of health care tasks places a variety of physical, cognitive, sensory/perceptual and emotional demands on people, whether they are caring for themselves

---

BOX 2-1
The Lopez Family

Ricardo Lopez, an 82-year-old retired teacher of Cuban descent, takes care of his wife Dolores, who in her mid-70s was diagnosed with Alzheimer's disease, approximately 7 years ago. The couple lives in a small one-bedroom apartment in Florida, within walking distance of a small local grocery store and pharmacy. Ricardo speaks both English and Spanish, and Dolores used to speak Spanish. Two years ago, she stopped talking and is now only able to make sounds whenever she gets emotional. This is very difficult for Ricardo to deal with, as he feels he has lost the ability to communicate with his wife; he misses her voice and their long talks. Dolores also shows other signs of mental and physical deterioration, and she depends on Ricardo to help her with all activities of daily living, such as feeding herself, bathing, dressing, and getting into and out of the bed or chair.

Ricardo is consumed with all aspects of Dolores's care and often neglects his own personal needs. He does not go to the doctor on a regular basis, because he does not have time or someone to take care of Dolores in his absence. He is in overall good health, but he has to monitor his blood pressure and diet.

Ricardo recently accepted the advice of a community social worker to have Dolores attend a day care program three times a week, which gives him some respite. Although getting her ready in the morning is very challenging, he does it because he feels that Dolores needs to be stimulated by engaging in social activities. She was a pianist and enjoys being around people and music.

or fulfilling the caregiver role. These demands can vary in complexity and the level of skill required. Health care tasks may also involve some type of equipment or technology, which presents its own set of demands, and may be performed in various environments that generate additional demands. (The family vignette in Box 2-1 illustrates some of this complexity.)

Cognitive abilities (e.g., memory, reasoning) and physical and motor functioning (which often decline with age) impact a person's ability to read and comprehend medication instructions, access medications, comply with medication regimens, and use technologies and assistive devices. Physical capabilities affect whether a caregiver can safely assist with such tasks as patient lifting and bathing. Sensory/perceptual capabilities determine whether someone can read the display on a medical device, such as an infusion pump, or hear an alarm, such as on an apnea monitor. Other

During the time that Dolores is at day care, Ricardo can go to the grocery store and pharmacy and do household chores. Although he has no formal training, he says, he does his best to keep the house clean. He tries to organize all of his errands and tasks to be done before the weekend, because on Saturday and Sunday he does not have any help. He spends most of that time preparing the week's meals for Dolores, with the idea that if he keeps her healthy, he can minimize the chances of her being hospitalized.

Last summer Dolores was hospitalized for almost a month for problems with her digestive system. This was very stressful for Ricardo, as he had to travel to and from the hospital and often had to stay with Dolores overnight. He is thankful to have the support of friends and some of Dolores's family members, such as her sisters and a niece. They don't visit often, but they do send home-cooked meals to help him.

Ricardo and Dolores do not have any children together, but Ricardo has a 58-year-old son who was recently hospitalized due to complications with a diabetic ulcer. Ricardo feels guilty that he is unable to visit his son as much as he would like, and he calls him every day to check up on him. Ricardo's son recently gave him a computer, and Ricardo has learned how to look up information and keep in contact with old friends who live in Spain and Mexico. At night he spends a few hours chatting online and keeping up with the news. For him, this is time he dedicates to himself, and he wishes he could learn more about how to use the computer.

SOURCE: Client at the University of Miami Miller School of Medicine.

characteristics and abilities, such as education, language/communication proficiency, health status, health literacy, health self-efficacy, knowledge of specific health conditions and treatments, culture, autonomy, social participation, personality, motivation, attitudes/beliefs, and trust are all important to the performance of health care tasks. In addition to the personal capabilities mentioned above, relevant attributes also include caregivers' skill level, technology literacy, attitude toward care recipients, coping ability, and ability to manage their workload.

Cognitive abilities influence a person's ability to process, comprehend, and integrate health information and to decide on and execute the appropriate response. For some user groups, the complex cognitive demands associated with current health care tasks and equipment/technologies may exceed user capabilities. Normal aging is associated with declines in "fluid abilities such as reasoning, attentional capacity and working memory" (Fisk et al., 2009). However, cognitive declines are possible at all ages as a result of illness, head trauma, the side effects of medication, or the complications of stress, learning disabilities, or developmental disabilities. In addition, cognitive abilities may wax and wane over time due to the effects of fatigue, pain, drugs, or disease progression. Care recipients (and even caregivers to the extent that fatigue and their own health challenges affect them) can be competent at times and impaired at others.

Physical impairments may affect mobility and gross motor movements, such as shifting the body from one posture or location to another, and declines in strength and stamina are common among people with diminished health. Limitations in manual dexterity may affect a person's ability to operate controls on equipment or open medication containers. Older adults often have slower walking speeds, and they may experience negative changes to the vestibular system that make balance less stable, increasing the risk of injury when caring for themselves (e.g., dressing, walking on uneven surfaces) or caring for others (e.g., helping a spouse move onto or off a bed or toilet) (Charness, 2010). Aging is often accompanied by decreases in ability to execute precise movements, which may make it difficult for older people to use small controls or use input devices, such as a keyboard, mouse, or touch screen. Chronic conditions, such as arthritis, may affect one's ability to execute movements precisely, operate controls, open containers, or grasp objects. These limitations are even more pronounced for people who have limb tremor or movement initiation disorders (e.g., Parkinson's disease).

Sensory/perceptual skills, critical to many tasks, are limited in many people. Recent data from the National Health Interview Survey indicate that, among adults ages 18 and older, about 15 percent have hearing impairments, 11 percent have some type of visual impairment, and 3.3 percent have combined vision and hearing impairments (U.S. Department of

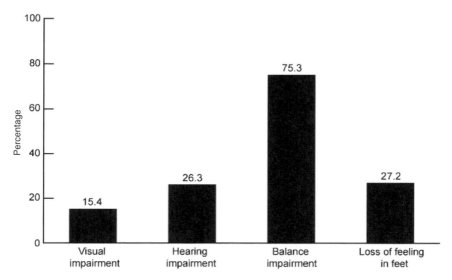

FIGURE 2-2 The prevalence of sensory impairments among people ages 70 and over, United States, 1999-2006.
SOURCE: Dillon et al. (2010).

Health and Human Services, 2009). These impairments, as well as additional impairments in balance and loss of feeling in feet, are more prevalent in older adults age 70 and over (see Figure 2-2). Declines in sensory abilities such as vision may make it difficult for people to read labels on medication containers or on controls of devices, and auditory declines may make alarm sensing and communication problematic.

Language and communications skills can have a profound impact on ability to access and implement care requirements and live independently at home. For many reasons, including the rise in non-English speakers,[3] many people may not easily express themselves well, comprehend complex instructions, or be able to use a health care device when provided with written instructions. It is estimated that 93 million U.S. adults have English literacy skills that are categorized as "basic" and "below basic." Rates of low literacy are higher among populations of lower socioeconomic status, older adults, and minorities (Kutner et al., 2006). Furthermore, for significant numbers of Americans, English language–only health care materials are inadequate. People with mental health problems are prone to

---

[3]Data from the 2000 U.S. census indicate that nearly 47 million people—or about 1 in 5 U.S. residents ages 5 and older—regularly speak a foreign language at home, representing an increase of 15 million people since 1990.

communication and language deficits, since, as a result of their conditions, they may have difficulties with memory, understanding, reasoning, talking, swallowing, and/or may have altered social skills and reduced nonverbal skills. Whether barriers such as weak language or cognitive skills can be surmounted by instructional materials that make greater use of symbols, diagrams, or video is not yet well understood (e.g., Morrell and Park, 1993).

The average age of the U.S. population is increasing because of relatively low birth rates coupled with declining death rates. Population projections indicate that by 2020, there will be an estimated 55 million people ages 65 and older and 6.6 million people ages 85 and older (Administration on Aging, 2009).

Older adults are more likely to have some type of disability. In addition, older adults experience increased activity limitations as they age as a result of chronic health conditions (see Figure 2-3). The older population is predominantly female (although this phenomenon is expected to be less

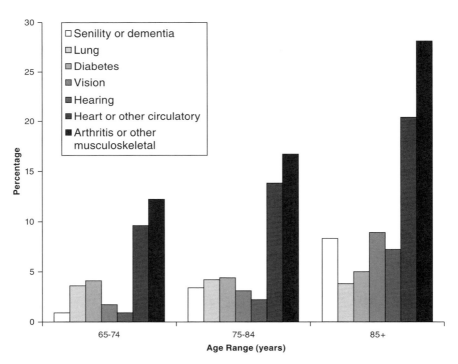

FIGURE 2-3 Older adults with limitations in activities.
SOURCE: Centers for Disease Control and Prevention (2009b).

pronounced in the future), and many of these women are likely to live alone.[4] Older adults as a whole have low health literacy, and the current cohort of elders is less likely to be familiar with computers and the Internet (Jones and Fox, 2009). Generally, older adults are less comfortable about adopting new technologies than are younger adults and have lower computer self-efficacy and less comfort with computers than other age groups (Nair, Lee, and Czaja, 2005; Czaja et al., 2006).

Educational achievement has increased over the past 70 years in the United States. The percentage of the population ages 25 and older that has completed 4 years of high school has risen from less than 40 percent in 1940 to nearly 90 percent in 2003. The proportion of the population that has completed 4 or more years of college has increased sixfold from 5 to over 30 percent (Stoops, 2004). Higher educational attainment is generally associated with higher income, better health, and greater longevity. These educational increases bode well for the ability of future generations to cope with complex health care regimens and equipment. However, it is important to recognize that educational disparities exist in all age groups.

Attitudinal variables also affect a person's performance of health care tasks. General attitudes toward health and health care have a strong influence on willingness to seek care and adherence to treatment protocols. Beliefs in one's ability to successfully carry out health care protocols and beliefs about the effectiveness of these protocols have a strong impact on treatment adherence and willingness to adopt behavioral changes. Trust is another important consideration. In today's world, this includes trust that one will have access to needed care, trust in caregivers, and trust in health care technologies. The distinction between distrust and overtrust should be recognized. Distrust, which can evolve from a number of attitudes including lack of confidence in knowledge or skills or concerns about privacy, can lead to the rejection of advice, use of an aid, or piece of technology. Conversely, overtrust can lead to complacency and failure to question or recognize malfunctions or misreadings under the presumption that equipment is working properly.

Ethnicity/Culture

Marked changes in the ethnic composition of the United States have occurred and are expected to continue over the coming decades. Overall, the Hispanic population is expected to double in size from 2000 to 2050, and the Asian population is projected to increase by 79 percent. Other ethnic minority groups, such as blacks and American Indians, will also

---

[4]In 2005, among people ages 85 and older, only 15 percent of women but 57 percent of men lived with their spouse (U.S. Census Bureau, 2007).

see moderate growth (Ortman and Guarmeri, 2009; U.S. Census Bureau, 2009). The older adult (ages 65+) minority populations are also projected to increase from 8.0 million in 2010 (20.1 percent of the elderly) to 12.9 million in 2020 (23.6 percent of the elderly) (Administration on Aging, 2009).

The prevalence of disease and disability and the risk factors, health behaviors, and access to and utilization of health services differ substantially by race and ethnicity as well as age. Many racial/ethnic minorities and individuals of lower socioeconomic status are less likely than whites and persons of higher socioeconomic status to have a usual source of care, to have access to quality care, and to engage in preventive health practices. These groups also tend to experience disproportionately some chronic illnesses and conditions, such as obesity, hypertension, and diabetes. For example, diabetes is more common among non-Hispanic blacks and Mexican Americans than among non-Hispanic whites (U.S. Department of Health and Human Services, 2010). There is also racial/ethnic variation in rates of disability (see Figure 2-4).

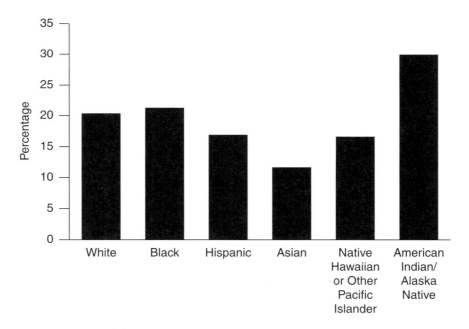

FIGURE 2-4 Disability rates among U.S. adults (≥ 18 years) by race and ethnicity, 2004-2006.
SOURCE: Centers for Disease Control and Prevention (2008).

With respect to technologies such as computers and the Internet, although use of these technologies by Hispanics and blacks is increasing, it still lags behind utilization rates of whites (Jones and Fox, 2009; Livingston, Parker, and Fox, 2009). This is important given the increased use of the Internet as a vehicle for delivery of health information and services.

For a racial/ethnic group whose primary means of communication is through a language other than English, translation of health materials originally written in English into a second language may be necessary. In this case, care should be taken to ensure that the translation is adequately performed and is sensitive to differences in culture (Taylor and Lurie, 2004). Lack of understanding of health documents or instructions may increase health disparities among racial/ethnic groups (U.S. Department of Health and Human Services, 2001).

Perceptions of power and cultural influences on attitudes about health and illness are also important to consider. Power differentials between care recipients and the health care system may be especially uncomfortable for minority racial and ethnic groups. Discomfort with this power difference arises from historical experiences and is reinforced by current practices (Valdez and Brennan, 2008). In addition, mental models about the nature of illness do not always transcend ethnic and racial boundaries. The majority population in the West believes in the use of allopathic medicine (i.e., that disease can be treated by drugs that have an antagonistic effect to the disease), but many cultures do not share this mental model. Mental models of illness vary among cultures and are informed by such factors as tradition, experiences, and religion (Valdez and Brennan, 2008).

Informal caregivers respond differently to the caregiving experience depending on their ethnic/cultural background. Implementing culturally competent interventions and care programs can help to overcome the cultural distance between caregivers, their care recipients, and associated communities and enhance health outcomes among diverse racial/ethnic groups (e.g., Gallagher-Thompson et al., 2003). These approaches include tailoring the language and images used in educational materials and brochures, becoming familiar with the histories and cultural norms of different populations, eliciting people's health beliefs and the context in which they experience illness, and developing mutually agreeable treatment plans (Gallagher-Thompson et al., 2003).

If issues related to power mismatch, mental models of illness, and language barriers are not addressed, racial/ethnic groups may refuse to follow health care procedures or use medical equipment or may fail to act when they do not understand health care tasks well. As a result, disparities in health status and health outcomes and rates of health care utilization could continue or increase (Valdez and Brennan, 2008).

Health Literacy

Currently, nearly half the U.S. population has difficulty understanding and using health information. Particularly vulnerable populations include elderly individuals, minority populations, people with chronic mental or physical health conditions, and people of lower socioeconomic status. Low health literacy has vast implications for home-based health care, having been linked to higher rates of hospitalization and use of expensive emergency services as well as lower use of preventive services (e.g., Baker et al., 2002).

Health literacy is defined in *Healthy People 2010* as "the degree to which individuals have the capacity to obtain, process, and understand basic health information and services needed to make appropriate health decisions" (U.S. Department of Health and Human Services, 2000, vol. 1, pp. 11-20). Health literacy includes the ability to understand instructions on prescription drug bottles and wording on appointment slips, medical education brochures, instructions and communications from doctors, medical consent forms, and health insurance plans, among others. Health literacy requires reading, listening, analytical and decision-making skills, and the ability to apply these skills to health situations.

Individuals and their family members at home often confront complex information and treatment decisions. They have to engage in such tasks as finding relevant health information, evaluating that health information for credibility and quality, analyzing relative risks and benefits of recommended treatment or health behaviors, calculating dosages, and interpreting test results. In order to accomplish these tasks, individuals need to be visually literate (able to understand graphs or other visual information), numerically or computationally literate (able to calculate or reason numerically), and analytically literate (able to integrate and apply relevant information). Oral language skills are important as well, as they enable individuals and their caregivers to articulate health concerns, describe symptoms and responses to treatment, ask pertinent questions, and understand spoken medical advice or treatment instructions. In an age of shared responsibility between consumers and providers of health care, individuals need strong decision-making skills. With the development of the Internet as a source of health information, health literacy has begun to include the ability to use a computer, search the Internet, and evaluate websites (U.S. Department of Health and Human Services, 2000).

INFORMAL CAREGIVERS

Rosalyn Carter is often quoted for her observation that there are only four types of people in the world: "those who have been caregivers; those who currently are caregivers; those who will be caregivers; and those who will need caregivers" (Carter, 1997). It follows that informal caregivers represent a broad and diverse group of individuals and are therefore difficult to characterize (see Table 2-1). Informal caregivers span the spectrum of age and are heterogeneous across multiple dimensions that include their relationship to and geographical proximity to the people for whom they provide care and the nature, duration, and intensity of the assistance they provide. They also vary in their level of competence and skill, their motivations for providing assistance, and the attitudes they bring to their role.

Prevalence of Informal Caregiving

Estimates of the number of informal caregivers in the United States vary widely across surveys. At one extreme is an estimate that 28.5 percent of the U.S. adult population, or 65.7 million people, provide unpaid care to an adult or child with special health care needs (National Alliance for Caregiving and American Association of Retired Persons, 2009). This figure is similar to the estimated 59 million adults with a disability in the United States found in the Behavioral Risk Factor Surveillance System survey (Centers for Disease Control and Prevention, 2006). A smaller estimate, reported by the Survey of Income and Program Participation, is that 28.8 million caregivers assist persons ages 15 and older with personal everyday needs (National Family Caregivers Association and Family Caregiver Alliance, 2006). A review of eight nationally representative surveys found published estimates ranging in magnitude from 2.7 to 36.1 million informal caregivers providing care to older disabled adults (Giovanetti and Wolff, 2010). Most prevalence estimates of caregivers from national surveys reflect ongoing assistance related to chronic disability. Intermittent episodes of caregiving are not well represented and are less well understood.

Children typically experience multiple acute illnesses that require assistance from adults, and children who have chronic disabilities require intensive and sometimes long-term support from their parents or other caregivers. The 2005-2006 National Survey of Children with Special Health Care Needs estimates that 13.9 percent of children under age 18 have special health care needs, defined in terms of use of services, therapies, counseling, or medications, or have functional limitations that persist for at least a year (U.S. Department of Health and Human Services, Health Resources and Services Administration, and Maternal and Child Health Bureau, 2008).

In some cases, grandparents have primary responsibility for the care of children. According to data from the 2000 U.S. census, 2.4 million individuals over age 30 were grandparent caregivers, defined as people who had primary responsibility for coresident grandchildren younger than age 18. The prevalence was particularly high among blacks (4.3 percent of the population age 30 or older) and American Indians and Alaska Natives (4.5 percent), compared with Hispanics (2.9 percent) and whites (1.1 percent, Simmons and Dye, 2003).

Recently it has also been recognized that some informal caregivers are children. One recent survey estimated that as many as 1.4 million children in the United States between the ages of 8 and 18 provide care for an older adult (Levine et al., 2005).

Because most surveys of caregivers are restricted to individuals who provide hands-on assistance with chronic illness and disability, gaps exist in knowledge of the numbers of other caregivers, such as individuals who assist from a distance or during time-limited episodes or who provide care to individuals at the end of life. In addition, recent events have resulted in unanticipated caregiving challenges, as veterans return from ongoing wars with multiple, interacting injuries or multiple traumas. The need for sustained caregiving for veterans is potentially immense, and the nature of the challenges for their informal caregivers is poorly understood.

Personal Characteristics

It is not surprising that the attributes of caregivers vary across surveys, given the wide variability in estimates of their numbers and the definitions employed. However, most data suggest that caregivers to older adults are typically female and are spouses or adult children of the people for whom they provide care and who either reside with or live in close proximity (e.g., National Alliance for Caregiving and American Association of Retired Persons, 2009). Approximately one-third to one-half of family caregivers to older adults are employed; employment rates are higher among caregivers who are adult children than for spouses, and higher among secondary caregivers than among those taking primary responsibility (Spillman and Pezzin, 2000). There is some evidence that blacks and Hispanics are more likely to be engaged in caregiving than are whites (Roth et al., 2009). As a group, caregivers are more likely to be of lower socioeconomic status (National Association for Caregiving and American Association of Retired Persons, 2004). The limited available information regarding child caregivers suggests that they also are more likely to come from households with lower incomes, less likely to reside in a two-parent home, and more likely to experience depression and anxiety when compared with their noncaregiving counterparts (Levine et al., 2005).

Roles and Responsibilities

Informal caregivers are involved in a wide range of household, personal care, and medically oriented tasks. The role that is perhaps most widely recognized is in assisting with personal care (activities of daily living, or ADLs: typically eating, dressing, bathing, transferring, toileting) and conducting household tasks (instrumental activities of daily living, or IADLs, such as shopping, transportation, meal preparation, money management, light housework, and laundry). Data from the National Long Term Care Survey and its Informal Caregivers Survey indicate that caregivers commonly assist with the full range of these tasks. In one study, primary caregivers helped chronically disabled older adults with shopping and/or transportation (85.3 percent), household tasks (77.7 percent), finances (49.4 percent), personal care and nursing (48.5 percent), and indoor mobility (35.1 percent) (Wolff and Kasper, 2006). These tasks commonly characterize long-term assistance provided to an older adult with a physical or cognitive disability.

In a 2009 survey conducted by the National Alliance for Caregiving (NAC) and the American Association of Retired Persons (AARP), the most common tasks performed by caregivers to children with special health care needs were reported as (National Alliance for Caregiving and American Association of Retired Persons, 2009)

- monitoring and reporting on condition severity (e.g., with school or government agencies, 85 percent),
- ensuring that people understand how to interact with and handle their child (84 percent),
- advocating for their child (72 percent),
- providing treatments and therapies (65 percent),
- administering medications or injections (64 percent),
- assisting with physical therapies/treatments (44 percent),
- preparing special diets (40 percent), and
- arranging paid services (39 percent).

Informal caregivers' involvement in health care delivery processes has been less systematically studied but is no less important. A substantial 43-53 percent of family caregivers perform medically oriented tasks in facilitating wound care, injections, equipment, or medication administration (Donelan, Hill, and Hoffman, 2002; Wolff and Kasper, 2006). Family caregivers who provide assistance to individuals with cognitive impairments, such as Alzheimer's, are widely acknowledged as taking responsibility for the full range of health care activities, including medical decision making. Caregivers commonly accompany care recipients to medical appointments and are actively engaged in medical communications (Schilling et al., 2002; Clayman et al., 2005; Wolff and Roter, 2008). The complexity of identifying and gaining access to health and social service support options that might be useful to family caregivers is daunting, even to experienced health professionals cast into the family caregiving role

(Kane, Preister, and Totten, 2005). The average informal caregiver faces significant challenges in optimizing formal support services to minimize the burdens of caregiving.

Ability to Provide Care

In addition to the range of physical, sensory, emotional, cognitive, perceptual, and intellectual attributes described earlier, several considerations affect informal caregivers' ability to provide care. Family dynamics and history, competing life demands, and available financial and social resources collectively influence the context of assistance and caregivers' motivation and capacity to provide high-quality care. The geographic proximity of informal caregivers to the person for whom they provide care is another important consideration. One study of living arrangements found that 24 percent of caregivers lived in the same house, 42 percent lived within 20 minutes, 19 percent lived between 20 and 60 minutes away, 5 percent lived 1 to 2 hours away, and 10 percent lived more than 2 hours away from the individual's home (National Alliance for Caregiving and American Association of Retired Persons, 2004). Geographic proximity affects the need to travel and the magnitude of psychological burdens experienced by caregivers, as well as their ability to supervise ongoing health-related activities, such as medication management.

The extent to which informal caregivers are prepared for the roles they assume varies considerably, but, for many people, preparation is minimal. According to one national survey, nearly one in five family caregivers who assist with medication management and one in three who assist with changing dressings or bandages received no instruction from a health care professional regarding how to perform these tasks (Donelan, Hill, and Hoffman, 2002). Caregivers' ability to cope with the challenges of caregiving in chronic illness may be enhanced by skills training designed to help prepare them to monitor the care recipient's behavior and progression of the disease and to provide appropriate assistance in response. One recent randomized clinical trial demonstrated the efficacy of a caregiver psychoeducational intervention on quality of life in multiple domains among white, black, and Hispanic caregivers of care recipients with dementia (Belle et al., 2006). Other intervention studies have shown that environmental modifications (Gitlin et al., 2009) and caregiver counseling (Mittelman et al., 2007) can reduce caregiver burden and delay institutionalization of the care recipient. Recognition that caregivers and care recipients reciprocally affect each other has led to the development of interventions that simultaneously target both caregiver and care recipient, with the aim of showing that dual treatment approaches are superior to treatments that focus on the caregiver only (Schulz et al., 2009). Intervention studies indicate that education and training can be valuable tools in enhancing caregiver functioning, but they have not yet been widely implemented in residential settings.

Monitoring of caregiver performance is a neglected area among both researchers and clinicians. With few exceptions (e.g., Gitlin et al., 2003), intervention studies that provide skills training to caregivers rarely assess the extent to which the intended skills are effectively implemented outside the treatment sessions, whether the learned skills are useful for newly emerging caregiver challenges, or how long skills learned as part of an intervention are used after the intervention is terminated. Similarly, clinicians who educate caregivers about care provision rarely assess the quality or appropriateness of caregiving outside the training session. For some types of care, care recipient status may be used as a proxy for caregiver performance, but this does not guarantee that the care provided by the caregiver was delivered as intended (Schulz and Tompkins, 2010). The costs of skills training and education for family members are covered during episodes of functional treatment for the care recipient (Gitlin et al., 2010); however, support for informal caregivers who themselves need assistance and support in order to continue to care for impaired family members is not reimbursed.

Detrimental Effects of Caregiving

Caregiving can be challenging for both people who provide care and people who receive it. For people who require it, receiving assistance from others may challenge their sense of independence; in some cases, the assumption of new roles and responsibilities within the family may result in conflict. One study of people ages 65 and older with physical disabilities whose spouses were their caregivers found that nearly 40 percent reported emotional distress from receiving the assistance, 50 percent reported being helped with activities unnecessarily, and 28 percent reported that they did not receive the help they needed (Newsom and Schulz, 1998).

Informal caregivers may experience a range of health and emotional morbidities associated with providing care. Studies have found that about two-thirds of all caregivers report stress or strain associated with the caregiving role (Schulz et al., 1997; Roth et al., 2009). Although relatively few studies have focused on the association between caregiving and health habits, researchers have found evidence for impaired health behaviors among caregivers engaged in heavy-duty caregiving (Schulz et al., 1997; Burton et al., 2003; Lee et al., 2003; Matthews et al., 2004). For some individuals, the experience of caregiving is sufficiently demanding that it may compromise their health and result in elevated stress hormones, physical illness, and psychological distress (Pinquart and Sörensen, 2003; Vitaliano, Zhang, and Scanlan, 2003). Measures of negative psychological effects, such as depression, stress, and burden, have been found to be more consistent than physical measures in indicating adverse consequences (Schulz et al., 1995, 1997; Teri et al., 1997; Marks, Lambert, and Choi, 2002; Pinquart and Sörensen, 2003).

Effects associated with caregiving are influenced by a range of contextual and personal characteristics, such as caregivers' age, socioeconomic status, and the availability of informal support: caregivers who are younger and have more economic and interpersonal resources report better health than do older caregivers, individuals of low socioeconomic status, and those with small support networks (Vitaliano et al., 2003). Some reviews suggest that the psychological effects of caregiving may be greater than the physical health effects, regardless of whether they are measured by self-report instruments or such measures as stress hormone levels (Vitaliano et al., 2003; Pinquart and Sörensen, 2007).

Although uncommon, elder abuse is by nature difficult to study and believed to be underdetected (Cooper, Selwood, and Livingston, 2009). Abusive arrangements have been shown to be more likely to occur among older adults who are physically dependent and cognitively impaired (Beach et al., 2005; Cooper, Selwood, and Livingston, 2009). One recent study of spousal caregivers in three U.S. communities found depression to be a risk factor for potentially harmful caregiver behaviors, which were defined as psychological (e.g., screaming, threatening with nursing home placement) and physical mistreatment of the care recipient (e.g., withholding food, hitting or slapping, shaking; Beach et al., 2005). Initial and intermittent assessment of caregivers would be beneficial, but little guidance regarding candidate assessment and situation intervention is available.

Interventions designed to diminish caregiver burden generally include education and training to help the caregiver understand the nature of a particular disease, its symptoms, and its progression. This type of information is often complemented with referral resources that provide additional information and services relevant to a particular health condition.

The effects of caregiving may extend to negative economic consequences. Middle-aged women at the peak of their earning power provide the majority of care to older disabled relatives (see Schulz and Martire, 2009, for a review), so caregiving may be combined with employment, childrearing, or both (Spillman and Pezzin, 2000). The increasing participation of women in the labor force, along with the increasing demand for care, raises important questions regarding how effectively and at what cost caregiving and employment may be combined. Caregiving may impose fairly significant burdens due to out-of-pocket costs (Covinsky et al., 1994). The most recent survey of caregivers by the NAC and AARP found that more than 6 in 10 informal caregivers with other jobs had made work accommodations that increased in proportion to the level of care needed by the person for whom they provided care (see Table 2-2).

TABLE 2-2 Work-Related Adjustments by Level of Burden (Base = Caregivers employed while caregiver)

Q41-Q47. IF WORKING WHILE A CAREGIVER: In your experience as both a worker and a caregiver, did you ever:

	Total	Level 1	Level 2	Level 3	Level 4	Level 5
In late, leave early, etc.	57%	40%	51%	63%	75%	83%
Took leave of absence	17%	8%	17%	14%	22%	41%
Went from full time to part time	10%	3%	7%	9%	15%	37%
Gave up work entirely	6%	1%	3%	4%	4%	35%
Lost any job benefits	5%	2%	2%	5%	9%	15%
Turned down promotion	4%	2%	3%	5%	6%	14%
Chose early retirement	3%	1%	1%	2%	3%	12%
None of the above	38%	57%	44%	31%	21%	8%

Base: 935 caregivers in the United States.
NOTE: The five levels refer to the level of burden of caregiving duties, based on the amount of time per week caregiver takes care of recipient and number and types of activities performed. Level 1 indicates lowest caregiving intensity, and Level 5 indicates the highest.
SOURCE: National Alliance for Caregiving and American Association of Retired Persons (2004, Table 9). Used by permission.

Evidence of health and economic consequences associated with caregiving suggests that it is an important public health issue in the United States (Talley and Crews, 2007). Recognition of these facts and the knowledge that caregivers represent a major national health resource resulted in the creation of the National Family Caregiver Support Program (Section 371 of the Older Americans Act) in 2001. This program, administered by the Administration on Aging, makes a range of services available to caregivers through Area Agencies on Aging and Aging and Disability Resource Centers. Services include information and assistance to caregiver services, counseling, support groups and training, respite care, and supplemental services. The program represents an important step in its explicit recognition of family caregivers. However, program funding has been fairly stable at a modest $150 million per year, and many advocates for caregivers feel that existing programs fall far short of what is needed (Riggs, 2003-2004).

FORMAL CAREGIVERS

Health professionals are defined here as individuals who receive compensation to provide health-related technical and supportive services. They include distinct groups that are certified and credentialed for their roles by virtue of education and training: physicians; nurses; physical, speech-language, and occupational therapists; social workers; dieticians; and pharmacists (see Table 2-3). Health professionals also include direct-care

TABLE 2-3 Types of Health Professionals Involved in Health Care Delivery in the Home, Ordered by Estimated 2018 Size of Workforce in the Home

Type of Provider	Estimated Total Quantity (000s)		Estimated Quantity in Homes (000s)	Mean Earnings ($)	
	2008	2018		Overall	In-Home Care
Home health aide	920	1,400	Most	9.84/hour	9.70/hour
Home aide/personal attendant	820	1,200	Most	9.22/hour	7.94/hour
Registered nurse	2,600	3,200	130	62,450/year	58,740/year
Licensed practical nurse	750	900	40	39,000/year	39,000/year
Social service assistant	352	432	Many	27,280/year	?
Physician (primary care)	661	806	Few	186,044/year	?
Pharmacist	270	316	Few	106,410/year	?
Physical therapist	186	242	Few	72,790/year	77,630/year
Social work	139	170	Few	46,650/year	46,930/year
Speech therapists	119	141	Few	62,930/year	77,030/year
Respiratory therapists	106	128	Few	52,200/year	?
Occupational therapists	105	131	Few	66,780/year	74,510/year
Dietician	60	66	Few	50,590/year	?

SOURCE: Bureau of Labor Statistics (2010a).

workers, who may be hired independently by individuals or their families or employed by home health, hospice, or other community-based agencies and who typically possess less formal education, certification, or credentialing: home care aides or personal care attendants, social service aides, or companions. In addition to providing direct health care services, health professionals supervise and educate individuals and families and provide technically skilled and supportive assistance that is unavailable or to augment assistance from families and friends.

Definitive estimates of the numbers of health professionals who deliver health care in the home do not exist. This workforce is difficult to quantify for several reasons. First, these professionals are remunerated by multiple funding streams, and they may be paid directly by care recipients or their families. Second, credentialing and licensure span numerous professional and paraprofessional organizations and typically vary by state. Third, since health care professionals may be employed in the home directly by individuals or families, their titles and job responsibilities may, at times, be poorly defined. The home health workforce that is certified and credentialed is composed primarily of nurses (registered nurses and licensed practical nurses). However, the dominant workers who provide health care in the home are home health aides, home aides/personal assistants, and social service assistants (see Tables 2-3 and 2-4).

Types of Professionals Providing Health Care in the Home

Direct-care workers who are employed in the home may be broadly categorized as home health aides and personal care aides or home care aides. These health professionals commonly assist with personal care activities, such as bathing, dressing, and performing daily tasks. They may also assist with food preparation or health care activities, such as wound care. These professional caregivers are believed to interact more than any others with individuals receiving care in the home; according to the Paraprofessional Health Care Institute (2010), they deliver 8 of every 10 hours of paid long-term services received in the home. About 88 percent of home care aides are women, which is even higher than their prevalence among informal caregivers (Yamada, 2002). Despite being the linchpin of health care in the home, direct-care workers have limited training, education, and credentialing requirements and may receive minimal or no oversight.

Home health aides employed by Medicare-certified home health and hospice agencies are required to have at least 75 hours of classroom and practical training and to pass a competency test covering 12 subject areas that include communication skills, reading and recording vital signs, infec-

TABLE 2-4 Roles of Health Professionals Relevant to Health Care in the Home

Type of Provider	Types of Job Responsibilities	Standards for Education, Licensure/Accreditation
Home health aide	Assist with personal care activities (e.g., bathing, dressing, negotiating daily tasks), light housekeeping, and health care activities, such as wound care, reading and recording vital signs, medications. Supervised by RNs or other home care professionals.	No high school diploma; 75-hour training program and state-competency evaluation if working for Medicare-Medicaid certified agency
Home aide/ personal attendant	Assist with personal care activities (e.g., bathing, dressing, negotiating daily tasks), household tasks. May assist with food preparation or health care activities, such as wound care.	No high school diploma required; no certification
Registered nurse (RN)	Provide skilled care, perform diagnostic tests and analyze results, operate medical equipment, administer treatments and medications, help establish treatment plans, supervise licensed practical nurses and other direct-care workers. Instruct care recipients and families how to perform self-care tasks. RNs may also be involved in coordinating care.	National Council Licensure Exam (NCLEX-RN); accredited program graduate (2-4 years duration beyond high school); state requirements vary
Licensed practical nurse (LPN)	Deliver routine care (e.g., administration of medication, wound care, and taking vital signs), collect samples for testing, perform routine laboratory tests, and may prepare injections, monitor catheters, dress wounds, and assist with hygiene and personal care. Supervised by RNs.	National Council Licensure Exam (NCLEX-PN); state-approved training program graduate (1-year duration beyond high school); state requirements vary

TABLE 2-4 Continued

Type of Provider	Types of Job Responsibilities	Standards for Education, Licensure/Accreditation
Advanced practical nurse	Utilize expanded skills, experience and knowledge in assessment, planning, implementation, diagnosis, and evaluation of care required. Few practice in the home setting.	Qualifications of a registered nurse plus trained at the graduate level and required to attain at least a master's degree
Social service assistant	Help determine eligibility, obtain access, and monitor use of social service programs.	High school diploma; no standard training or certification
Physician	Diagnose and treat injuries and disease, oversee care. Examine patients; obtain medical histories; order, perform, and interpret diagnostic tests; counsel care recipients on lifestyle and self-care activities. Few physicians practice in the home but they are most often responsible for initiation of health care services, prescription medications, and health care procedures. Home health care is initiated with physician prescription; home health care recipients must be under care of a physician.	Medical school (4 years) from accredited program in addition to bachelor degree; 3-8 year internship/residency; U.S. Medical Licensing Examination (USMLE) and board certification from American Board of Medical Specialists
Pharmacist	Dispense prescription drug medications, counsel care recipients and their families on use of prescription drugs and over-the-counter medications, advise physicians about medication therapy. Some pharmacists advise care recipients, provide specialized services related to specific conditions or diseases, assist with billing to third-party payers.	Doctor of pharmacy (4 years) from approved program in addition to bachelor degree; North American Pharmacist Licensure Exam (NAPLEX); other exams vary by state

continued

TABLE 2-4 Continued

Type of Provider	Types of Job Responsibilities	Standards for Education, Licensure/Accreditation
Physical therapist	Promote mobility and restoration or maintenance of functioning by engaging care recipients in a range of activities, such as therapeutic exercise, functional training, and teach them to use assistive and adaptive devices and equipment. Jobs may be physically demanding.	Graduate of an accredited postbaccalaureate program plus state requirements that typically include licensure examination
Social worker (medical/public health)	Help care recipients cope with and solve life issues by providing psychosocial support or assessing, coordinating, and monitoring services.	Bachelor degree; state licensure varies but typically includes supervised experience
Speech therapist	Assess, diagnose, and treat disorders related to swallowing, voice, speech, language fluency, and communication. Help care recipients to make sounds, increase their written or oral communication, with alternative communication methods, such as the use of automated devices or sign language. May help care recipients to swallow without choking or inhaling food by strengthening muscles or relying on compensatory strategies.	Graduate of an accredited postbaccalaureate program; national certification examination; state licensure varies but typically includes 300-375 hours of supervised clinical experience and 9 months experience
Respiratory therapist	Evaluate and treat breathing and cardiopulmonary disorders. Respiratory therapists typically treat care recipients with oxygen, chest physiotherapy, aerosol medications, or ventilators. Those employed by home health agencies inspect and maintain equipment, educate care recipients in the use of medications and equipment. Supervised by physicians.	Associate degree from accredited program, plus certification exam; licensure varies by state

continued

TABLE 2-4 Continued

Type of Provider	Types of Job Responsibilities	Standards for Education, Licensure/Accreditation
Occupational therapist	Help care recipients with mental, physical, or emotional deficits to compensate for loss of functioning, with the goal of maximizing independence, productivity, and quality of life. Help them develop, recover, and maintain their ability and skills using a range of techniques, computer programs, and adaptive or assistive devices.	Graduate of an accredited postbaccalaureate program plus national certification examination; state licensure requirements vary
Dietician	Plan food and nutrition programs, promote health with recommended dietary modifications, and evaluate and counsel individuals. Few dieticians practice in the home, but success of dietary treatment regimens hinge on care recipients' and families' adherence and implementation in the home environment.	Bachelor degree; state licensure requirements vary but may include certification exam; continuing education required

SOURCE: Bureau of Labor Statistics (2010b).

tion control, body functions, and basic nutrition, among others.[5] Some states require more training, but approximately half of all states require no more than the minimum (Institute of Medicine, 2008); home health aides are allowed to work up to 4 months before completing this training. Home health aides are supervised by registered nurses or speech, occupational, or physical therapists, who are also involved in care.

Personal and home care aides are typically employed and supervised by individuals and families who are also responsible for deciding whether the worker adequately demonstrates basic competencies; they are not typically supervised by licensed health care professionals (e.g., nurses or therapists). Although some states require training and certification for personal and home care aides, the extent of such requirements is highly variable (U.S. Department of Health and Human Services, 2006). Some states impose

---

[5]See Home Health Aide Training. 2006. 42 C.F.R 484.36.

no training or credentialing requirements on personal and home care attendants.

Nurses constitute the largest single occupation involved in the provision and oversight of skilled health care in the home. Two broad categories of nurses commonly practice in the home: registered nurses and licensed practical nurses. Although advanced practice nurses are important to the nursing workforce, they much less frequently practice in the home setting. The education, training, and certification required to practice, as well as the scope of practice, vary considerably across these three categories of nurses, as shown in Table 2-4. Of the three categories, licensed practical nurses have the most limited scope of practice and are supervised by registered nurses or advanced practice nurses.

Registered nurses, in an effort to ensure quality of clinical care, record medical histories and symptoms, perform diagnostic tests and analyze results, operate medical equipment, administer treatments and medications, and help establish treatment plans. Registered nurses also supervise licensed practical nurses and other direct-care workers and play an important educational role by instructing care recipients and families how to perform self-care tasks. Registered nurses may also be involved in coordinating care.

Licensed practical nurses provide direct care, such as administration of medication, wound care, and measurement of vital signs, such as height, weight, and blood pressure. They may also collect samples for testing, perform routine laboratory tests, prepare injections, monitor catheters, dress wounds, and assist with hygiene and personal care. Licensed practical nurses may help educate care recipients and their family members in following a treatment plan.

The presence of *advanced practice nurses* in the home lags behind other practice settings. Reasons for this disparity include lack of a well-defined role for advanced practice nurses in the home (Milone-Nuzzo and Pike, 2001), restrictive reimbursement mechanisms, and regulatory challenges pertaining to the scope of practice for advanced practice nurses in home care.[6] Although limited, empirical studies that have examined the impact of advanced practice nurses suggest beneficial effects for the cost and quality of care provided in the home to specific patient populations, as well as for postacute patients transitioning from the hospital back to the community (Brooten et al., 1986, 2001, 2002; Naylor et al., 1999).

Aside from nurses and direct-care workers, few other health professionals practice in the home (see Table 2-3). Nevertheless, the involvement of

---

[6]See, for example, interpretive guidelines such as *Medicare Home Health Conditions of Participation and Guidance to Surveyors* (http://cms.gov/manuals/Downloads/som107ap_b_hha. pdf [March 31, 2011]) that clarify 42 CFR Part 484, Conditions of Participation for home health agencies.

several types of health care providers—notably therapists, physicians, and pharmacists—merits comment, in that their involvement has substantive relevance to the quality of health care delivered in the home. For example, physical, occupational, and speech therapists have been valuable members of home care teams for decades. Importantly, physicians typically oversee, monitor, and adjust care recipients' overall plan of care; Medicare stipulates that home health care recipients must be "under the care of a physician." Likewise, although few pharmacists practice in the home, many of them provide medical devices and supplies that are used in the home, and they offer training, albeit usually informal.

Unfortunately, adverse complications of prescription drug underuse, overuse, and misuse are common (Gurwitz et al., 2003). A greater degree of coordination between pharmacists and physicians and a focus on educating care recipients have been shown to improve outcomes, such as successful glucose control among diabetics (Rothman et al., 2003). Yet with rare exceptions, most physicians and pharmacists do not have broad exposure to home environments. House call programs, under which very frail older adults receive primary care in their homes and care coordination across all treatment settings, are one such exception. Care coordination is provided by a physician- or nurse practitioner–directed team of health care professionals with geriatrics training who make in-home visits and are available around the clock to carry out plans of care tailored to the beneficiary's individual needs (Andrews, 2010).

Recruitment and Retention

The hiring of direct-care workers independently by individuals or their families has been described as a huge, private pay "grey market" operating off the books (Seavey, 2007). These providers may be identified through an informal network of friends, family members, churches, and other social groups that are either aware of people looking for employment or have had positive personal experience with an individual whom they refer. The dilemma this presents is that prospective employers (the individuals needing care or family members) may not know if the worker's training and experience matches their needs and may be unable to conduct an appropriate background check or otherwise confirm credentials and trustworthiness.

A number of factors challenge retention and recruitment of direct-care workers. As shown in Table 2-3, the mean hourly wage of home health aides and personal and home care aides in 2008 was $9.70/hour and $7.94/hour, respectively (Bureau of Labor Statistics, 2010a), the lowest wage earned among all categories of health professionals presented. Although some direct-care workers (25 percent) have completed some college (Wright, 2005), a substantial proportion have not received a high school diploma (Montgomery et al., 2005; Seavey, 2007). Given low wages and low levels of educational attainment, it is not surprising that many direct-care providers in all settings are among the working poor (U.S. Department of Health and Human Services, Health Resources and Service Administration, and Maternal and Child Health Bureau, 2004). They are more likely than other workers to live in poverty, to rely on food stamps, and to lack health insurance (U.S. Government Accounting Office, 2001). As many as one in four direct-care workers are single parents of dependent children (Wright, 2005; Smith and Baughman, 2007).

Several other factors impede recruitment and retention of direct-care workers, including perceptions of lack of respect, lack of control over the workplace, and limited opportunities for professional growth that contribute to low job satisfaction (Parsons et al., 2003; Castle et al., 2007). Although exact estimates vary widely, direct-care worker turnover rates are extremely high, ranging from 40 to 75 percent per year (Paraprofessional Health Care Institute, 2005; Lacey and McNoldy, 2007). Direct-care work often is physically demanding. Job-related injury rates are high, with reported workplace injuries among direct-care workers that result in time away from work four times the average rate of all occupations (Bureau of Labor Statistics, 2007). Since many direct-care workers are employed outside the formal health care system, workplace injury reporting may fall outside existing surveillance systems, raising the likelihood of underestimates.

Lack of training or commitment to long-term career success has the potential to detract from the caring attitude and knowledgeable care essential for direct-care workers to deliver optimal care. For example, since most direct-care workers are female, there may be an assumption that they can expertly perform such tasks as shopping for and preparing healthy foods for restricted diets, although they may have never learned or personally experienced either. Perhaps more problematic is that without guidelines for practice, unsupervised direct-care workers may practice beyond their scope, inadvertently endangering the individuals in their care due to their insufficient knowledge or skill in identifying emerging health crises, making appropriate clinical decisions, or knowing when to summon assistance. A lack of professional supervision may likewise endanger direct-care workers whose actions (or inaction) may result in occupation-related illness or injury. Furthermore, they may not be aware of how to handle on-the-job injury or to collect workers' compensation if they are injured in the work setting (Institute of Medicine, 2008).

There is a well-documented shortage of nurses, and evidence suggests that home care nurses are among the least satisfied with their profession (Sochalski, 2004). In one article, input into decision making and freedom to make important health care and work decisions were consistently highly ranked in relation to job satisfaction (Flynn, 2003; Flynn, Carryer, and Budge, 2005). Commonly cited reasons for possibly leaving their jobs include burdensome paperwork, excessive workload, and lack of role in organizational decision making (Smith-Stoner, 2004; Ellenbecker and Byleckie, 2005; Ellenbecker, Boylan, and Samia, 2006). Features of the work environment central to job satisfaction among home care nurses include design of the work hours, job structure, opportunities for career advancement, and access to continuing education and professional development (Cushman et al., 2001; Kimball and O'Neill, 2002). Flynn and Deatrick (2003) found that insufficient time with and access to front-line managers was a significant contributor to stress and job dissatisfaction in home care nurses.

Professional Practice Issues

Relative to health professionals employed in traditional clinical environments, those who practice in the home have greater independence and autonomy. Control over practice decisions, flexibility, and independence (clinical autonomy) have been reported to be key driving forces in attracting and keeping nurses in home health care (Anthony and Miline-Nuzzo, 2005; Tullai-McGuinness, Madigan, and Anthony, 2005) and are likely to be relevant issues for all health care professionals who practice in the home.

However, with this autonomy comes the potential for social and professional isolation from peers. Delivering health care in the home requires independence and critical thinking to solve problems as they arise, and other clinicians often are not available to provide advice or assistance. Health professionals are susceptible to compassion fatigue, but they rarely have access to peer support or emotional guidance because of the autonomous nature of their practice (Abendroth and Flannery, 2006). Electronic record-keeping, telecommunication, and agency policies may further limit in-person interactions and impede collegiality. This problem may be seen as an opportunity for good user-centered design of electronic networks to alleviate some of the isolation among formal caregivers working in homes.

Because health care professionals are usually educated in, and typically practice in, institutional or ambulatory health care settings, they may lack familiarity with issues encountered in the home. This disconnect between health care professionals who practice in the home and their counterparts raises the potential for communication breakdown and conflict that may detract from quality of care and safety and may exacerbate professionals' feelings of isolation, lack of support, and misunderstanding. From a professional practice standpoint, there is less opportunity for supervision, and it is more difficult to build in quality controls.

Given extensive autonomy and independence, it is paradoxical that health professionals who practice in the home often struggle with a lack of professional identity (Humphrey and Milone-Nuzzo, 2009). Unlike their colleagues in other settings, most professionals who practice in the home do not have active professional organizations. Few professional organizations impose certification exams or standards for employment that are specific to the home environment. For health care professionals in other settings, professional organizations serve as a mechanism for career development and advancement, along with commensurate salary increases. These benefits are largely unavailable for professionals working in the home environment. Lack of formal credentialing, in combination with logistical challenges associated with supervision in the home, raises the potential for quality of care to be compromised.

Occupational Hazards

The home is, in many ways, more challenging as a workplace than formal ambulatory or institutional health care environments designed and constructed for health care delivery. The physical environment is much more varied and may include logistical or physical impediments, and even hazards, for the administration of health care. Health professionals may encounter distractions, hazardous household conditions, physical discomfort from carrying equipment, heavy lifting, travel requirements, and even violence in neighborhoods and homes (Markkanen et al., 2007).

Although environmental issues are broadly relevant to everyone involved in health care in the home (and are discussed in detail in Chapter 6), several issues are unique to health care professionals. Health care professionals who practice in the home are more susceptible to a range of injuries and hazards because, unlike medical facilities, the home environment is more variable and generally not designed for the delivery of health care services. For example, although such tasks as lifting, pushing, and pulling are often performed by health care professionals, in the home they have less human assistance, usually no ergonomically designed equipment, and the environment is typically less appropriate (e.g., small spaces, crowded rooms) than in institutional health care facilities. Consequently, tasks may be performed in awkward positions or involve more strain and exertion— and may thereby result in injury. Formal caregivers whose jobs involve substantial time on personal care tasks, such as transferring, bathing, and dressing, have been found to incur among the highest rates of musculoskeletal injuries (Orr, 1997; Pohjonen, Punakallio, and Louhevaara, 1998; Galinsky, Waters, and Malit, 2001).

Health care professionals who practice in the home work primarily out of their cars or use public transportation and have no formal workstation (Markkanen et al., 2007). Most agencies provide "trunk kits" to professional staff that include extra supplies, protective equipment, and other items in order to reduce the need to return to the office to retrieve something necessary to complete an expected or unexpected visit. Because they repeatedly get into and out of the car (or other vehicle), often carrying equipment and supplies, these individuals are at risk for discomfort in and injury to the neck, lower back, shoulders, and hips (Sitzman, Pett, and Bloswick, 2002; Askew and Walker, 2008). The average home health care bag was found to weigh approximately 20 pounds in one study (Lee et al., 2006). Another study found that 60 percent of home care nurses experience discomfort from transporting their nursing bag (Sitzman, 2005). In addition to their bags, health professionals often must transport medical devices and technologies and various supplies, as well as paperwork, teaching materials, references such as a drug compendium, and anything else needed for an efficient and effective visit. Although these professionals are encouraged to complete all documentation in the home during the visit, this is not always possible and can necessitate writing, making phone calls, and using other technology in the uncomfortable conditions of an automobile.

Occupational hazards associated with provision of health care in the home extend well beyond physical stresses. For example, a report by the National Institute for Occupational Safety and Health details a broad range of issues that may be encountered in the delivery of health care in the home. In addition to musculoskeletal disorders, caregivers are exposed to blood-borne pathogens and needlestick injuries, various chemicals, unsanitary environments, violence and firearms, animals, weather-related hazards such as ice-covered sidewalks, and vehicular injuries related to long commutes to the worksite (Centers for Disease Control and Prevention, 2010).

COMMUNICATION BETWEEN FORMAL AND INFORMAL CAREGIVERS

The ability of professional caregivers to engage with family members, understand their strengths, respect their cultural norms and values, and foster their competence as informal caregivers is a critical dimension of practice. Because the typical home health care visit is one hour or less (Madigan, 2007), it is incumbent upon home health care professionals to be skilled at preparing family members to function effectively in their absence. Teaching is such an important aspect of providing home care that Medicare considers teaching as a skilled service—one that can be done only by a licensed health care professional. Despite the practical importance of establishing a productive partnership with care recipients and their informal caregivers, most formal caregivers are exposed to limited, if any, formal educational curriculum addressing effective strategies to include families in health decision making, prepare them to facilitate use of medical or adaptive technologies, or evaluate and support family caregivers' needs related to care provision (Reinhard et al., 2008; Yaffe and Jacobs, 2008).

The partnership between care recipients, families, and health care providers is not always positive. For example, family members of hospitalized patients often receive insufficient information and perceive lack of respect from hospital-based health professionals (Azoulay et al., 2000; Heyland et al., 2002; Teno et al., 2004).

One study of home health care recipients found that communication between clinicians and informal caregivers was not adequate around the discharge process (the termination of home health services). Nearly 40 percent of these informal caregivers reported learning that the home care services would end around the time of the last visit by the formal caregiver (Levine et al., 2006). This gave the family no time to prepare for the transition.

Cultural competence is important, as professional caregivers and care recipients are often from different backgrounds and may differ in expectations and preferences. The health care professional must respect, acknowledge, and address care recipients' and families' preferences and beliefs so as to effectively garner their support in adhering to their treatments (Lowe and Archibald, 2009; Teal and Street, 2009).

An exemplary effort to further best practices for health care professionals to support informal caregivers is a partnership—funded by the John A. Hartford Foundation and the Jacob and Valeria Langeloth Foundation, among the AARP Foundation, the *American Journal of Nursing*, the Council on Social Work Education, the Family Caregiver Alliance, and the Rutgers Center for State Health Policy—to advance competencies in this area specifically for nurses and social workers (Kelly, Reinhard, and Brooks-Danso, 2008). The effort outlines nursing and social work–specific competencies in six domains: (1) cultural competence and appreciation for diversity in people's attitudes and values; (2) communication—respect and compassion for both care recipients and their family caregivers; (3) assessment of family knowledge, skills, and needs; (4) intervention planning and implementation; (5) education; and (6) interdisciplinary teamwork (Damron-Rodriguez, 2008). This model could serve for other professional groups, including direct-care workers, physicians, and pharmacists.

Communication is important between caregivers in the home and primary care providers. Caregivers would like to have more regular communication with the care recipient's primary care provider (Fairchild et al., 2002). Given the complex health conditions of many people receiving health care in the home, coordination of health care services across settings and providers of care is important (Bodenheimer, 2008). Such coordination may be possible with developments in communications systems, medical technologies, and training. As we detail in the next chapters, human factors can play an increasingly important role in ensuring that systems, technologies, and training are all accessible to and usable by diverse populations.

REFERENCES

Abendroth, M., and Flannery, J. (2006). Predicting the risk of compassion fatigue: A study of hospice nurses. *Journal of Hospice and Palliative Nursing, 8*(6), 346-356.

Administration on Aging. (2009). *A profile of older Americans.* Available: http://www.aoa.gov/AoARoot/Aging_Statistics/Profile/2009/2.aspx [July 2010].

Andrews, M. (2010, September 13). House calls ready to go national. *Los Angeles Times.* Available: http://articles.latimes.com/2010/sep/13/health/la-he-house-calls-20100913 [April 2011].

Anthony, A., and Milone-Nuzzo, P. (2005). Factors attracting and keeping nurses in home care. *Home Healthcare Nurse, 23*(6), 372-377.

Askew, R., and Walker, J.T. (2008). Ergonomics for home care providers. *Home Healthcare Nurse, 26*(7), 412-417.

Azoulay, E., Chevret, S., Leleu G., Pochard, F., Barboteu, M., Adrie, C., Canoui, P., Le Gall, J.R., and Schlemmer, B. (2000). Half the families of intensive care unit patients experience inadequate communication with physicians. *Critical Care Medicine, 28*, 3044-3049.

Baker, D.W., Gazmararian, J.A., Williams, M.V., Scott, T., Parker, R.M., Green, D., Ren, J., and Peel, J. (2002). Functional health literacy and the risk of hospital admission among Medicare managed care enrollees. *American Journal of Public Health, 92*, 1278-1283.

Beach, S.R., Schulz, R., Williamson, G.M., Miller, L.S., Weiner, M.F., and Lance, C.E. (2005). Risk factors for potentially harmful informal caregiver behavior. *Journal of the American Geriatrics Society, 53*(2), 255-261.

Belle, S.H., Burgio, L., Burns, R., et al. (2006). Enhancing the quality of life of dementia caregivers from different ethnic or racial groups: A randomized, controlled trial. *Annals of Internal Medicine, 145*(10), 727-738.

Bodenheimer T. (2008). Coordinating care: A perilous journey through the health care system. *New England Journal of Medicine, 358*, 1064-1071.

Brault, M.W. (2008). *Americans with disabilities: 2005 household economic reports, current population reports.* Washington, DC: U.S. Census Bureau. Available: http://www.census.gov/prod/2008pubs/p70-117.pdf [April 2011].

Brooten, D., Kumar, S., Brown, L., et al. (1986). A randomized clinical trial of early discharge and home follow-up of very low birthweight infants. *New England Journal of Medicine, 315*, 934-939.

Brooten, D., Youngblut, J.M., Brown, L., et al. (2001). A randomized trial of nurse specialist home care for women with high risk pregnancies: Outcomes and costs. *American Journal of Managed Care, 7*, 793-803.

Brooten, D., Naylor, M.D., York, R., et al. (2002). Lessons learned from testing the quality cost model of advanced practice nursing (APN) transitional care. *Journal of Nursing Scholarship, 334*, 369-375.

Bureau of Labor Statistics. (2007). *Nonfatal occupational injuries and illnesses requiring days away from work.* Washington, DC: Author.

Bureau of Labor Statistics. (2010a). *May 2009 national occupational employment and wage estimates United States, 2010.* Available: http://www.bls.gov/oes/current/oes_nat.htm [March 31, 2011].

Bureau of Labor Statistics. (2010b). *Occupational handbook, 2010-2011 edition.* Available: http://www.bls.gov/oco [March 31, 2011].

Burton, L.C., Zdaniuk, B., Schulz, R., Jackson, S., and Hirsch, C. (2003). Transitions in spousal caregiving. *Gerontologist, 43*(2), 230-241.

Carter, R. (1997, February 13). *Remarks, as Honorary Chair of the Last Acts.* Available: http://gos.sbc.edu/c/carter.html [April 2011].

Castle, N.G., Enberg, J., Anderson R., and Men, A. (2007). Job satisfaction of nurse aides in nursing homes: Intent-to-leave and turnover. *The Gerontologist, 47*(2), 193-204.

Centers for Disease Control and Prevention. (2006). *Disability and health state chartbook: Profiles of health for adults with disabilities* (LCCN: 2006-238868). Atlanta, GA: Author. Available: http://www.cdc.gov/ncbddd/disabilityandhealth/chartbook/ [April 2011].

Centers for Disease Control and Prevention. (2008). Racial/ethnic disparities in self-rated health status among adults with and without disabilities: United States, 2004-2006. *Morbidity and Mortality Weekly Report, 57*(39), 1069-1073.

Centers for Disease Control and Prevention. (2009a). *Chronic disease prevention and health promotion.* Available: http://www.cdc.gov/chronicdisease/resources/publications/AAG/chronic.htm [July 2009].

Centers for Disease Control and Prevention. (2009b). *National health interview survey, 2003-2007, table 1. Frequency distributions of number of limitations in activities of daily living (ADLs) by age: United States, 2003-2007.* Hyattsville, MD: U.S. Department of Health and Human Services.

Centers for Disease Control and Prevention. (2010). *NIOSH hazard review: Occupational hazards in home healthcare.* Washington DC: National Institute for Occupational Safety and Health. Available: http://www.cdc.gov/niosh/docs/2010-125/pdfs/2010-125.pdf [April 2011].

Charness, N. (2010). The health care challenge: Matching care to people in their home environments. In National Research Council, *The role of human factors in home health care: Workshop summary* (pp. 73-117). S. Olson, Rapporteur. Committee on the Role of Human Factors in Home Healthcare. Committee on Human-Systems Integration, Division of Behavioral and Social Sciences and Education. Washington, DC: The National Academies Press.

Clayman, M., Roter, D., Wissow, L., and Bandeen-Roche, K. (2005). Autonomy-related behaviors of patient companions and their effect on decision-making activity in geriatric primary care visits. *Social Science and Medicine, 60*(7), 1583-1591.

Cooper, C., Selwood, A., and Livingston, G. (2009). Knowledge, detection, and reporting of abuse by health and social care professionals: A systematic review. *American Journal of Geriatric Psychiatry, 17*(10), 826-838.

Covinsky, K.E., Goldman, L., Cook, E.F., et al. (1994). The impact of serious illness on patients' families. *Journal of the American Medical Association, 272*(23), 1839-1844.

Cushman, M.J., Ellenbecker, C.H., Wilson, D.L., et al. (2001). Home healthcare nurses: Why they leave and why they stay. *Caring, 20*(10), 62-67.

Czaja, S.J., Charness, N., Fisk, A.D., et al. (2006). Factors predicting the use of technology: Findings from the Center for Research and Education on Aging and Technology Enhancement (CREATE). *Psychology & Aging, 21*, 333-352.

Damron-Rodriguez J. (2008). Developing competence for nurses and social workers: Quiz 46. *American Journal of Nursing, 108*, 40-46.

Dillon, C.F., Gu, Q., Hoffman, H.J., and Ko, C-W. (2010). *Vision, hearing, balance, and sensory impairment in Americans aged 70 years and over: United States, 1999-2006.* NCHS Data Brief, Number 31. Available: http://www.cdc.gov/nchs/data/databriefs/db31.pdf [April 2011].

Donelan, K., Hill, C., and Hoffman, C. (2002). Challenged to care: Informal caregivers in a changing health system. *Health Affairs (Millwood), 21*(4), 222-231.

Economic Systems Inc. (2008). *A study of compensation payments for service-connected disabilities: Volume I, executive report*. Falls Church, VA: U.S. Department of Veterans Affairs.

Ellenbecker, C.H., and Byleckie, J.J. (2005). Home healthcare nurses' job satisfaction scale: Refinement and psychometric testing. *Journal of Advanced Nursing, 52*(1), 70-78.

Ellenbecker, C.H., Boylan, L.N., and Samia, L. (2006). What home healthcare nurses are saying about their jobs. *Home Healthcare Nurse, 24*(5), 315-324.

Fairchild, D.G., Hogan, J., Smith, R., et al. (2002). Survey of primary care physicians and home care clinicians: An assessment of communication and collaboration. *Journal of General Internal Medicine, 17*(4), 253-257.

Fisk, A.D., Rogers, W.A., Charness, N., Czaja, S., and Sharit, J. (2009). *Designing for older adults: Principles and creative human factors approaches* (2nd ed.). Boca Raton, FL: CRC Press.

Flynn, L. (2003). Agency characteristics most valued by home care nurses: Findings of a nationwide study. *Home Healthcare Nurse, 21*(12), 812-817.

Flynn, L., and Deatrick, J.A. (2003). Home care nurses' descriptions of important agency attributes. *Journal of Nursing Scholarship, 35*(4), 385-390.

Flynn, L., Carryer, J., and Budge, C. (2005). Organizational attributes valued by hospital, home care, and district nurses in the United States and New Zealand. *Journal of Nursing Scholarship, 37*(1), 67-72.

Freedman, V.A., Schoeni, R.F., Martin, L.G., and Cornman, J.C. (2007). Chronic conditions and the decline in late-life disability. *Demography, 44*(3), 459-477.

Galinsky, T., Waters, T., and Malit, B. (2001). Overexertion injuries in home health care workers and the need for ergonomics. *Home Health Care Services Quarterly, 20*(3), 57-73.

Gallagher-Thompson, D., Haley, W., Guy, D., et al. (2003). Tailoring psychological interventions for ethnically diverse dementia caregivers. *Clinical Psychology: Science and Practice, 10*(4), 423-438.

Giovanetti, E.R., and Wolff, J.L. (2010). Cross-survey differences in national estimates of numbers of caregivers to disabled older adults. *Milbank Quarterly, 88*(3), 310-349.

Gitlin, L.N., Winter, L., Corcoran, M., and Hauck, W. (2003). Effects of the home environmental skill-building program on the caregiver-care recipient dyad: 6-month outcomes from the Philadelphia reach initiative. *Gerontologist, 43*(4), 532.

Gitlin, L.N., Hauck, W., Dennis, M.P., et al. (2009). Long-term effect on mortality of a home intervention that reduces functional difficulties in older adults: Results from a randomized trial. *Journal of the American Geriatrics Society, 57*(3), 476-481.

Gitlin, L.N., Winter, L., Dennis, M.P., et al. (2010). Targeting and managing behavioral symptoms in individuals with dementia: A randomized trial of a nonpharmacological intervention. *Journal of the American Geriatrics Society, 58*(8), 1465-1474.

Gurwitz, J., Field, T., Harrold, L.R., Rothschild, J.M., Debellis, K., Seger, A.C., Fish, L.S., Garber, L., Kelleher, M., and Bates, D.W. (2003). Incidence and preventability of adverse drug events among older persons in the ambulatory setting. *Journal of the American Medical Association, 289*(9), 1107-1116.

Heyland, D., Rocker, G., Dodek, P., Kutsogiannis, D.J., Konopad, E., Cook, D.J., Peters, S., Tranmer, J.E., and Callaghan, C.H. (2002). Family satisfaction with care in the intensive care unit: Results of a multiple center study. *Critical Care Medicine, 30*, 1413-1418.

Humprey, C.J., and Milone-Nuzzo, P. (2009). *Characteristics of formal caregivers*. Presentation to the Committee on the Role of Human Factors in Home Healthcare, Session 1: People Who Receive and Provide Home Healthcare, October 1, National Academy of Sciences, Washington, DC.

Institute of Medicine. (2008). *Retooling for an aging America: Building the health care workforce.* Committee on the Future Health Care Workforce for Older Americans. Board on Health Care Services. Washington, DC: The National Academies Press.

Jones, S., and Fox, S. (2009). *Pew Internet Project data memo, re: Generations online in 2009.* Available: http://www.pewinternet.org/~/media//Files/Reports/2009/PIP_Generations_2009.pdf [March 31, 2011].

Kane, R., Preister, R., and Totten, A.M. (2005). *Meeting the challenge of chronic illness.* Baltimore, MD: Johns Hopkins University Press.

Kelly, K., Reinhard, S.C., and Brooks-Danso, A. (2008). Professional partners supporting family caregivers. *American Journal of Nursing, 108*(9), 6-12.

Kimball, B., and O'Neill, E. (2002). *Health care's human crisis: The American nursing shortage.* Princeton, NJ: Robert Wood Johnson Foundation. Available: https://folio.iupui.edu/bitstream/handle/10244/471/NursingReport.pdf?sequence=2 [April 2011].

Kutner, M.A., Greenberg, E., Jin, Y., and Paulsen, C. (2006). *The health literacy of America's adults: Results from the 2003 National Assessment of Adult Literacy.* Washington, DC: National Center for Education Statistics.

Lacey, L., and McNoldy, T.P. (2007). *Turnover rates in North Carolina home health and hospice agencies.* North Carolina Center for Nursing-Quick Facts. Available: http://www.hwic.org/pdf/homehealth_turnover.pdf [March 31, 2011].

Lee, E.J., Haddock, M., Yu, S., Back, C., and Yassi, A. (2006). Developing and evaluating a nursing bag system for home care nurses using a participatory ergonomics approach. *Home Healthcare Nurse, 24*(9), 591-597.

Lee, S., Colditz, G.A., Berkman, L.F., and Kawachi, I. (2003). Caregiving and risk of coronary heart disease in U.S. women—A prospective study. *American Journal of Preventive Medicine, 24*(2), 113-119.

Levine, C., Hunt, G.G., Halper, D., Hart, A.Y., Lautz, J., and Gould, D.A. (2005). Young adult caregivers: A first look at an unstudied population. *American Journal of Public Health, 95*(11), 2071-2075.

Levine, C., Albert, S. M., Hokenstad, A., Halper, D.E., Hart, A.Y., and Gould, D.A. (2006). "This case is closed": Family caregivers and the termination of home health care services for stroke patients. *Milbank Quarterly, 84*(2), 305-331.

Livingston, G., Parker, K., and Fox, S. (2009). *Latinos online, 2006-2008: Narrowing the gap.* Washington DC: Pew Hispanic Center, Pew Research Center.

Lowe, J., and Archibald, C. (2009). Cultural diversity: The intention of nursing. *Nursing Forum, 44*(1), 11-18.

Madigan, E.A. (2007). A description of adverse events in home healthcare. *Home Healthcare Nurse, 25*(3), 191-197.

Markkanen, P., Quinn, M., Gallign, C., Chalupka, S., Davis, L, and Laramie, A. (2007). There's no place like home: A qualitative study of the working conditions of home health care providers. *Journal of Occupational and Environmental Medicine, 49*(3), 327-337.

Marks, N.F., Lambert, J.D., and Choi, H. (2002). Transitions to caregiving, gender, and psychological well-being: A prospective U.S. national study. *Journal of Marriage and Family, 64*(3), 657-667.

Matthews, J.T., Dunbar-Jacob, J., Sereika, S., Schulz, R., and McDowell, B.J. (2004). Preventive health practices: Comparison of family caregivers 50 and older. *Journal of Gerontological Nursing, 30*(2), 46-54.

Milone-Nuzzo, P., and Pike, A. (2001). Advanced practice nurses in home care: Is there a role? *Journal of Home Health Management and Practice, 13*(5), 349-355.

Mittelman, M.S., Roth, D.L., Clay, O.J., and Haley, W.E. (2007). Preserving health of Alzheimer caregivers: Impact of a spouse caregiver intervention. *American Journal of Geriatric Psychiatry, 15*(9), 780-789.

Montgomery, R.J.V., Holley, L., Deichert, J., and Kosloski, K. (2005). A profile of home care workers from the 2000 census: How it changes what we know. *Gerontologist, 45*(5), 593-600.

Morrell, R.W., and Park, D.C. (1993). The effects of age, illustrations, and task variables on the performance of procedural assembly tasks. *Psychology and Aging, 8*(3), 389-399.

Nair, S.N., Lee, C.C., and Czaja, S.J. (2005). Older adults and attitudes towards computers: Have they changed with recent advances in technology? *Proceedings of the 49th Annual Meeting of the Human Factors and Ergonomics Society* (pp. 154-157), Orlando, FL.

National Alliance for Caregiving and American Association of Retired Persons. (2004). *Caregiving in the U.S. 2004*. Washington, DC: Author.

National Alliance for Caregiving and American Association of Retired Persons. (2009). *Caregiving in the U.S. 2009*. Available: http://www.caregiving.org/data/Caregiving_in_the_US_2009_full_report.pdf [March 31, 2011].

National Family Caregivers Association and Family Caregiver Alliance. (2006). *Prevalence, hours and economic value of family caregiving, updated state-by-state analysis of 2004 national estimates*. Kensington, MD: Author.

Naylor, M.D., Brooten, D., Campbell, R., Jacobsen, B.S., Mezey, M.D., Pauly, M.V., and Schwartz, J.S. (1999). Comprehensive discharge planning and home follow-up of hospitalized elders. *Journal of the American Medical Association, 281*(7), 613.

Newsom, J.T., and Schulz, R. (1998). Caregiving from the recipient's perspective: Negative reactions to being helped. *Health Psychology, 17*(2), 172-181.

Orr, G.B. (1997). Ergonomics programs for health care organizations. *Occupational Medicine, 12*(4), 687-700.

Ortman, J., and Guarneri, C. (2009). *United States population projections: 2000 to 2050*. Washington, DC: U.S. Census Bureau. Available: http://www.census.gov/population/www/projections/analytical-document09.pdf.

Paraprofessional Healthcare Institute. (2005). *Role of training in improving recruitment and retention of direct care workers in long-term care*. Bronx, NY: Author.

Paraprofessional Healthcare Institute. (2010). *Direct-care workers at a glance*. Available: http://phinational.org/policy/about-the-workforce/at-a-glance/ [March 31, 2011].

Parsons, S.K., Simmons, W.P., Penn, K., and Furlough, M. (2003). Determinants of satisfaction and turnover among nursing assistants. The results of a statewide survey. *Journal of Gerontological Nursing, 29*(3), 51-58.

Pinquart, M., and Sörensen, S. (2003). Differences between caregivers and noncaregivers in psychological health and physical health: A meta-analysis. *Psychology & Aging, 18*(2), 250-267.

Pinquart, M., and Sörensen, S. (2007). Correlates of physical health of informal caregivers: A meta-analysis. *Journals of Gerontology Series B: Psychological Sciences & Social Sciences, 62B*(2), 126-137.

Pohjonen, T., Punakallio, A., and Louhevaara, V. (1998). Participatory ergonomics for reducing load and strain in home care work. *International Journal of Industrial Ergonomics, 21*, 345-352.

Reinhard, S., Brooks-Danso, A., Kelly, K., and Mason, D.J. (2008). How are you doing? *American Journal of Nursing, 108*(9 Suppl), 4-5.

Riggs, J.A. (2003-2004). A family caregiver policy agenda for the twenty-first century. *Generations, 27*(4), 68-73.

Roth, D.L., Perkins, M., Wadley, V.G., Temple, E.M., and Haley, W.E. (2009). Family caregiving and emotional strain: Associations with quality of life in a large national sample of middle-aged and older adults. *Quality of Life Research, 18*(6), 679-688.

Rothman R, Malone, R., Bryant B., Horlen C., and Pignone M. (2003). Pharmacist-led, primary care-based disease management improves hemoglobin A1c in high-risk patients with diabetes. *American Journal of Medical Quality, 18*(2), 51-58.

Scherer, M., Jutai, J., Fuhrer, M., Demers, L., and Deruyter, F. (2007). A framework for modelling the selection of assistive technology devices (ATDs). *Disability and Rehabilitation Assistive Technology, 2*(1), 1-8.

Schilling, L., Scatena, L., Steiner, J., Albertson, G.A., Lin, C.T., Cyran, L., Ware, L., and Anderson, R.J. (2002). The third person in the room: Frequency, role, and influence of companions during primary care medical encounters. *Journal of Family Practice, 51*(8), 685-690.

Schulz, R., and Martire, L.M. (2009). Caregiving and employment. In S.J. Czaja and J. Sharit (Eds.), *Aging and work: Issues and implications in a changing landscape.* Baltimore, MD: Johns Hopkins University Press.

Schulz, R., and Tompkins, C.A. (2010). Informal caregivers in the United States: Prevalence, characteristics, and ability to provide care. In National Research Council, *The role of human factors in home health care: Workshop summary* (pp. 118-144). S. Olson, Rapporteur. Committee on the Role of Human Factors in Home Health Care. Committee on Human-Systems Integration, Division of Behavioral and Social Sciences and Education. Washington, DC: The National Academies Press.

Schulz, R., O'Brien, A.T., Bookwala, J., and Fleissner, K. (1995). Psychiatric and physical morbidity effects of dementia caregiving: Prevalence, correlates, and causes. *The Gerontologist, 35*(6), 771-791.

Schulz, R., Newsom, J., Mittelmark, M., Burton, L., Hirsch, C., and Jackson, S. (1997). Health effects of caregiving: The caregiver health effects study: An ancillary study of the cardiovascular health study. *Annals of Behavioral Medicine, 19*(2), 110-116.

Schulz, R., Czaja, S.J., Lustig, A., Zdaniuk, B., Martire, L.M., and Perdomo, D. (2009). Improving the quality of life of caregivers of persons with spinal cord injury: A randomized controlled trial. *Rehabilitation Psychology, 54*(1), 1-15.

Seavey, D. (2007). *Written statement before the Subcommittee on Workforce Protections, Committee on Education and Labor, U.S. House of Representatives hearing on "H.R. 3582: The Fair Home Health Care Act."* Available: http://www.directcareclearinghouse.org/download/Seavey%20Written%20Statement%20FINAL%20Oct%2007.pdf [April 2011].

Simmons, T., and Dye, J.L. (2003). *Grandparents living with grandchildren: 2000.* Census 2000 brief. Washington, DC: Economics and Statistics Administration.

Sitzman, K. (2005). Bag and supply transport tips. *Home Healthcare Nurse, 23*(1), 49.

Sitzman, K.L., Pett, M.A., and Bloswick, D.S. (2002). An exploratory study of nurse bag use by home visiting nurses. *Home Healthcare Nurse, 20*(4), 237-243.

Smith, D.L. (2008). Disparities in health care access for women with disabilities in the United States from the 2006 National Health Interview Survey. *Disability and Health Journal, 1*(2), 79-88.

Smith, K., and Baughman, R. (2007). Caring for America's aging population: A profile of the direct care workforce. *Monthly Labor Review, 130*(9), 20-26.

Smith-Stoner, M. (2004). Home care nurses' perceptions of agency and supervisory characteristics: Working in the rain. *Home Healthcare Nurse, 22*(8), 536-546.

Sochalski, J. (2004). Building a home healthcare workforce to meet the quality imperative. *Journal for Healthcare Quality, 26*(3), 19-23.

Soni, A. (2009). *The five most costly children's conditions, 2006 estimates for the U.S. civilian noninstitutionalized children, ages 0-17.* Statistical brief, AHRQ #242. Rockville, MD: Agency for Healthcare Research and Quality.

Spillman, B., and Pezzin, L. (2000). Potential and active family caregivers: Changing networks and the "sandwich" generation. *Milbank Quarterly, 78*(3), 347-374.

Stoops, N. (2004). *Educational attainment in the United States: 2003.* Washington, DC: U.S. Census Bureau.

Talley, R.C., and Crews, J.E. (2007). Framing the public health of caregiving. *American Journal of Public Health, 97*(2), 224-228.

Taylor, S., and Lurie, N. (2004). The role of culturally competent communication in reducing ethnic and racial healthcare disparities. *American Journal of Managed Care, 10*, SP1-SP4.

Teal, C.R., and Street, R.L. (2009). Critical elements of culturally competent communication in the medical encounter: A review and model. *Social Science and Medicine, 68*(3), 533-543.

Teri, L., Logsdon, R.G., Uomoto, J., and McCurry, S.M. (1997). Behavioral treatment of depression in dementia patients: A controlled clinical trial. *Journals of Gerontology: Series B: Psychological Sciences and Social Sciences, 52B*(4), P159-P166.

Teno, J.M., Clarridge, B.R., Casey, V., Welch, L.C., Wetle, T., Shield, R., and Mor, V. (2004). Family perspectives on end-of-life care at the last place of care. *Journal of the American Medical Association, 291*, 88-93.

Tullai-McGuinness, S., Madigan, E.A., and Anthony, M.K. (2005). Exercise of autonomous home care practice: The relationship with nurse characteristics. *Home Healthcare Nurse, 23*(6), 378-384.

U.S. Census Bureau. (2007). *Statistical abstract of the United States: 2007.* Washington, DC: Author.

U.S. Census Bureau. (2009). *Statistical abstract of the United States: 2009.* Washington, DC: Author.

U.S. Department of Health and Human Services. (2000). *Healthy people 2010 volume 1.* Washington, DC: U.S. Government Printing Office.

U.S. Department of Health and Human Services. (2001). *Quick guide to health literacy.* Available: http://www.health.gov/communication/literacy/quickguide/ [March 31, 2011].

U.S. Department of Health and Human Services. (2006). *States' requirements for Medicaid-funded personal care service attendants.* (OEI-07-05-00250, revised December 2006). Available: http://oig.hhs.gov/oei/reports/oei-07-05-00250.pdf [April 2011].

U.S. Department of Health and Human Services. (2009). *Summary health statistics for U.S. adults: National health interview survey, 2008.* Hyattsville, MD: National Center for Health Statistics. Available: http://www.cdc.gov/nchs/data/series/sr_10/sr10_242.pdf [March 31, 2011].

U.S. Department of Health and Human Services. (2010). *Summary health statistics for U.S. adults: National Health Interview Survey, 2009.* Series 10, No. 249, Vital Health and Statistics. Available: http://www.cdc.gov/nchs/data/series/sr_10/sr10_249.pdf [April 2011].

U.S. Department of Health and Human Services, Health Resources and Services Administration, and Maternal and Child Health Bureau. (2004). *Nursing aides, home health aides, and related health care occupations: National and local shortages and associated data needs.* Washington, DC: National Center for Health Workforce Analyses, Bureau of Health Professions, Health Resources, and Services Administration. Available: http://bhpr.hrsa.gov/healthworkforce/reports/nursinghomeaid/nursinghome.htm [March 31, 2011].

U.S. Department of Health and Human Services, Health Resources and Services Administration, and Maternal and Child Health Bureau. (2008). *The National Survey of Children with Special Health Care Needs chartbook 2005-2006.* Available: http://mchb.hrsa.gov/cshcn05/ [May 3, 2010].

U.S. Government Accounting Office. (2001). *Nursing workforce: Recruitment and retention of nurses and nurse aids is a growing concern.* Testimony before the Committee on Health, Education, Labor and Pensions, U.S. Senate. Available: http://www.gao.gov/new.items/ d01750t.pdf [April 2011].

Valdez, R., and Brennan, P. (2008). *Medical informatics.* New York: Springer.

Vitaliano, P.P., Zhang, J., and Scanlan, J.M. (2003). Is caregiving hazardous to one's physical health? A meta-analysis. *Psychological Bulletin, 129*(6), 946-972.

Wolff, J., and Roter, D. (2008). Hidden in plain sight: Medical visit companions as a quality of care resource for vulnerable older adults. *Archives of Internal Medicine, 168*(13), 1409-1415.

Wolff, J.L., and Kasper, J.D. (2006). Caregivers of frail elders: Updating a national profile. *Gerontologist, 46*(3), 344-356.

Wright, B. (2005). *Direct care workers in long-term care. Research report.* Washington DC: AARP Public Policy Institute. Available: http://www.governor.wa.gov/ltctf/ workgroup/20070912/DirectCareWorkersinLTC_AARP_052005.pdf [April 2011].

Yaffe, M., and Jacobs, B. (2008). Education about family caregiving: Advocating family physician involvement. *Canadian Family Physician, 54*(10), 1355-1364.

Yamada, Y. (2002). Profile of home care aides, nursing home aides, and hospital aides: Historical changes and data recommendations. *Gerontologist, 42*(2), 199-206.

3

What Is Human Factors?

Human factors, with its emphasis on user- or person-centered design, can help to ensure that health care in the home suits the people, the tasks, and the environments involved and that the care provided is safe, effective, and efficient. According to the International Ergonomics Association, "[Human factors] is the scientific discipline concerned with the understanding of interactions among humans and other elements of a system, and the profession that applies theory, principles, data, and other methods to design in order to optimize human well-being and overall system performance" (International Ergonomics Association, 2010).

Human factors is therefore concerned with applying what is known about human behavior, abilities, limitations, and other characteristics to the design of systems, tasks/activities, environments, and equipment/technologies. It is also concerned with the design of training programs and instructional materials that support the performance of tasks or the use of technology/equipment.

The focus of human factors is on how people interact with tasks, with equipment/technologies, and with the environment, in order to understand and evaluate these interactions. The goals of human factors are to optimize human and system efficiency and effectiveness, safety, health, comfort, and quality of life. To date, there has been only limited application of human factors knowledge and methods to health care in the home. This report is designed to call attention to the resulting missed opportunities and the great potential advantages of bringing a human factors approach into the center of planning for high-quality and safe home health care.

In this chapter, we discuss some of the tools and methods of human factors and how their application could improve the design and implementation of home health care.

A HUMAN FACTORS MODEL

Figure 3-1 presents a model of the human factors of health care in the home, based on a systems approach (e.g., Lawton and Nahemow, 1973; Meister, 1989; Czaja et al., 2001; Czaja and Nair, 2006). The components of this system are the person(s) involved in health management (e.g., care recipients and caregivers), the tasks in which they are engaged (e.g., blood glucose monitoring, assistance with activities of daily living), the equipment/technology that they are using to perform these tasks (e.g., blood glucose meter, computer, lifting device), and the environments in which these interactions occur (physical, social, community, and policy environments).

As depicted in the model, people have different characteristics, skills/abilities, education, health conditions, preferences, and attitudes that they

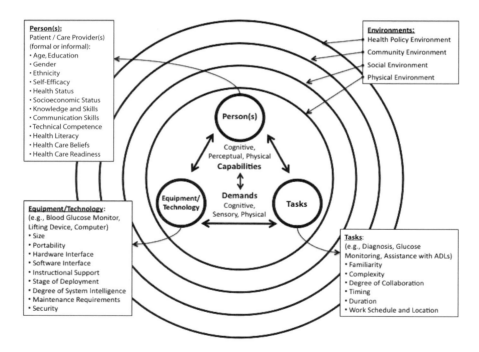

FIGURE 3-1 Model of human factors of health care in the home.
SOURCE: Czaja and Nair [adapted from Czaja et al. (2001)].

bring to the home health care experience. As a result, they vary with respect to their cognitive, perceptual, and physical capabilities with which to interact with tasks and equipment/technology. Interactions are represented by the double arrows in the model. Tasks and equipment/technology also have different characteristics. The type and magnitude of cognitive, sensory, and physical demands placed on people by these tasks and equipment/technology vary and are directly related to personal capabilities. The multiple environments in which the person(s), tasks, and equipment/technology reside interact with each other and are represented by overlapping circles in the model. These environments also have different characteristics and place varying enablers and barriers on a person's successful completion of tasks and use of equipment/technology. It is also important to note that systems are dynamic and the attributes of the people, tasks, equipment/technology, and environments change over time.

A diabetes management example can be used to illustrate the model. In this case, we examine the interactions involved when an older man with diabetes uses a glucometer in his home to track his glucose level with the goal of maintaining his serum blood glucose within recommended limits in order to prevent complications. The man performing the task may have low health literacy, visual problems, and some mild cognitive impairment, and his caregiver may be his wife, who is close to him in age. The person components of the interactions may also include a nurse at a distant clinic who monitors the medical data of the care recipient via telemonitoring[1] and a nurse and home health aide who visit weekly to check on the general health status of the care recipient, measure his vital signs, and assist with personal care. In terms of tasks, the man may be required to monitor his glucose according to a prescribed protocol. Both he and his wife may take several medications on varying schedules. The wife may need to help her husband with various activities and operate the telemonitoring equipment. Use of both the glucometer and the telemonitoring equipment requires the ability to read labels and displays, operate controls, calibrate the equipment, and understand and remember operating procedures. The environment also plays an important role. In this case, the couple may live in a small apartment in a rural location with unreliable Internet access. However, they may have neighbors who check on them and children who visit regularly. A basic tenet of human factors is that "optimization" of this system requires understanding the characteristics of and interactions among *all* of the components of the system. As illustrated in this example, even relatively modest home health care systems can be complex and may

---

[1]Telemonitoring may involve a personal computer with Internet or e-mail connectivity to send data electronically to the clinic.

involve several people who must interact with a variety of technologies to perform an array of tasks.

Ultimately, the interactions and the degree of "fit" among each of these system components influence the efficiency, effectiveness, and safety of the system and the degree to which the goals of the system can be met. In this example, if the fit is adequate, the man's diabetes will be successfully managed and he will be able to remain at home. If the fit is poor, he may develop complications that require him be hospitalized. This would increase his risk for comorbidities, such as infection, and also result in a dramatic increase in the cost of care. Misfits among system components may occur at a number of points in the system interactions. For example, the man may not be able to adhere to his medication schedule. He and his wife may have problems using the glucometer and become frustrated and so discontinue using it. They also may have difficulty communicating such problems to caregivers and/or medical providers. The nurse may not be able to adequately monitor the husband's progress due to problems with the telemonitoring technology or Internet access in the neighborhood. The home health aide may not have adequate training or may be frustrated and/or stressed because of her workload or difficulties accessing the couple's home. Clearly this is a complex system with many risks for misfit or failure. These risks could be avoided or minimized and the chances for success maximized with the integration of human factors considerations into the design of the system.

HUMAN FACTORS METHODS

Research Methods

Human factors specialists often engage in research to gain a basic understanding of or new knowledge about people and behavior. As with other disciplines, they use a variety of research methods that range from highly controlled laboratory experiments, to less controlled observational studies in real-world contexts, to simulation and modeling. When engaging in research, they also use a variety of data collection techniques that include objective measurement of performance or physiological indices; subjective ratings of satisfaction, comfort, or workload; observational checklists; and interview methods. As with any discipline, the research method chosen and the type of data collected depend on the nature of the problem and other issues, such as feasibility, cost, and time constraints.

For example, in order to design cognitive aids to support the ability of people to engage in Internet-based health information seeking, it is important to understand the cognitive abilities that are required to perform this task successfully. This would typically involve conducting research in a laboratory setting to investigate the relationship between cognition and information-seeking performance. The research protocol is likely to entail assessing the cognitive abilities of study participants using standard measures of cognition; having the participants perform a sample set of health information search tasks; asking the participants to rate the level of difficulty of the tasks and identify the sources of difficulty; and examining the relationship between the measures of cognition and measures of performance (e.g., task duration or errors). Another example is an observational study, in which the goal is to understand if the prevalence of Internet-based health information seeking varies among age or ethnic subgroups. In this case, telephone or mail surveys or real-time tracking of Internet behavior might be used to gather the needed information. Sometimes the information gathered about behavior is used to develop mathematical models or simulations, which can then be used in the design of tasks or technologies. For example, biomechanical models are often used to evaluate or compare physical demands of tasks or environments. These models might be used to predict the amount of stress on the spines of caregivers to help in the design or selection of mechanical aids for transferring care recipients from a bed to a wheelchair or shower.

System Design and Evaluation

User-Centered Design

Optimally, human factors methods and principles are involved in all aspects of the design process, including the predesign analysis, design expression and prototyping, testing, and evaluation (see Figure 3-2). Human factors methods should also be employed in the evaluation of existing systems and system elements, for example, the evaluation of emergency room protocols after some highly consequential errors, such as patient safety violations, occur, or as part of official "postmarket surveillance" activities required by the U.S. Food and Drug Administration for some medical devices on the market.

Human factors specialists use a variety of methods to support the design process. The overriding principle is to center the design process on the person or persons in the system; in other words, human factors practitioners adopt a user-centered design approach. User-centered design, as a design philosophy, has been around for several decades (e.g., Norman and Draper, 1986; Norman, 1988; Morales, Casper, and Brennan, 2007) and has been shown to increase user safety, performance, efficiency and effectiveness, cost-effectiveness, and user satisfaction. In fact, user-centered design has been elevated to a standard (International Organization for Standardization, 2010 [ISO 9241-210:2010]).

Generally, user-centered design involves understanding user needs, task/

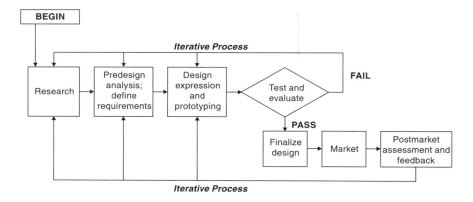

FIGURE 3-2 Conceptual model of the design process.

activity flows and environments, focusing early and continually on users, basing the design of the user interface on known human behavior principles, usability testing and empirical measurement, participatory design in which users are actively involved throughout the process (Wickens et al., 2004), and iterative design.

The term "iterative" applied to the design process refers to the fact that the process should not be a one-way linear progression from concept to product. As needs are determined and design features conceptualized, it is useful to develop prototypes of the design at each point in its development and to test these prototypes with the intended user population. Often the information gained from such prototyping and testing will need to be fed back to inform changes in design that will improve the product or system. This repeated prototyping, testing, and revisiting of the design, shown by the recursive arrows in Figure 3-2, is the best way to ensure good fit with user needs, expectations, and capabilities. Even after the product or system is marketed, it is useful to solicit and analyze feedback on it from users to inform updates or new designs.[2]

User and Environment Analyses

The design of a system or equipment/technology generally begins with an analysis of the potential user groups (which may include care recipients, informal and formal caregivers, and professional health care providers) to understand their characteristics, needs, preferences, and goals with respect

---

[2]A more extensive description of prototyping and some of its uses can be found in National Research Council (2007, pp. 235-239).

to a system/device. The user-needs analysis usually includes such characteristics as age, education, gender, culture and ethnicity, physical and cognitive abilities, relevant skills, language, and literacy, among others. It also involves descriptions of the users' needs and preferences, goals, and past experiences. Gathering this information might involve conducting interviews with potential users to understand their goals and objectives with respect to a particular system or system component, such as a device, where it will be used, how often it will be used, experiences with similar devices, etc. It is important to recognize that, for health care in the home, the users are heterogeneous and include people who engage in self-care or receive care and both lay and professional caregivers who vary widely in their skills, abilities, and characteristics (see Chapter 2).

It is also important to gather information on the characteristics of the environment in which the system/device will be used. As noted in Figure 3-1, the environment is multifaceted and not restricted to its physical characteristics. Thus, information should be gathered on all aspects of the environment relevant to the system/device: the immediate physical environment (e.g., home, work, school, travel), the social environment (e.g., family, friends, colleagues, neighbors), the community environment (e.g., weather, sidewalks, parks, shops, transportation), and policy environments (e.g., building codes, social services, insurance policies, reimbursement mechanisms; see Chapter 6).

Task Analysis

Task analysis is a fundamental method in human factors and is used in the design of systems, devices/technologies, training protocols, instruction manuals, jobs or activities, and activity environments. It is also used in the evaluation of existing systems to help identify design problems and sources of mismatches between system demands and user-group capabilities. The basic elements of a task analysis include defining the task or activities that a person will be performing, dividing these activities into subtasks or steps, and specifying the sensory/perceptual, cognitive, and physical demands associated with these subtasks (Chapanis, 1996). It also typically involves identifying the equipment/technology that may be involved in the performance of these activities and the demands associated with the environment in which the activities will occur. The results of task analyses are typically used to develop system requirements for the design/redesign of systems, as well as to develop checklists, training procedures, and performance aids (see Chapter 4).

A task analysis begins with a "task description," which involves a description of the overall system objectives and of the tasks/activities required by the person to meet these objectives and the linkages among these tasks. Following the task description, the task demands for each task level, whether they are physical, sensory/perceptual, cognitive, social, or emotional, are specified. These demands are then compared with the capabilities of the planned user population to determine where errors and inefficiencies are likely to arise. The result is a list of potential mismatches keyed to each task and subtask, which is the basis for deriving design requirements for a usable system.

The current standard task analysis methodology is hierarchical task analysis (HTA), although many methods are available. HTA starts from system goals and uses a systematic goal decomposition methodology until a sufficient level of detail is reached to solve the problem at hand. The result of the analysis is generally a hierarchical structure that can be represented either graphically or in an outline-like formatted table that organizes tasks as sets of actions used to accomplish higher level goals. Chapter 4 presents several examples of this methodology.

In health care, many tasks, especially those relying on the use of technology, draw heavily on cognitive capabilities with users required to receive, understand, evaluate, and act on information. For these, one might perform a cognitive task analysis, which can be conceptualized as task analysis applied to the cognitive domain. In this case the demands focus on the knowledge structures (e.g., domain knowledge of a disease or medications, basic knowledge of information-seeking strategies) and the cognitive processes (e.g., working memory, reasoning) that underlie decisions that must be made by the person. Often, the analysis is performed by assuming a computational model of the relevant cognitive processes, and the specific analysis approaches depend on the model adopted.

Many techniques are used for the collection of task data, including observation, interviews, questionnaires, and review of instruction manuals. A task analysis might also involve the use of verbal or "think-aloud" protocols, in which people are asked to verbalize what they are doing and the steps they are taking when engaging in a task or an activity or immediately on completion of that activity (National Research Council, 2007). The human factors literature is often used to find the range of capabilities in the appropriate population to compare with the task demands. The success of task analysis applied to health care in the home depends on the analyst's human factors expertise, domain knowledge regarding health care and health management in the home, accurate knowledge and descriptions of activities and activity requirements, and knowledge of user capabilities and other characteristics.

Usability Testing

A critical human factors method that is particularly appropriate for the design of components of health care systems is user testing. These tests may take the form of focus groups or usability testing with early mock-ups or mid-stage prototypes or final system components. Often in usability testing, a variety of prototypes or mock-ups are used. For example, in the early stages of usability testing, two-dimensional representations of a device or user interface (a graphical, nonfunctioning version of a system) or storyboards (that describe in a series of images the steps involved in execution of a task) may be used, whereas working prototype devices or fully interactive systems may be used in later stages of testing. Frequently, especially in software engineering, human factors specialists use iterative prototyping, involving a series of tests with rough prototypes and short revision cycles (National Research Council, 2007).

In usability testing it is important to ensure that the participants are representative of the anticipated user groups and that the data collection techniques capture both the demands associated with the activities they will be performing and the relevant environmental contexts. This is especially important with respect to health care systems for the home, for which the potential user groups are broad and diverse. Failing to understand the appropriate range of user abilities, needs, and preferences and the characteristics of and demands imposed by the tasks, equipment/technologies, and environments often results in technology-centered, rather than user-centered, designs that are much more likely to fail (Norman, 1988; Reason, 1990; Casey, 1993; see medical examples in Morrow, North, and Wickens, 2006, pp. 259-265).

Usability metrics include measures of effectiveness (e.g., percentage of tasks completed, ratio of successes to failures, number of applications or features of a product/device used), efficiency (e.g., time to complete a task, time to learn, number of errors, number of help requests), and user satisfaction (e.g., ratings of usefulness, usability, satisfaction with features, number of times user expresses frustration) (Wickens et al., 2004).

Sources of Human Factors Data

Human factors specialists rely on a variety of sources of information to guide their involvement in the design process. This may initially include review of the existing literature, data compendiums, and design standards and guidelines. Several peer-reviewed journals are devoted to the topic of human factors, including *Human Factors, Human Factors in Manufacturing, Ergonomics, Applied Ergonomics, Ergonomics in Design, International Journal of Industrial Ergonomics, Journal of Cognitive Engineering and*

Design Making, and *Journal of Experimental Psychology: Applied.* Databases that contain information on human capabilities are also available (e.g., Boff and Lincoln, 1988; Boff, Kaufman, and Thomas, 1994; Wickens et al., 2004; Salvendy, 2006; Fisk et al., 2009).

The Human Factors and Ergonomics Society (HFES) offers best practice documents. For example, HFES 300, *Guidelines for Using Anthropometric Data in Product Design,* provides guidance for using data on the dimensions of the human body in the design process. The document provides human dimension data and explains proper techniques for applying these data, which may vary depending on the complexity of the population to be accommodated. The guide describes basic and advanced methods for applying anthropometric data, illustrated with examples, and explains the methods' advantages and disadvantages. The guide includes a long list of resources and references (Human Factors and Ergonomics Society, 2004). In addition, a number of design standards and guidelines are available to guide the design process of medical devices and systems (see Chapter 5).

APPLICATION OF HUMAN FACTORS

Human factors methods and knowledge can be applied to any stage of design or implementation of a system. This includes the initial design of systems and system components to avoid problems and deficiencies, as well as the diagnosis and identification of problems with existing systems. Thus, the concepts and methods of human factors have broad applicability to health care in the home.

For example, human factors techniques can be applied to the design of health care equipment and technologies, such as medication dispensers, glucometers, nebulizers, blood pressure monitors, telemedicine technologies, and software interfaces for Internet health applications. These techniques can also be applied to the design of instruction manuals and training programs to ensure that individuals or their caregivers have the information and skills they need to operate equipment and perform health care tasks. Human factors techniques can be used to inform the design of a home environment to ensure that lighting, layout, and space are adequate for the tasks being performed or the design of a neighborhood to help ensure that there is adequate and effective signage. Human factors approaches are also relevant to the design of jobs for health care workers. For example, human factors methods can be used to determine workflow, to coordinate work, to maintain scheduling and communication protocols, and to determine work requirements to ensure worker productivity, safety, and health. Human factors can have input into the broader organizational environment to help design and implement safety programs, certification protocols, or program evaluation methods.

Human factors techniques can also be used to help understand the sources of human errors and safety violations in the health care domain. In fact, the goals of human factors are commensurate with the goals stated in the report *Crossing the Quality Chasm* (Institute of Medicine, 2001) for health system reform: safety, effectiveness, patient-centeredness, timeliness, efficiency, and equality. There are numerous examples in the health care domain in which the application of human factors has resulted in reduced errors and cost, increased safety, efficiency, and effectiveness, and personal satisfaction. These examples include efforts to enhance safety and reduce medical errors (e.g., Karsh et al., 2006), medication management (e.g., Lin, Vincente, and Doyle, 2001; Murray et al., 2007), communication among health care providers (e.g., Donchin et al., 2003; Leonard, Graham, and Bonacum, 2004), and the workflow of health care workers (e.g., Carayon and Gurses, 2005). Human factors methods have also been applied to the design of medical equipment and devices (e.g., Lin et al., 1998; Ginsburg, 2005), technology systems to support health management (e.g., Czaja, Sharit, and Nair, 2008; Sharit et al., 2008), and environments in which health care occurs (e.g., Donchin et al., 2003).

From a human factors perspective, optimization of a system's effectiveness and reduction of adverse outcomes require that all of the components of a system be considered in the design process. This is in contrast to a more traditional reductionist approach, which focuses on one component of a system in isolation from the other components. Using a traditional approach, the focus is typically on the physical or technical components of a system, with little regard for the human. For example, glucometer or medication instructions may be designed without considering how the persons using these instructions might vary in terms of age, cognitive and sensory capabilities, English literacy, health literacy, or stage of illness acceptance.

If there is a mismatch between an individual's capabilities and those required to perform a task, it is likely that the individual will fail to complete that task successfully or will make errors that may pose a threat to health and well-being. For example, such errors could include lapses in performing health promotion and disease prevention behaviors, not adhering to a prescribed treatment, ignoring warning signs of complications, and not sharing important information about health history, symptoms, or response to treatment with caregivers. Other examples include potentially life-threatening events, such as misreading output from health monitoring equipment, altering equipment settings, turning off alarms, sustaining injuries due to poor body mechanics during lifting and transfers, or continuing intravenous (IV) antibiotic infusion in a person who is showing signs of allergic reaction.

There are many types of human error, and the causes and consequences of these errors vary. Although some errors may be inconsequential, others may result in preventable disease (i.e., physical or psychological illness or injury), inadequate disease detection and treatment (i.e., too little, too much, or too late), poor symptom control, development of complications, excessive use of health resources, long-term disability, psychological distress, and even death. Some errors and their consequences are preventable via good device or environmental design, whereas others must be handled through procedural or administrative solutions or through user education and training.

In general, optimal system design and error prevention require knowledge about the people, tasks, technologies/equipment, and environments that are involved in the system. They also require knowledge of whether the fit among these system elements is adequate.

In summary, applying human factors knowledge and techniques to the design of health care systems intended for use in the home can make the systems safer, more effective, and more efficient. By optimizing the relationships among the people, the health care tasks and technologies, and the environments in which health care occurs and ensuring that the demands placed on users by the system are within those individuals' capabilities, these goals can be achieved.

REFERENCES

Boff, K.R., Kaufman, L., and Thomas, J. (1994). *Handbook of perception and human performance. Volume II. Cognitive processes and performance.* New York: John Wiley and Sons. Available: http://www.dtic.mil/cgi-bin/GetTRDoc?AD=ADA289587&Location=U2&doc=GetTRDoc.pdf [April 2011].

Boff, K.R., and Lincoln, J.E. (1988). *Engineering data compendium of human perception and performance. Volume 1.* Available: http://www.dtic.mil/cgi-bin/GetTRDoc?AD=ADB345187&Location=U2&doc=GetTRDoc.pdf [April 2011].

Carayon, P., and Gurses, A. (2005). Nursing workload and patient safety in intensive care units: A human factors engineering evaluation of the literature. *Intensive and Critical Care Nursing, 21,* 284-301.

Casey, S. (1993). *Set phasers on stun, and other true tales of design, technology, and human error* (2nd ed.). Santa Barbara, CA: Aegean.

Chapanis, A. (1996). *Human factors in systems engineering.* New York: John Wiley and Sons.

Czaja, S.J., and Nair, S.N. (2006). Human factors engineering and systems design. In G. Salvendy (Ed.), *Handbook of human factors and ergonomics* (3rd ed). New York: John Wiley and Sons.

Czaja, S.J., Sharit, J., Charness, N., and Fisk, A.D. (2001). The Center for Research and Education on Aging and Technology Enhancement (CREATE): A program to enhance technology for older adults. *Gerontechnology, 1,* 50-59.

Czaja, S.J., Sharit, J., and Nair, S.N. (2008). Usability of the Medicare health web site. *Journal of the American Medical Association, 300,* 790.

Donchin, Y., Gopher, D., Olin, M., et al. (2003). A look into the nature and causes of human errors in the intensive care unit, 1995. *Quality & Safety in Health Care, 12*(2), 143-147.

Fisk, A.D., Rogers, W., Charness, N., Czaja, S.J., and Sharit, J. (2009). *Designing for older adults: Principles and creative human factors approaches* (2nd ed.). Boca Raton, FL: CRC Press.

Ginsburg, G. (2005). Human factors engineering: A tool for medical device evaluation in hospital procurement decision-making. *Journal of Biomedical Informatics, 38*(3), 213-219.

Human Factors and Ergonomics Society. (2004). *Guidelines for using anthropometric data in product design.* Santa Monica, CA: Author.

Institute of Medicine. (2001). *Crossing the quality chasm: A new health system for the 21st century.* Committee on the Quality of Health Care in America. Washington, DC: National Academy Press.

International Ergonomics Association. (2010). *What is ergonomics?* Available: http://www.iea.cc/01_what/What%20is%20Ergonomics.html [March 30, 2011].

International Organization for Standardization. (2010). ISO 9241-210:2010 *Ergonomics of human-system interaction Part 210: Human-centered design for interactive systems.* Available: http://www.iso.org/iso/iso_catalogue/catalogue_tc/catalogue_detail.htm?csnumber=52075 [April 2011].

Karsh, B., Holden, R., Alper, S.J., and Or, C.K.L. (2006). A human factors engineering paradigm for patient safety—Designing to support the performance of the health care professional. *Quality and Safety in Health Care, 15*(Suppl I), i59-i65.

Lawton, M.P., and Nahemow, L. (1973). Ecology and the aging process. In C. Eisdorfer and M.P. Lawton (Eds.), *The psychology of adult development and aging.* Washington, DC: American Psychological Association.

Leonard, M., Graham S., and Bonacum, D. (2004). The human factor: The critical importance of effective teamwork and communication in providing safe care. *Quality and Safety in Health Care, 13*(Suppl 1), i85-i90.

Lin, L., Isla, R., Doniz, K., Harkness, H., Vicente, K.J., and Doyle, D.J. (1998). Applying human factors to the design of medical equipment: Patient-controlled analgesia. *Journal of Clinical Monitoring and Computing, 14*(4), 253-263.

Lin, L., Vicente K.J., and Doyle, D.J. (2001). Patient safety, potential adverse drug events, and medical device design: A human factors engineering approach. *Journal of Biomedical Informatics, 34*(4), 274-284.

Meister, D. (1989). *Conceptual aspects of human factors.* Baltimore, MD: Johns Hopkins University Press.

Morales R.M., Casper, G., and Brennan P.F. (2007). Patient-centered design. The potential of user-centered design in personal health records. *Journal of the American Health Information Management Association, 78*(4), 44-46, quiz 49-50.

Morrow, D., North, R., and Wickens, C.D. (2006). Reducing and mitigating human error in medicine. In R. Nickerson (Ed.), *Reviews of human factors and ergonomics, Volume 1* (pp. 254-296). Santa Monica, CA: Human Factors and Ergonomics Society.

Murray, M.D., Young, J., Hoke, S., et al. (2007). Pharmacist intervention to improve medication adherence in heart failure: A randomized trial. *Annals of Internal Medicine, 146*(10), 714-725.

National Research Council. (2007). *Human-system integration in the system development process; A new look.* Committee on Human-System Design Support for Changing Technology, R.W. Pew and A.S. Mavor, Eds. Committee on Human Factors, Division of Behavioral and Social Sciences and Education. Washington, DC: The National Academies Press.

Norman, D.A. (1988). *The psychology of everyday things.* New York: Basic Books.

Norman, D.A., and Draper, S.W. (1986). *User-centered system design: New perspectives on human-computer interaction.* Hillsdale, NJ: Lawrence Erlbaum Associates.

Reason, J. (1990). *Human error.* Cambridge, UK: Cambridge University Press.

Salvendy, G. (2006). *Handbook of human factors and ergonomics* (vol. 3). Hoboken, NJ: John Wiley and Sons.

Sharit, J., Hernández, M.A., Czaja S.J., and Pirolli, P. (2008). Investigating the roles of knowledge and cognitive abilities in older adult information seeking on the web. *ACM Transactions on Computer-Human Interaction, 15*(1), 3.

Wickens, C.D., Gordon, S.E., and Liu, Y. (2004). *An introduction to human factors engineering.* Upper Saddle River, NJ: Pearson Prentice Hall.

4

Health Care Tasks

Tasks involved in caring for oneself or others at home may be quite simple, such as taking brisk walks to promote cardiovascular fitness or applying a wrist splint to relieve discomfort from carpal tunnel syndrome. At the other extreme, health care tasks may be far more complex, such as recovery from major surgery or acclimating to new chronic care regimens. Complex health care tasks often require nuanced understanding of a health condition and its treatment as well as the ability to manage symptoms, detect complications, provide hands-on care, offer emotional support, and communicate effectively with health care providers to participate in decisions and manage logistical aspects of health care.

This chapter describes the wide range of tasks related to health care that, with increasing frequency, take place in the home. It describes the demands of those tasks as well as the varying capabilities of caregivers to handle the task demands. Boxes 4-1 and 4-2 provide family vignettes to illustrate varying task demands as well as capabilities.

The chapter also presents methods of analyzing health-related tasks and suggests how the analytic methods may be modified to suit the special considerations associated with home care. Two variants of task analysis are presented, reflecting human factors approaches that enable identification of the capabilities and information that are necessary for performing specific tasks safely and effectively and the factors related to task execution that may be amenable to intervention. An example of a simplified task analysis is offered to illustrate how use of this technique, even at a basic level, can provide health care system and technology designers, evaluators, and train-

BOX 4-1
The Burns Family

Ray Burns is a 59-year-old maintenance supervisor who quit smoking 2 years ago. Forty pounds overweight, he was recently diagnosed with Type 2 diabetes and sleep apnea. Ray reluctantly uses a CPAP (continuous positive airway pressure) machine at night to control his apnea. He has recently acknowledged that his excess weight and lack of regular exercise are threatening his long-term health, and he is serious about renewing the more disciplined approach to diet and exercise that served him well in his youth. He has joined a weight loss group at work and is learning to make healthier choices, monitor his conditions, follow prescribed treatment, and maintain supplies of medications and batteries, test strips, and tubing for his medical devices. He has settled into a daily routine that includes measuring his blood glucose level at home and during the day at work, downloading each reading onto his computer, and generating a trend report to send by e-mail to his doctor. Ray welcomes the structure and encouragement provided by the weight loss program. By adhering to his current diet and exercise plan, he hopes to eliminate his diabetes medication altogether.

Ray's parents live nearby and are quite frail. Ray's father, Ed, requires constant supervision due to a stroke he sustained 3 years ago. Ed is a tall and stout man who needs assistance with bathing, dressing, walking, and transfers from bed to chair. Because of difficulty swallowing, he requires tube feedings. Ray's mother, Dorothy, is small in stature and has emphysema and severe arthritis, so she can help her husband dress, but she cannot help with more strenuous tasks, like bathing and transferring. Ed and Dorothy receive 6 hours daily of in-home services from the Program for All-inclusive Care of the Elderly (PACE). *Personal care aides help Ed bathe, and an occupational therapist monitors his functional status, oversees his exercise program, and evaluates his use of assistive devices. A nurse recently set up an electronic monitoring system for both Ed and Dorothy, enabling family members and PACE staff to track their medication taking remotely. She is also helping Dorothy use the nebulizer and oxygen concentrator that were recently prescribed. Either Ray or his wife Patricia stops by every day to help with tube feedings and oversee Ed and Dorothy's medication routine.

---

*PACE is a capitated system for delivery of in-home, clinical, and adult day care services to nursing home–eligible older adults living in the community (Mukamel et al., 2007).
SOURCE: Clinical experience of committee member Judith Matthews.

BOX 4-2
The Miller Family

Two weeks ago, Lisa gave birth to a son with a congenital heart defect. Lisa is home now, but the baby remains in a neonatal intensive care unit (NICU) an hour away, recovering from cardiac surgery. Her husband, Tom, took a leave of absence from work and has been at the hospital almost constantly, but Lisa must remain at home because her cesarean incision became infected. The home health nurse who visits for wound care helps her frame questions for the NICU staff, with whom Lisa talks several times a day using a webcam-equipped laptop to see how the baby is doing.

When Lisa first got home from the hospital, she quickly learned from the visiting nurse how to monitor the healing of her cesarean incision, pack the wound, change the dressing, and take her antibiotic as prescribed. To prepare for the baby's eventual discharge from the hospital, she and Tom are trying to learn all they can about his condition, treatment, and prognosis. Luckily, they have been able to access quite a bit of information on the Internet. Using the webcam to see and hear their baby or talk with staff of the NICU keeps them apprised of his status when they cannot be at his side.

Lisa and Tom, initially naive about their infant's heart condition, have learned to ask the NICU staff for more elaborate explanations and to validate the information they have found on the Internet. Lisa keeps a journal chronicling her virtual visits to the NICU as well as Tom's accounts of his visits there. This keeps events from blurring in Lisa's mind, and she thinks it will be helpful for future reference.

SOURCE: Clinical experience of committee member Judith Matthews.

---

ers with critical information to improve the execution of health care and health management tasks in the home.

TYPES OF TASKS

Health-related tasks involve many aspects of daily function, including personal hygiene and nutrition, safety and comfort, physical fitness, sleep quality, stress management, as well as the planning and coordination to accomplish these personal tasks. *Health care–specific tasks* may entail obtaining routine health examinations, screenings, and immunizations, instituting prescribed treatment, monitoring disease progression and treatment response, and implementing personal care or therapeutic regimens that accommodate functional impairment and disability. Table 4-1 outlines some health care tasks in four categories: (1) health maintenance—promoting general health and well-being, preventing disease or disability; (2) episodic care—optimizing outcomes of health events that pertain to pregnancy, childbirth, and mild or acute illness or injury; (3) chronic care—managing ongoing treatment of chronic disease or impairment; and (4) end-of-life care—addressing physical and psychological dimensions of dying.

Health Maintenance

People of all ages are advised to engage in various self-help and self-care behaviors that may enhance their general health and well-being or enable early detection and treatment of disease (Zayas-Cabán and Brennan, 2007). These important behaviors include consuming a balanced diet, being physically active, and getting adequate sleep for one's age or stage of development. Additional personal health habits involve proper hand washing and personal hygiene, appropriate use of vitamin and mineral supplements, adherence to safe sex practices, and avoidance of smoking, illicit drug use, and excessive alcohol consumption. Age- and gender-appropriate physical and oral health examinations, immunizations, and screenings at recommended intervals are disease prevention measures. Using protective gear while driving (e.g., car seats, booster seats, seatbelts, motorcycle helmets), performing hazardous work (e.g., earplugs, headgear, eyewear, clothing, shoes), or engaging in recreational activity (e.g., bicycle helmets, mouth guards, other protective sports gear) is yet another way for people to be proactive about their health.

Activities of Daily Living

Basic activities of daily living (ADLs) are among tasks performed regularly by or for all community-residing individuals. Although this classification of tasks was originally developed to assess independence among persons in institutional settings (The Staff of the Benjamin Rose Hospital, 1959), it is commonly used to describe the functional capabilities of non-institutionalized individuals. ADLs pertain to personal care and include bathing, grooming, dressing, feeding, toileting and continence, ambulation, and transfers (i.e., moving from one surface to another, such as from bed to chair or wheelchair to toilet). Although it is developmentally appropriate for infants and toddlers to require help with ADLs, assistance with these activities may be required by people of any age who have physical, cognitive, sensory/perceptual, or emotional impairments.

TABLE 4-1 Health Care Tasks in the Home

Category	Examples
Health maintenance	Personal hygiene
	Diet and nutrition management
	Vitamin and supplement management
	Exercise regimen
	Stress management
	Sleep management (appropriate for age or stage of development)
	Safe sex practices
	Avoidance of smoking, excessive alcohol consumption, illicit drug use
	Use of protective equipment (e.g., gloves, seat belts, bicycle and motorcycle helmets)
	Regular medical and dental examinations, screenings, immunizations, and care
Episodic care	Medication management for minor illnesses
	First aid provision for minor injuries
	Wound care
	Burn care
	Recovery from serious injuries
	Recovery from major incidents (e.g., heart attack, stroke)
	Recovery from surgeries
	Allergy treatment
	Pregnancy management and postpartum recovery
Chronic care	Diabetes management
	Asthma management
	Apnea management
	Nutritional therapy
	Home infusion therapy
	Respiratory therapy
	Home dialysis
	Chronic obstructive pulmonary disease (COPD) care
	Tracheostomy care
	Decubitus ulcer (pressure sore) care
	Stoma (e.g., colostomy, ileostomy, ureterostomy) care
	Catheterization and related care
	Rehabilitation regimens prescribed by physiatrists or physical, occupational, vocational, or speech therapists
	Psychotherapeutic regimens
End-of-life care	Pain management
	Symptom management
	Care recipient and family counseling

Instrumental Activities of Daily Living

Additional tasks essential to day-to-day living are called the instrumental activities of daily living, or IADLs (Lawton and Brody, 1969). These involve tasks related to independence, including household management, meal preparation, cleaning, laundry, shopping, and handling of personal finances. Performance of these types of household activities may be hampered temporarily or permanently by disabling health conditions.

Care of Injury, Illness, or Impairments

Tasks necessitated by injuries, illnesses, or impairments affect the rhythm of everyday life for millions of people. Some health care tasks are simple and intrude little on normal day-to-day life. Others are highly disruptive, at least temporarily if not permanently, and require clinical competencies that were once strictly within the purview of health care providers in hospitals, clinics, or doctors' offices. These tasks may be anticipated, or they may arise unexpectedly. They may diminish in intensity over time, or they may require prolonged performance.

Whether a father administers phototherapy at home using a bili light to resolve jaundice in his newborn, a mother performs tracheostomy care for her school-age child with bronchopulmonary dysplasia, or a woman empties the drainage tubes extending from her abdominal incision, the people who perform these and other condition-specific health care tasks at home do so for many reasons. Their efforts may be directed toward managing symptoms, controlling or curing disease, or monitoring response to prescribed treatment. The tasks may also involve assessment of possible complications or implementation of elaborate ADL and IADL routines necessitated by severe disability.

Episodic Care

Episodic care is medical treatment needed for a short-term condition, illness, or injury. Episodic care may require care recipients or caregivers to quickly learn care procedures and operation of medical equipment, and it may require temporary home adjustments to adapt to short-term needs or activity limitations. Episodic care does not require long-term lifestyle changes, although, for example after a stroke or heart attack, episodic care may transition to chronic care. Some examples of tasks for episodic care include medication management, pain management, wound and skin care for incisions and lacerations that require cleansing and dressing changes, adherence to standard precautions for infection control (Siegel et al., 2007), sanitation or sterilization of equipment, and performance of physical, occupational, and speech therapies for maintaining or restoring function.

Chronic Care

Chronic care is needed to deal with long-term, ongoing conditions or diseases (e.g., asthma, congestive heart failure, cystic fibrosis, kidney disease, diabetes, impairments) and may require lasting adjustments by all household members. Chronic care is complex, and, in order to be effective and safe, it frequently requires careful planning. It often requires learning and continuing to perform new procedures and equipment operation. It may require both the care recipient and others in the household to make long-term changes in lifestyle (e.g., diet, exercise, activities of daily living, household responsibilities) and to continuously monitor the care recipient's condition. It also is likely to require the care recipient and informal caregivers to establish and maintain effective long-term relationships with professional caregivers. Chronic care is often more challenging and stressful than episodic care because of its greater effects on daily living and its continuing burden.

Although many of the tasks mentioned above for episodic care exist for chronic care, such care often requires regular sustained tasks and tasks involving medical devices. Some examples of tasks for chronic care include provision of nutritional support delivered enterally (e.g., via a nasogastric or gastrostomy tube into the stomach or via a jejunostomy tube into the small intestine) or parenterally (i.e., intravenously); intravenous infusion therapies (e.g., prescription medication, fluid replacement, Epogen therapy, and blood products); care required for oxygen and other respiratory therapies, including cleaning and storage of equipment (e.g., oxygen tanks and concentrators, nebulizers, positive airway pressure [CPAP and BiPAP] masks and machines); management of mechanical ventilation equipment; tracheostomy care and suctioning for removal of airway secretions; care for a stoma (e.g., colostomy, ileostomy, ureterostomy) and the apparatus used to collect body waste (i.e., feces or urine); diapering, enema administration, clean catheterization, or indwelling or suprapubic catheter care; management of continuous vacuum drainage systems; and implementation of psychotherapeutic regimens.

End-of-Life Care

The term "end-of-life care" is applicable only when it is known (at least to the caregivers) that the care recipient is dying, and care is provided in the context of this knowledge. This care is often palliative, designed to maintain the care recipient's comfort and reduce pain and distress, although in some cases active treatment is continued. Many of the tasks of end-of-life care are the same as those of chronic care, but the conditions under which they are performed are different. The caregivers must provide care under the emotional burden of knowledge that death is approaching, and difficult decisions about treatment must often be made. Unique tasks include counseling of the family and the care recipient.

Coordination of Care

Tasks for coordinating care are logistical in nature: scheduling medical or dental appointments, arranging for transportation, ordering prescriptions and other medical supplies, renting or purchasing medical equipment, arranging for pick-up or delivery of supplies or equipment, managing health-related finances, and maintaining personal health records. In addition, informal caregivers must interact, to varying degrees, with physicians and other health care professionals about care recipient status and care needs, hire nurses and aides, communicate and negotiate with other family members about care decisions, and provide companionship and emotional support to recipients. Informal caregivers are also called on to coordinate services from various health and human service agencies and make decisions about service needs and how to access them (Bookman and Harrington, 2007).

Skills for Coordinating

Attending to personal health at home requires skills for garnering resources, organizing health care tasks, and communicating effectively with the other people involved (in person, by telephone, or by some electronic means). In contrast to clinical environments in which health care management is largely the province of health care providers, primary responsibility for managing health care at home is borne by care recipients or their family members. Some people manage care systematically and are articulate when dealing with their health, whereas others are disorganized and communicate poorly. Moreover, people who handle other aspects of daily life quite well may find it difficult, at least initially, to transfer these skills to their handling of health matters at home.

Coordinating services needed to support care recipients in the home or as they transition from one care setting to another is particularly challenging for caregivers (Levine et al., 2010). Even seasoned health professionals with detailed knowledge of and experience with health care systems find care coordination for family members a formidable challenge (Kane, Preister, and Totten, 2005). The intensity of tasks associated with coordination of care has been described as contributing to a blurring of the boundaries between informal and professional caregivers, as family members begin to assume professional attitudes toward the care of their loved ones to ensure their needs are best met (Allen and Ciambrone, 2003).

Formal Caregivers as Role Models

Formal caregivers often demonstrate and supervise repeated practice of proper techniques for previously untrained persons. Personnel in home visiting programs routinely show individuals and members of their households how to modify daily living activities to accommodate functional limitations, perform medical procedures or therapies, watch for changes in health status, and troubleshoot clinical or technical problems that arise. Formal caregivers expend considerable effort bolstering the health management capabilities of persons who care for themselves or provide assistance to others as informal caregivers. They do so by offering guidance and encouragement while modeling and reinforcing behaviors, thereby enabling persons without prior health training to anticipate, prevent, or address health-related problems on their own. By observing formal caregivers communicating with others on their behalf, care recipients and informal caregivers can gain confidence in their own ability to coordinate care among providers.

TASK DEMANDS ON CAPABILITIES

The array of tasks performed as part of health care as well as daily living involves many domains of human capability. Indeed, embedded in these health-related tasks are myriad subtasks that place demands on the physical, cognitive, sensory/perceptual, emotional, and communication capabilities of those performing them and require flexibility in execution. The examples here illustrate how multiple domains of human capability may be activated simultaneously in accomplishing even seemingly simple tasks, such as bathing, check writing, and taking medication as well as caring for surgical incisions at home.

Bathing independently involves multiple actions that require balance, strength, and flexibility for coordinated movement of the limbs and trunk, especially for quick recovery from slips or trips on hard and wet surfaces. It requires executive cognitive function and psychomotor skills that enable performance of each step in logical sequence and with insight into one's limitations and risk of falling, thus underscoring the important interaction among the person, the environment, and the bathing task itself (Murphy, Gretebeck, and Alexander, 2007).

Although often mundane and influenced by cultural expectations for role and gender, IADLs are actually quite complex and require capabilities in several domains. For example, bill paying goes well beyond the physical act of paying with cash or credit card, writing a check in the correct amount, or making a payment online. It requires capabilities in the cognitive domain (organizing bills received, remembering to pay them when due, interpreting invoice information, computing balances, and determining whether sufficient funds are available), the physical domain (manipulating the cash, check, credit card, or electronic device used for payment), the sensory/perceptual domain (seeing and reading statements for the bill and source of funds for payment), and the communication domain (dealing with vendors and account representatives in person, online, in writing, or by phone).

Taking medication, whether prescribed by licensed health professionals or self-prescribed, is among the most common health care behaviors performed by individuals of all ages. For many people, adhering to a medication regimen is difficult, often due to its complexity or inconvenient timing, or as a result of simple forgetfulness, belief that the regimen lacks therapeutic benefit (Osterberg and Blaschke, 2005), or cognitive decline (Stilley et al., 2010). Successful medication taking involves the correct person receiving the correct dose administered using the appropriate technique at the right time under the proper conditions (e.g., with food, while sitting up, or before cleansing and dressing a painful wound). Medications may enter the body in various ways—by topical application, oral or rectal administration, subcutaneous or intramuscular injection, inhalation, or peripheral or central venous infusion, among others. Lippa, Klein, and Shalin (2008) provide an example of the cognitive complexity of self-management of diabetes, including discussion of medication management and other tasks. Thus, psychomotor skills, as well as adequate vision, tactile sensation, knowledge, memory, and judgment, are needed to administer medications safely and effectively, regardless of who performs the task.

Caring for a surgical incision at home following a total knee replacement is an example of an episodic care task that involves many capability domains. This task can be divided into many subtasks that include placing wound dressing supplies and a trash receptacle within reach, washing hands before and after the procedure, positioning the knee for full view of the wound, donning gloves, removing and disposing of the soiled dressing, cleansing the incision, applying fresh bandages, wrapping the knee with gauze to secure the dressing in place, and, finally, removing the gloves and disposing of them properly (physical capabilities). In addition to these psychomotor skills, sufficient health literacy is needed to understand the care instructions, follow the steps involved in changing the dressing in proper sequence, gauge whether healing is occurring as expected, and solve any problems that arise (cognitive capabilities). Vision is needed to inspect the incision for signs of infection and healing, and touch and smell enable detection of excessive warmth, swelling, or foul odor that may indicate infection or poor healing (sensory/perceptual capabilities). Stress imposed by emotional or physical discomfort, limited mobility, disruption in usual routines, and uncertainty about return to normal function activates one's repertoire of coping strategies (emotional capabilities), and the ability to report progress or concerns to health care providers (communication capabilities) may influence the rate and course of recuperation.

APPLYING A HUMAN FACTORS APPROACH

The diversity of persons engaged in health care in the home and the heterogeneity of health-related tasks performed in the context of home and family present many challenges for achieving an ideal fit between task demands and human capabilities. When task demands exceed an individual's physical, cognitive, emotional, sensory/perceptual, or communication ability to perform the task, the potential for adverse outcomes increases. Identifying precisely where mismatches exist—that is, where there is lack of fit between what is required to perform safe, efficient, and effective care and the capabilities of the people who provide that care—makes possible the crafting of a plan for tailored intervention. Such a plan could include hands-on training, assistive devices, additional caregivers, and use of various printed, audiovisual, or interactive (telehealth) tools that provide guided prompting or access to professional and peer support. Human factors approaches can help delineate where targeted intervention can enable safer and more efficient and effective task completion.

In order to reduce the probability of errors and improve the efficiency of care, it is first necessary to assess both the task demands and the capabilities of the individuals performing the tasks to determine where potential mismatches occur and, second, to design the system or the processes to reduce the mismatch.

Assessment Tools

A number of tools are available for assessing functional capabilities of individuals, providing objective data to assist with targeting individualized rehabilitation needs or planning for specific in-home services, such as meal preparation, nursing care, homemaker services, personal care, or continuous supervision. These functional assessment tools are often used by clinicians to focus on a person's baseline capabilities, facilitating early recognition of changes that may signify a need either for additional resources or for a medical work-up (Gallo and Paveza, 2006). In research, these tools are frequently used to describe sample characteristics or to enable longitudinal evaluation of the impact of a disease or treatment on functional status.

One such instrument is the Lawton Instrumental Activities of Daily Living Scale, which is typically used to assess independent living skills among adults and measures eight domains of function (Lawton and Brody, 1969). Another functional assessment tool used to measure capacity to execute basic activities of daily living in the adult population is the Katz Index of ADLs (Katz et al., 1970; Katz, 1983), which assesses level of performance in six functions: bathing, dressing, toileting, transferring, continence, and feeding. Additional tools exist for measuring the functional status of children, particularly relative to their capacity and readiness for learning.

A number of other clinical and research tools exist that permit assessment, in general, of individuals' cognitive and physical function, emotional status, and level of preparedness for the health care and health management tasks they need to assume. An important limitation of all these measures, including those of ADL and IADL capabilities, is that they commonly do not evaluate the extent of correspondence between specific capabilities of the individual and the capabilities needed to perform each of the specific tasks and subtasks required for managing his or her health at home. Gaining a more nuanced appreciation of the specific capabilities required for specific tasks or subtasks is needed, and human factors offers established techniques for accomplishing this objective.

Application of Task Analysis

Task analysis, as explained in the following sections, involves human factors methodology developed for this purpose. Although comprehensive description of all task analysis techniques is beyond the scope of this chapter, the goal here is to illustrate the usefulness and importance of the task analysis approach.

The effectiveness in executing a given task—that is, low error rate and high efficiency—for most health-related activities at home is predicated on the condition that the capabilities of the individual, or actor, performing the task meet or exceed those demanded by the task. Any discrepancy must be mitigated by one of several solutions, including training the users, deploying individuals with greater capabilities, or introducing technology or other changes to transform a demanding task into an easier one requiring lower levels of user capability. Improving the skills of individuals or their caregivers may not always be feasible, but technology or task redesign can simplify a task or reduce the need for special skills. Technology can support tasks that are otherwise difficult to perform or minimize the probability of errors and adverse events.

Overview of Task Analysis

Task analysis is a tool used in human factors engineering to help optimize the functioning of a system. In order to develop specifications for viable systems or procedures, it is important to understand the demands of the tasks as well as potential pitfalls that may lead to adverse situations. The purpose of task analysis is to identify the prerequisites, demands, resources, workflow issues, and potential error-prone situations involved in execution of a task. Task analysis comprises a collection of formal methods that enable systematic analysis of the actions and interactions involved in order to minimize omission of specific steps and the potential for erroneous actions.

Development of the task analysis methodology was initially motivated by the need for formal human factors methods in industry and the military, for which the value of maximizing safety and performance is particularly high. In aviation, nuclear plants, or military operations, failures in task execution by humans and machines can lead to catastrophic effects (Fitts and Jones, 1947). Task analysis has since been extended to a variety of applications, ranging from health care to computer interfaces (Dix et al., 2004). The results of these analyses are typically used to develop system requirements for the design or redesign of systems, and also to develop checklists and training procedures. For example, task analysis has been used to study system interactions with people who have physical or cognitive impairments, and the results of the analysis have been used to develop training programs tailored to the needs of these individuals. Currently, the success of task analysis applied to health care in the home depends on the analyst's human factors expertise, domain knowledge regarding health care and health management at home, understanding of tasks and task demands, and direct experience with task performance (Drury, 2010).

A typical task analysis process has three stages: (1) acquisition of information, (2) analysis of the data, and (3) development of a representation of the results that can be used to guide the design of devices, processes, or selection of personnel.

Gathering data enables the analyst to break the task into its components and characterize each of these in turn. Task analysis conducted with any degree of rigor first entails developing descriptions of the tasks based on use cases, or scenarios, such as that depicting the Burns family in this chapter (see Box 4-1). The task description specifies the objective to be achieved by performing the task, what is required of the actor (task demands) regardless of who performs it, the system or environmental feedback resulting from task performance, and the interrelationship among subtasks. It further specifies where errors and inefficiencies are likely to occur when capabilities fall short of task demands. There are two general approaches to data acquisition: (1) empirical observations and (2) logical decomposition of the task objectives and characterization of any available contextual information. In general, the most complete and reliable task analysis process relies to some extent on both approaches if empirical data are available. If any of the tasks cannot be performed without use of some type of technology and the technology is not available for task observation, then the analysis may be based entirely on the logical approach or on observation of the task performance on a similar system or on a prototype. In these situations, the task analysis results will inform the subsequent design of technological solutions.

Task Analysis and Home Health Care

Classification of tasks is an important component of both the task analysis process and the development of solutions, and it supports two goals: (1) systematically classifying and creating an ontology of tasks usually leads to more complete sets of tasks and (2) determining similarity among tasks suggests the possibility of finding similarity among solutions. The first formal step in the analysis of the needs and requirements of persons managing health care at home is to identify the critical tasks that are required to maintain independence and maximize quality of life. Several studies have deployed empirical approaches to determine sets of tasks that are important to different populations at home (Clark and Rakowski, 1983; Wilkins, Bruce, and Sirey, 2009). The set of tasks identified by each study generally depended on the specific goals of the study, as well as on the populations evaluated and other factors. The different lists comprise tasks that vary in level of detail. These lists informed the taxonomy shown in Table 4-1.

Given the diversity of health care that occurs in the home, an analyst must consider a wide range of situations. Even if a particular intervention is designed for a caregiver who is present with the care recipient, the task analysis process must consider the possibility of remote caregivers' involvement as well. Remote caregivers, such as adult children who live far from aging parents, may play key roles in care coordination, socialization, and many other aspects of care. Advances in technology present increasing opportunities for remote caregivers to provide support to individuals at home (see Chapter 5).

Although the general approach in task analysis is agnostic as to who performs the task (Drury, 2010), in the domain of health care in the home the specific components of the tasks may depend on the particular actor, or person performing the task. For example, the task of bathing another person, as might be performed by a parent caring for an adult child recovering from a traumatic injury, would be different from the task of bathing oneself. Thus, for many tasks in the home care domain, it is necessary to consider task demands in relation to the capabilities of the specific actor who performs the task. This actor may be an individual capable of self-care, an individual in need of assistance (care recipient), an informal caregiver (on-site or remote), a formal caregiver (on-site or remote), or some combination of these.

Another important aspect of tasks that needs to be considered in the task analysis process for home care involves estimates of the utility of specific tasks. In contrast to a typical industrial situation in which task utilities are frequently implicit, in the home situation, not all health-related tasks competing for resources are equally important. For example, some tasks are essential for survival, whereas other tasks merely enhance quality of life. Determination of utility is important for resource allocation and prioritization of different tasks. In a resource-limited situation, the more critical tasks must be performed first. When safety and accurate decision making rather than resource scarcity are at issue, greater emphasis needs to be placed on subtasks that are critical.

The empirical approach to task analysis can include observational studies, questionnaires, analysis of errors, or any combination of these. A simple task analysis of medical device use may include identification of the subtasks involved in performance of a task (i.e., task decomposition), the information required by the user to complete each, the feedback that the device or environment provides, and the potential problems that could arise if the task were not carried out properly. For example, Rogers et al. (2001) performed a task analysis of using a blood glucose meter, which found that setting up and checking the meter and testing blood involved 52 subtasks; Table 4-2 lists only the 10 subtasks associated with using the lancing device. The analysis showed that many of these subtasks required knowledge of how to handle the device and knowledge of correct procedures for lancing a finger. This result suggests a significant need for effective device instructions and, for at least some users, training.

A classic example based on self-report questionnaires and videotaped observation is a study by Czaja, Weber, and Nair (1993) in which task analysis was applied to bathing, one of the basic activities of daily living. Bathing was recognized as a problem for frail older adults (i.e., 23 percent of older adults living at home at the time needed help with bathing—Dawson, Hendershot, and Fulton, 1987), but the key factors were not known. Using task analysis in conjunction with an empirical approach, these investigators identified specific functional problems (e.g., difficulty reaching or lifting) and suggested possible solutions (e.g., grab bars). An alternative way to collect specific activity-related information involves systematic exploration of the relationship among three different classes of descriptors, namely person, task, and environment (Strong et al., 1999). This classification of input information is useful in that it guides consideration of various aspects that are likely to affect performance. The result of this exploration, however, is generally equivalent to a competent task analysis.

TABLE 4-2 Results of a Task Analysis for Using a Lancing Device

Subtask No.	Subtask	Task/Knowledge Requirements	Feedback	Potential Problems
1	Remove the lancing device cap	Correct procedure	Tactile	Lancing device cap not removed
2	Insert a sterile lancet in the lancet holder	How to insert lancet	Tactile	Lancet inserted incorrectly; sharps injury
3	Twist off the lancet protective cap	How to remove protective cap	Tactile	Protective cap not removed
4	Replace the lancing device cap	How to replace lancing device cap	Tactile	Lancing device cap not replaced or replaced incorrectly
5	Cock the lancing device	How to cock the lancing device	Lancing device clicks when cocked [audible]	Lancing device not cocked
6	Wash your hands	Correct procedure	None	Hands not washed; possible infection
7	Hang your arm at your side for 10-15 seconds	Correct procedure; proper length of time	None	Don't hang arm at side; unable to get good blood flow to fingers
8	Hold the lancing device against the side of a finger	Correct location to prick finger	Tactile	Lancing device not held against finger; unable to get blood
9	Press the release button	Location of release button	Tactile (feel finger pricked)	Unable to prick finger
10	Squeeze the finger to obtain a large, hanging drop of blood	Correct procedure	Blood produced [visual]	Not enough blood produced; blood is smeared rather than hanging

SOURCE: Rogers et al. (2001).

Hierarchical Task Analysis

Hierarchical task analysis is the task analysis methodology used most frequently in industrial settings. Although developed originally for the chemical industry (Annett and Duncan, 1967), it has been applied in a variety of situations ranging from aviation to the training of individuals with cognitive impairments. A comprehensive description of hierarchical task analysis can be found in Shepherd (2001) and Annett (2003), but in this chapter we present the basics of the approach and use two examples to illustrate its application. Using hierarchical task analysis can help identify possible conditions that could lead to adverse events and can support the development of physical or cognitive assistive devices that would help in the execution of these tasks or the development of training procedures. Hierarchical task analysis starts from a set of main goals and "uses a systematic goal decomposition methodology until a sufficient level of detail is reached" (Drury, 2010). The result of the analysis is generally a hierarchical structure that can be represented either graphically (e.g., in block diagrams or signal flow graphs) or in an outline-like formatted table.

The first example of a hierarchical task analysis is for washing hands, from a project that focused on the development of cognitive aids to enable individuals with mild cognitive impairment to perform a variety of simple tasks (Mihailidis et al., 2008; Hoey et al., 2010). The project envisioned a system of video cameras and sensors that would depend on adaptive artificial intelligence algorithms to infer an individual's actions and provide guidance if needed. The development of the system required fairly detailed task analysis in order to infer the correctness of each action and its sequences.

The results of task decomposition for hierarchical task analysis to the task of washing hands are shown in Figure 4-1. In Figure 4-1a, the main task is divided into a set of component tasks, but the order of execution is not a part of this representation. If this decomposition were used only to prescribe a procedure for training, it would be sufficient to arrange the component tasks in a single linear sequence. However, the cognitive assistive application would require the system to include all valid paths, because it would be inappropriate to generate corrective feedback in situations in which the actor happened to choose a different but also valid sequence.

Rather than specifying exponentially more complex plans, it is better to represent the results of task decomposition in terms of a state diagram that is similar to those used in link analysis (Drury, 1990; Stanton, 2006; Wolf et al., 2006). An example of the state-transition diagram (state-space representation) is shown in Figure 4-1b. Each node in this graph represents either an activity, such as a component task, or a state that resulted from completing predecessor tasks. Any sequence from "Start" to "Finish" in this diagram is a valid sequence that would result in a successful completion of the task. By traversing the different paths, it is possible to examine each state and action for the user capabilities and task demands.

The state transition-based representation is also very useful in detecting possible sequencing errors. One way to determine all possible errors due to sequencing is to create a complete graph, that is, connect each node to all

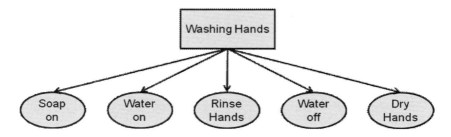

a. The first level of task decomposition for hierarchical task analysis for washing hands.

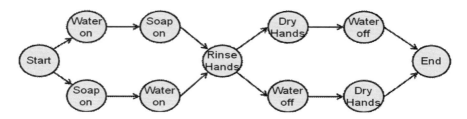

b. A state-transition diagram of task decomposition for hierarchical task analysis for washing hands.

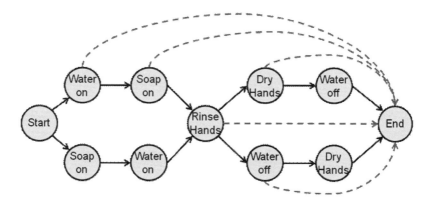

c. A state-transition diagram of task decomposition for hierarchical task analysis for washing hands with possible erroneous transitions indicated by dashed lines.

FIGURE 4-1 Task decomposition for hierarchical task analysis of the task of washing hands.
SOURCE: Adapted from Hoey et al. (2010). See Hoey et al. (2010) for more details on how these results can be used in the design of assistive systems.

other nodes, identify which of these transitions are erroneous, and estimate the seriousness of the error. The graph in Figure 4-1c illustrates a small subset of the possible errors using dashed lines. The seriousness of the errors can be illustrated by comparing forgetting to dry hands with forgetting to rinse off the soap and turn off the water.

The discussion thus far has treated task analyses and their results as being deterministic. While this is appropriate when determining procedures for controlled situations (such as in many industrial, military, and medical applications), for health care in the home situations, the tasks, as well as their sequencing, need to be described in probabilistic terms, in which the execution of different components, their success, and their order are uncertain and therefore better described by their probabilities. This can be easily implemented in a graph-based representation similar to that used for link analysis in industrial applications. The probabilistic representation would enable the development of technology-based aids that would, in addition to providing guidance to the individual, enable the system to make inferences about his or her capabilities.

Lane, Stanton, and Harrison (2006) have demonstrated a more complex example of task decomposition for hierarchical task analysis applied to administration of medications in hospital settings (Lane, Stanton, and Harrison, 2006). The resulting hierarchy of tasks is shown in Figure 4-2. For the sake of clarity, this diagram shows only the coarsest decomposition of the tasks at the highest levels of the hierarchy. Although this specific analysis involves hospital settings, it may be adapted for similar analyses in residential environments. The analysis in this case was performed using logical analysis in combination with practical experience by a trained pharmacy technician and was then reviewed by two nurses. This example illustrates that errors in medication administration may occur in a number of ways, even if there is no mismatch between task demands and an actor's abilities, and that errors can be anticipated using hierarchical task analysis in conjunction with expert assessments and models of human cognitive abilities.

Cognitive Task Analysis

As illustrated by the examples given above, in many health care situations in the home, the most critical user capabilities are cognitive rather than physical or sensory/perceptual. Although the importance of other user capabilities is hard to overestimate, many home care tasks depend heavily on the cognitive functions and processes of the individual performing them. The goal of the cognitive task analysis is to ensure that the actor has the required prior knowledge, necessary real-time information, cognitive skill, and sufficient resources (such as time) to perform the task. The

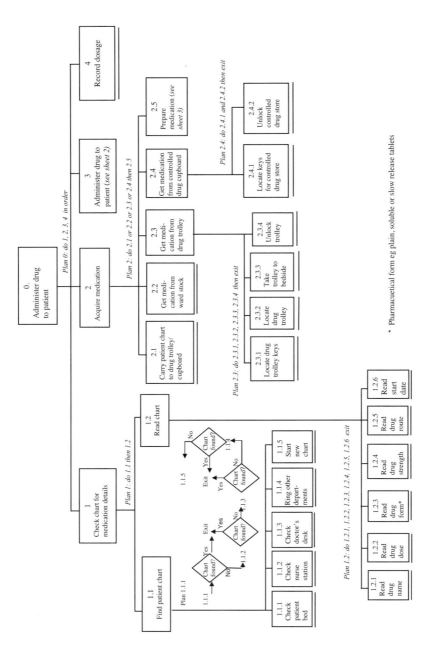

FIGURE 4-2 Example of a result of task decomposition for hierarchical task analysis for medication administration in a hospital setting.
SOURCE: Reprinted from Lane, Stanton, and Harrison (2006).

match between task demands and the actor's capabilities can be determined through use of cognitive task analysis. Cognitive task analysis may be considered task analysis applied to the cognitive domain, with the added difficulty that not all actions and component tasks are directly observable and some must therefore be inferred from performance or by using a variety of knowledge elicitation techniques.

The products of cognitive task analysis are the knowledge structures and the cognitive processes that underlie individuals' decisions and actions. Knowledge structures are methods for representing concepts and the relationships among them, such as domain knowledge of a disease or medication or basic knowledge of information-seeking strategies. For example, in order to adhere to a medication regimen, a care recipient and/or caregiver must know the conditions that call for drug administration (e.g., "evening before dinner," "high blood pressure," "high glucose concentration"). In particular, performance of activities associated with, for example, an adolescent with Type 1 diabetes requires considerable knowledge of a variety of interrelated concepts ranging from the significance of glucose concentration and the requirements for glucose monitoring to maintenance and troubleshooting of the monitoring equipment.

Knowledge structures comprising concepts and associated relationships may be represented as ontologies (Gruber, 1993) or semantic networks.[1] These network-like representation techniques applied to cognitive task analysis are often referred to as concept maps (Novak, 1990; Castellino and Schuster, 2002). Like semantic networks, concept maps are used frequently to characterize complex knowledge structures using graphs, with concepts as nodes and connections between nodes indicating relationships between two connected concepts. For example, physical exercise and glucose level are linked in the case of a diabetic individual, and this link must be incorporated into his own and his caregivers' knowledge structure.

Cognitive processes are typically covert computation-like operations, such as storing items in working memory or reasoning, that a care recipient or caregiver must perform to accomplish a task. Examples of cognitive processes include searching memory for appointments or medications, directing one's attention to the particular source of visual or auditory information, recognizing alerts, etc. A subset of these processes is associated with perception, but a number of the more complex cognitive processes, such as planning, problem solving, and decision making, are generally subsumed under the term "executive function."

As for any type of task analysis, in cognitive task analysis, the development of knowledge structures (such as concept maps or semantic networks)

---

[1]Software tools have been developed to support generation and use of ontologies and concept maps, for example, IHMC CmapTools (http://cmap.ihmc.us/).

and specification of the underlying cognitive processes require an analyst to collect data regarding the specific tasks and contexts to be included and analyzed. The acquisition of this knowledge may require deploying a number of diverse data-gathering techniques that facilitate extraction of information from the individuals involved in executing the task. These data elicitation approaches typically include interviews, self-reports, unobtrusive observations, and automated data capture by sensors and computers. Each of these data acquisition techniques has its advantages and disadvantages. Because of the covert nature of cognitive processes, the analyst must carefully structure any interviews to reduce subjective effects due to the interviewers' biases and preconceived notions.

One useful approach to cognitive task analysis is to hypothesize a computational model of the relevant cognitive processes (e.g., perception, memory, decision making) and then construct a program to perform the task. Although the specific aspects of such analysis depend on the particulars of the adopted model, this general approach is likely to lead to a more complete characterization of the task and the task requirements.

One example of a model that enables cognitive task analysis in a similar manner to hierarchical task analysis is GOMS (Card, Moran, and Newell, 1983) and its derivatives. GOMS is a human information processing model that stands for Goals, Operators, Methods, and Selection rules. Much like hierarchical task analysis, the application of GOMS leads to a decomposition of cognitive tasks into component tasks until the desired level of analysis is reached. Many other models of cognitive processes can be used to characterize individuals' cognitive activities and therefore can be used for cognitive task analysis (Crandall, Klein, and Hoffman, 2006). With advances in sensing and inference technology, cognitive task analysis will be increasingly useful in guiding the design of human-system interfaces and cognitive aids.

Applications of the Results of Task Analysis

Task analysis is a powerful, though sometimes complex, human factors technique that can be used for gaining a nuanced understanding of what is required to perform the array of health-related tasks that are increasingly performed at home and for detecting when individuals lack the capabilities necessary to perform these tasks safely, efficiently, and effectively. The invaluable insights gained through this technique can be used to improve the systems, processes, and training needed to support health care and health management in the home. By taking into account the factors that influence task performance, core elements of system design can be tailored to accommodate the expected users and minimize or eliminate the mismatch between task demands and human capabilities.

The results of task analyses can inform design modifications of medical devices and health information technologies used in the home, either during their initial development or for subsequent versions of these products. By helping designers to anticipate where target user groups may commit errors with or misuse their systems, the results of task analysis can facilitate timely alteration of design specifications, ideally prior to usability testing and commercial deployment. Likewise, these findings can inform device labeling, thereby increasing the likelihood that labels will be intuitive, or user-friendly, for diverse populations whose ability to see, read, hear, and understand instructional cues or label content may vary widely.

Training of individuals to perform various health-related tasks at home can also be strengthened by applying the results of task analysis. Thorough understanding of what it takes to perform health-related tasks properly in the home environment, coupled with broad appreciation of the varying amount of preparation people may have to assume such responsibility, supports development of training materials at several levels. Although many training materials are available, particularly on websites and in print format, they tend to be prescriptive, focusing more on what must be done and less on the capabilities essential to the task. They also tend to be condition-specific, of varying quality, and difficult to locate.

Most importantly, performance supports or job aids informed by task analysis can be developed to guide people who have little or no preparation for performing the task or who suffer cognitive declines. These aids can range from sketches that depict essential components or steps of the task to textual or audiovisual materials that convey the same information in a language and vocabulary that is easily understood by persons with low health literacy. Such aids can also help address variations in cognitive abilities due to the effects of fatigue, pain, drugs, or disease progression. We expect that the results of task analysis will shortly become a key tool for developing intelligent, networked cognitive assistive devices that will compensate for the cognitive limitations of the care recipients and their caregivers.

Checklists developed from task analyses are a particularly effective kind of performance aid for prompting correct execution of health-related tasks. Checklists that may be useful for home-based health care can be divided into two types (Gawande, 2009):

- READ-DO: a step-by-step list of procedures to be followed in sequence. This type of checklist is best suited for tasks involving details that people may not remember, particularly when under emotional stress. Examples of these tasks are wound care, infusion pump use, and automatic external defibrillator (AED) operation.
- DO-CONFIRM: a list of tasks that actors check off as or after they complete them. These lists are most appropriate when a number

of people perform jobs separately or asynchronously and use the checklist afterward to confirm that the job was done correctly. An example of this type of list might be used to guide transitions of care from hospital to home, which involves a number of people with responsibilities for various tasks.

For persons who are not health care providers but whose experience or education has prepared them to some extent to perform the task, greater visual detail or more complex language may be used for training. Among formal caregivers new to health care in the home, training may need to emphasize insightful appraisal of their own capabilities and those of others (e.g., persons whom they supervise, such as people who receive care, family members, and coworkers on their team) and promote strategies for enhancing task performance. For formal caregivers with extensive experience providing health care in the home, training in the form of continuing education can incorporate methods for promoting these same assessment and tailored intervention skills. Health professional education and training programs for direct-care workers in health care in the home can likewise benefit from curricula infused with information gained from task analysis.

An example of the use of task analysis to support the efficient and effective selection of devices for home health care can be developed from Table 4-2, showing the subtasks involved in using a lancing device to obtain blood for monitoring glucose levels. A task analysis for use of the lancing device could be developed and included in a device database, like the one recommended in Chapter 7. Then, if assessment instruments were readily available to evaluate the capabilities of care recipients, as also recommended in Chapter 7, such an evaluation could be done on each recipient before a care plan is developed.

Then, whenever a provider was considering recommending (for example) that lancing device for a care recipient, the task demands of the device and of alternative devices performing the same function could be retrieved from the database and compared with the care recipient's capabilities. This would allow the provider to determine whether that device or some other would be the best fit and whether the care recipient would need training, support, or assistance in using the device that is finally chosen. A skilled person, perhaps an appropriately trained occupational therapist, would be needed to evaluate the information on task demands and recipient capabilities, but a new task analysis would not be needed for each device/ user analysis.

As an experience base developed, device designers could obtain feedback on the mismatches commonly found between the devices they have marketed and the actual capabilities of those who need to use the devices, informing the design of future devices to ensure their usability by the population in need of them.

In summary, human factors approaches applied to the ever-increasing array of health-related tasks performed in the home can be used to improve the systems, processes, and training available for their successful completion. This is not to say that a task analysis is done for each and every care recipient and caregiver. We recognize that would be prohibitively expensive and probably unnecessary. Ideally, task analyses are developed for specific tasks (e.g., glucose monitoring) and would specify the subtasks and capabilities needed to perform the task. Developers could use these analyses, in conjunction with other knowledge from human factors research, to recognize potential limitations in user capabilities and to improve the design of medical technologies as well as medical procedures and trainings that better leverage existing capabilities to complete tasks. These analyses should then be refined as the tools, technologies, and procedures associated with the tasks are designed, developed, or changed. In-home assessment tools could draw on these analyses to measure if potential task performers have the capabilities to perform the tasks. When they do not, a professional, such as an occupational therapist, can consider the options for matching tasks and performers: adapting devices or their operational requirements, choosing different devices, training, professional support, etc.

REFERENCES

Allen S., and Ciambrone, D. (2003). Community care for people with disability: Blurring boundaries between formal and informal caregivers. *Qualitative Health Research, 13*(2), 207-226.

Annet, J. (2003). Hierarchical task analysis. In E.E. Hollnagel (Ed.), *Handbook of cognitive task design* (pp. 12-36). Mahwah, NJ: Lawrence Erlbaum Associates.

Annett, J., and Duncan, K.D. (1967). Task analysis and training design. *Occupational Psychology, 41*, 211-221.

Bookman, A., and Harrington, M. (2007). Family caregivers: A shadow workforce in the geriatric health care system? *Journal of Health Politics and Policy Law, 32*(6), 1005-1041.

Card, S.K., Moran, T.P., and Newell, A. (1983). *The psychology of human-computer interaction.* Hillsdale, NJ: Lawrence Erlbaum Associates.

Castellino, A., and Schuster, P. (2002). Evaluation of outcomes in nursing students using clinical concept map care plan. *Nurse Educator, 27*(4), 149-150.

Clark, N.M., and Rakowski, W. (1983). Family caregivers of older adults: Improving helping skills. *Gerontologist, 23*(6), 637-642.

Crandall, B., Klein, G., and Hoffman, R.R. (2006). *Working minds: A practitioner's guide to cognitive task analysis.* Cambridge, MA: MIT Press.

Czaja, S.J., Weber, R.A., and Nair, S.N. (1993). A human factors analysis of ADL activities: A capability-demand approach. *Journal of Gerontology, 48*, 44-48.

Dawson, D., Hendershot, G., and Fulton, J. (1987). *Aging in the eighties: Functional limitations of individuals age 65 years and over.* Available: http://www.cdc.gov/nchs/data/ad/ad133acc.pdf [March 31, 2011].

Dix, A., Finlay, J., Abowd, G., and Beals, R. (2004). *Human computer interaction*. Englewood Cliffs, NJ: Prentice Hall.

Drury, C. (2010). *Frameworks for understanding home caregiver tasks*. Paper presented at the Workshop on the Role of Human Factors in Home Healthcare, National Academy of Sciences, Washington, DC.

Drury, C.G. (1990). Methods for direct observations of performance. In J. Wilson and E.N. Corlett (Eds.), *Evaluation of human work: A practical ergonomics methodology* (2nd ed., pp. 45-68). London: Taylor and Francis.

Fitts, P.M., and Jones, R.E. (1947). Analysis of factors contributing to 460 "pilot error" experiences in operating aircraft controls. *Aero Medical Laboratory, Air Materiel Command, Wright Patterson Air Force Base* (Vol. Memorandum Report TSEAA-694-12), Dayton, OH.

Gallo, J.J., and Paveza, G.J. (2006). Activities of daily living and instrumental activities of daily living assessment. In J.J. Gallo, T. Fulmer, and G.J. Paveza (Eds.), *Handbook of geriatric assessment* (4th ed., pp. 193-240). Sudbury, MA: Jones and Bartlett.

Gawande, A. (2009). A challenge for practitioners worldwide: Why safe surgery saves lives. *Journal of Perioperative Practice, 19*(10), 312.

Gruber, T. (1993). A translation approach to portable ontology specifications. *Knowledge Acquisition, 5*, 199.

Hoey, J., Poupart, P., von Bertoldi, A., et al. (2010). Automated handwashing assistance for persons with dementia using video and a partially observable markov decision process. *Computer Vision and Image Understanding, 114*, 503-519.

Kane, R., Preister, R., and Totten, A.M. (2005). *Meeting the challenge of chronic illness*. Baltimore, MD: Johns Hopkins University Press.

Katz, S. (1983). Assessing self-maintenance: Activities of daily living, mobility and instrumental activities of daily living. *Journal of the American Geriatrics Society, 31*(12), 721-726.

Katz, S., Down, T.D., Cash, H.R., and Grotz, R.C (1970). Progress in the development of the index of ADL. *The Gerontologist, 10*(1), 20-30.

Lane, R., Stanton, N.A., and Harrison, D. (2006). Applying hierarchical task analysis to medication administration errors. *Applied Ergonomics, 37*(5), 669-679.

Lawton, M.P., and Brody, E.M. (1969). Assessment of older people: Self-maintaining and instrumental activities of daily living. *The Gerontologist, 9*(3), 179-186.

Levine, C., Halper, D., Peist, A., et al. (2010). Bridging troubled waters: Family caregivers, transitions, and long-term care. *Health Affairs, 29*(1), 116-124.

Lippa, K.D., Klein, H.A., and Shalin, V.L. (2008). Everyday expertise: Cognitive demands in diabetes self-management. *Human Factors, 50*(1), 112-120.

Mihailidis, A., Boger, J.N., Craig, T., and Hoey, J. (2008). The coach prompting system to assist older adults with dementia through handwashing: An efficacy study. *BMC Geriatrics, 8*, 28.

Mukamel, D.B., Peterson, D.R., Temkin-Greener, H., et al. (2007). Program characteristics and enrollees' outcomes in the program for all-inclusive care for the elderly (PACE). *Milbank Quarterly, 85*(3), 499-531.

Murphy, S.L., Gretebeck, K.A., and Alexander, N.B. (2007). The bath environment, the bathing task, and the older adult: A review and future directions for bathing disability research. *Disability and Rehabilitation, 29*(14), 1067-1075.

Novak, J.D. (1990). Concept maps and vee diagrams: Two metacognitive tools for science and mathematics education. *Instructional Science, 19*, 29-52.

Osterberg, L., and Blaschke T. (2005). Adherence to medication. *New England Journal of Medicine, 353*(5), 487-497.

Rogers, W.A., Mykityshyn, A.L., Campbell, R.H., and Fisk, A.D. (2001). Analysis of a "simple" medical device. *Ergonomics in Design: The Quarterly of Human Factors Applications, 9*(1), 6-14.

Shepherd, A. (2001). *Hierarchical task anlysis.* London: CRC Press.

Siegel, J.D., Rhinehart, E., Jackson, M., and Chiarello, L. (2007). *2007 guideline for isolation precautions: Preventing transmission of infectious agents in healthcare settings.* Atlanta, GA: Centers for Disease Control and Prevention.

Stanton, N. A. (2006). Hierarchical task analysis: Developments, applications, and extensions. *Applied Ergonomics, 37,* 55-79.

Stilley, C.S., Bender, C.M., Dunbar-Jacob, J., Sereika, S. and Ryan, C.M. (2010). The impact of cognitive function on medication management. *Health Psychology, 29*(1), 50-55.

Strong, S., Rigby, P., Stewart, D., et al. (1999). Application of the person-environment-occupation model: A practical tool. *Canadian Journal of Occupational Therapy, 66*(3), 122-133.

The Staff of the Benjamin Rose Hospital. (1959). Multidisciplinary studies of illness in aged persons. II. A new classification of functional status in activities of daily living. *Journal of Chronic Diseases, 9*(1), 55-62.

Wilkins, V.M., Bruce, M.L., and Sirey, J.A. (2009). Caregiving tasks and training interest of family caregivers of medically ill homebound older adults. *Journal of Aging & Health, 21*(3), 528-542.

Wolf, L., Potter P., Sledge J.A., et al. (2006). Describing nurses' work: Combining quantitative and qualitative analysis. *Human Factors: The Journal of the Human Factors and Ergonomics Society, 48,* 5-14.

Zayas-Cabán, T., and Brennan, P.F. (2007). Human factors in home care. In P. Carayon (Ed.), *Handbook of human factors and ergonomics in health care and patient safety.* Mahwah, NJ: Lawrence Erlbaum Associates.

5

Health Care Technologies in the Home

Hospital patients today are being discharged sooner than in the past, sometimes with complex continuing care plans that require the use of medical technologies in the home for an extended period following discharge, if not permanently. Some of these technologies are simple, and others are quite sophisticated and require that care recipients and/or their caregivers be trained in their use; retraining is also often needed. Evidence from the Agency for Healthcare Research and Quality suggests that, for some individuals, electronic tools may become important adjuncts to treatment, improving medication adherence or enabling delivery of mental health interventions, such as cognitive behavioral therapy on demand (Gibbons et al., 2009).

Care recipients and health care consumers are generally becoming more engaged in managing their own health and health care. Self-help and wellness books regularly make the bestseller lists, online health information seeking has increased dramatically over the last decade, and people are purchasing various devices and software to monitor and maintain their own health (e.g., to measure their blood sugar, check their blood pressure, log exercise). Some types of medical devices have become de facto consumer products, and more and more individuals expect to be able to choose products that suit their lifestyles and are convenient and easy to use.

In effect, health care requires the use of technology, both by formal and informal caregivers and by care recipients. Much of the medical equipment now used in homes was designed by device manufacturers to be used only in clinical settings and by trained health care professionals (U.S. Food and Drug Administration, 2010). Its migration to the home poses many challenges to both caregivers and care recipients. This is because the equipment generally was not designed with their capabilities and limitations in mind, and because the home environment differs in significant ways from the controlled environment of the hospital or clinic. These developments also pose a challenge to the medical device industry, which must take into account these factors when designing medical technology which may be used in the home.

Technology relevant to health care can be separated into two major categories: medical devices and health information technologies (HIT). The dividing line between these two categories is becoming less clear as technology evolves (similar to the case of voice and data in telecommunications; see Federal Telemedicine News, 2010, April 25). This chapter describes issues, challenges, and relevant research related to these technologies.

MEDICAL DEVICES

Medical devices in the United States are regulated by the U.S. Food and Drug Administration (FDA). The Center for Devices and Radiological Health (CDRH) of the FDA defines a medical device as "an instrument, apparatus, implement, machine, contrivance, implant, in vitro reagent, or other similar article that is . . . intended for use in the diagnosis of disease or other conditions, or in the cure, mitigation, treatment or prevention of disease" (21 U.S.C. 321, Federal Food, Drug, and Cosmetic Act, 2005, Section 201(h)). The FDA's Home Health Care Committee, recognizing the need for a definition of home medical device, drafted a definition that takes into account device use in a nonclinical environment under the direction of nonprofessional users. As of this writing, however, this definition is still under review, and the FDA solicited industry input on its wording at a May 2010 public meeting.

The FDA divides medical devices into three classes based on a number of factors, including the degree of risk a device presents to the patient. Only devices that pose a significant degree of risk require that developers/manufacturers complete a 510(k) premarket notification submission that documents, in great detail, an assessment of the risks associated with the device and describes the actions taken by the developer to address each risk identified. Although the determination of the class to which a particular device is assigned is not always simple, in general, the device classes are as follows:

1. Class I—devices with a minimum potential for harm to the user and generally simpler than Class II and Class III devices. They are

usually exempt from good manufacturing practice requirements,[1] and almost all Class I devices are exempt from the FDA's 510(k) premarket notification requirements. Such devices are subject only to general controls by the FDA, such as manufacturer registration, branding and labeling requirements, and general reporting procedures. Devices in this category include elastic bandages, canes, weight scales, flow meters, and other simple devices used in the home or in clinical environments.

2. Class II—devices that involve some risk to the user. Most Class II devices require a 510(k) premarket notification submission. These devices require more than general controls by the FDA to ensure safety and effectiveness, such as meeting special labeling requirements and mandatory performance standards and being subject to postmarket surveillance. Most devices in this category are noninvasive and include blood pressure cuffs, catheters, heating pads, powered wheelchairs, and many other electrically powered home care and clinical use devices.

3. Class III—devices in this class present the highest potential risk to the user and require a 510(k) premarket notification submission and additional scientific review to ensure device safety and effectiveness. Many of the devices in this category are invasive, such as pacemakers, heart valves, other implantable devices, or high-risk medical devices, such as defibrillators.

Medical Device Use in the Home

Over the past decade and a half, the range of types and level of complexity of medical devices used in the home have increased dramatically. Prior to this time, it was common to see fairly simple equipment for first aid (thermometers, bandages, heating pads) and medication administration (e.g., dosing cups, pill splitters) in the home, along with various assistive technologies (e.g., hearing aids, reaching tools), durable medical equipment, such as wheelchairs, walkers, and crutches, and prosthetic or orthotic devices (e.g., artificial limbs, shoe inserts). Oxygen concentrators, nebulizers, and CPAPs were also in use.

Now medical equipment that previously was used only in the hospital or clinic is finding its way into the home (see Table 5-1). Home dialysis is

---

[1]The FDA has many good manufacturing practices (GMPs), which are well known to device developers and pharmaceutical companies and relate to every aspect of the design, development, and manufacturing practices. These are generally regulatory documents. For example, 21 CFR Part 210/211 are the Pharmaceutical Industry GMPs, and 21 CFR Part 820 is the Good Manufacturing Practice for Medical Devices—Quality System Regulation.

TABLE 5-1 Types of Health Care Devices and Technologies Used in the Home

Category	Device or Technology
Medication administration equipment	Dosing equipment (cups, eyedroppers, blunt syringes) Nasal sprays, inhalers Medication patches Syringes/sharps
Test kits	Pregnancy test Male/female stress hormone test Cholesterol test Allergy test Bladder infection test HIV test Hepatitis C test Drug, alcohol, nicotine test
First aid equipment	Bandages Ace bandage, compression stocking Snakebite kit Heating pad Traction Ostomy care Tracheotomy care Defibrillator
Assistive technology[a]	Eyeglasses Hearing aid Dentures (full or partial) Prosthetic device Orthotic device, including braces Cane or crutches Walker Wheelchair Scooter
Durable medical equipment	Hospital bed Specialized mattress Chair (e.g., geri-chair or lift chair) Lift equipment Commode, urinal, bed pan
Meters/monitors	Thermometer Stethoscope Blood glucose meter Blood coagulation (PT/INR) meter Pulse oximeter Weight scale Blood pressure monitor Apnea monitor Electrocardiogram (ECG) monitor Fetal monitor

TABLE 5-1 Continued

Category	Device or Technology
Treatment equipment	IV equipment Infusion pumps Dialysis machines Transcutaneous electrical nerve stimulation (TENS) systems
Respiratory equipment	Ventilator, continuous positive airway pressure (CPAP), bi-level positive airway pressure (BiPAP), and demand positive airway pressure (DPAP) equipment Oxygen cylinder Oxygen concentrator Nebulizer Masks and canulas Respiratory supplies Cough assist machine Suction machine Manual resuscitation bags
Feeding equipment	Feeding tubes (nasogastric, gastrostomy, jejunostomy) Enteral pump
Voiding equipment	Catheter Colostomy bags
Infant care	Incubator Radiant warmer Bilirubin lights Phototherapy Apnea monitor
Telehealth equipment	Cameras Sensors Data collection and communication equipment (e.g., computer, smart phone) Telephone or Internet connections

[a]**Assistive technology** or **adaptive technology** is an umbrella term. Given various definitions of the term, an assistive technology is essentially anything (e.g., item, piece of equipment, device, or system) that can help an individual do anything that he/she would be unable to do otherwise, or have difficulty doing otherwise.
SOURCE: Story (2010).

becoming more common, for example, and such devices as apnea monitors, infusion pumps, ventilators, and left ventricular assist devices (the latter used to provide circulatory support before cardiac transplantation) are being used—to a great extent independently—by care recipients at home. Similarly, more complex diagnostic and testing devices are being made available for use at home or "on the go," so that people can monitor their own cholesterol, blood glucose levels, and even blood coagulation (if they take blood-thinning medications) wherever they are. For example, see the vignette in Box 5-1 for use of both conceptually simple devices (e.g., weight scale) and more conceptually complex ones (e.g., pulse oximeter) in the management of congestive heart failure.

Access to medical equipment has also changed significantly in recent years. It was once limited to the modest array of devices available over the counter or equipment obtainable from health care professionals or durable medical equipment providers, often only by prescription, but this is no longer the case. Care recipients can now purchase many medical devices, medications, assistive technologies, and health information technologies from a variety of sources via the Internet, including sources like Craigslist and eBay. In some cases, devices purchased through these sources may not be up to date, may not come with instructions, and indeed may not be appropriate or even work correctly. There is little or no customer support for devices purchased through many third-party sources.

Currently, few regulations address medical device use in the home. In April 2010, the FDA announced a Home Use Device Initiative that would more closely scrutinize medical devices being approved for home use. As part of this initiative, the FDA is developing a guidance document that would assist device manufacturers in understanding the complexities of developing devices for home use instead of, or in addition to, clinical use. The guidance is to focus on existing standards, the unique characteristics of the physical environment, and the unique characteristics of the untrained user when designing and testing a device for home use. In addition, the FDA cautioned manufacturers that knew their devices were being used in the home but not labeled as such and were causing injury or death: their subsequent premarket applications would either have to include the proper user testing and design needed for home use or would have to declare that the device would be specifically labeled "not for home use" (U.S. Food and Drug Administration, 2010).

General Problems with Device Use in the Home

Problems with medical device use in the home can be expected to mimic, to some extent, those found in hospitals and clinics, but they may be more likely to have negative consequences. This is because the capabilities

BOX 5-1
The Stames Family

Martin Stames, 70 years old, has had congestive heart failure for 7 years. He lives with his wife, Nanako, who is retired, in rural Michigan about 35 miles from the hospital where he has been admitted several times for acute episodes of congestive heart failure. Martin and Nanako have an adult son, Dennis, and a daughter, Lynn, who are supportive but do not live close by.

Martin was discharged to nursing care at home after his most recent hospitalization. Based on an initial screening and home visit by the nurse case manager, Martin was enrolled in telehealth services, which allow him to monitor his vital signs using a blood pressure cuff, weight scale, and fingertip pulse oximeter that are provided and send the data daily via a small portable computer telehealth unit to his visiting nurse. Using the same telehealth unit, he can participate in an educational program designed to help him better manage his condition.

The nurse installed the telehealth unit with help from a support person back at the office. Martin mastered the home-unit user interface easily, despite having never used a computer before.

Some of the medical devices, however, posed difficulties. Martin has some difficulty weighing himself with the scale provided when he is fatigued. Stepping up onto the scale and maintaining his balance are challenging for him, unless his wife is close by to assist. Martin learned to take his blood pressure with the standard blood pressure cuff provided, but he does not fully understand what the readings mean.

The educational software is not always appropriate to Martin's needs. For example, the software has provided little help in terms of interpreting his blood pressure. It asked if his blood pressure was within its normal range but did not provide feedback as to whether his answer was correct. Often it was not, which triggered a phone call from the nurse to provide additional training about blood pressure. Nanako commented to the nurse that on some days Martin has difficulty remembering this sort of information.

Martin completed 55 sessions over 59 days, missing days when a winter storm caused him to be without telephone service for 2 days and for 3 days when he did not transmit his weight because his wife was out of town and he could not weigh himself without her assistance. Missed sessions triggered contacts from the nurse.

SOURCE: Clinical profile of participants in telehealth study evaluated by committee member Daryle Gardner-Bonneau.

and limitations of untrained users in the home are quite different, as are the environments in which the devices are used.

Problems with device use often manifest themselves through human errors. As mentioned in Chapter 2, there are many types of human error, and the causes and consequences of errors vary. Some errors and their consequences are preventable via good design and selection of the device, whereas others must be handled through procedural or administrative solutions or through user education and training. Senders (1994) describes an error taxonomy with five categories that is useful in describing human error in medical device use:

1. Input error based on misperception. The user misperceives data displayed on a medical device and performs an incorrect action based on that misperception (e.g., misperceiving the infusion rate on an infusion pump display and acting based on the incorrectly perceived data).
2. Mistake. The user correctly perceives the data but forms and carries out an incorrect intention (e.g., a user of a blood pressure cuff correctly perceives his blood pressure reading as 210/96 but does not realize that he should call his health care provider immediately, instead of taking an extra dose of blood pressure medication).
3. Execution error or slip. The user correctly perceives the data and forms the correct intention but performs an incorrect action (e.g., a device user presses the "increase volume" button on a device instead of the "decrease volume" button, which the user intended).
4. Endogenous error. These are errors that arise from processes internal to the user of which he or she may not even be aware (e.g., biases and assumptions that may not be appropriate in a given circumstance, errors caused by becoming distracted or interrupted during use of a medical device). An actual case serving as an example (described in U.S. Food and Drug Administration, 2010) involved a care recipient who received a new infusion pump and was not trained in its use. He assumed it was programmed in the same way as the old pump and acted accordingly. As a result, his medication was delivered too quickly.
5. Exogenous error. These are errors that arise from situations, conditions, or processes external to the user and include the following four subcategories:
   • Errors of omission—leaving out one in a sequence of steps required to operate a device because, for example, the step has been omitted or deemphasized in instructional materials or the device allows the step to be omitted with no immediate consequences. Also reported in U.S. Food and Drug Administration

(2010) was the case of a care recipient who failed to remove the cap from the infusion line of an infusion pump after inserting a new infusion cassette, blocking the medication flow. She was hospitalized as a result.

- Errors of insertion—adding an inappropriate step to a process.
- Errors of repetition—repeating a step inappropriately (may occur because the device user has lost his or her place in a complex sequence of steps, for example).
- Errors of substitution—using an inappropriate object, action, place, or time instead of the appropriate one (e.g., using a glucometer test strip other than the one specified for the device, using a diagnostic device within 1 hour after eating instead of the necessary 2 hours).

Potential use errors during medication administration include giving the wrong drug, at the wrong time, through the wrong route, or through improper execution of the procedure. In operating a device to provide treatment, users might make errors due to missing a step in a procedure, inserting or substituting a step, or repeating a step they already executed because they were distracted.

It is easy to see why the number of errors as well as the severity of their consequences might be greater for untrained caregivers and care recipients operating medical devices. These individuals usually do not have the education and training of health care professionals, so they are more apt to misperceive visual information or audible signals and more likely to make incorrect judgments and take inappropriate actions based on those data. Even if untrained users can correctly perform the activities involved in operating a device, they may not understand the implications of the information they receive, given their level of knowledge about health care in general and the specific circumstances.

Some errors and their consequences may be minimized through design of the device, and this is the preferred method when it can be achieved, whereas other errors must be reduced through procedural or administrative solutions. In comparison, user education and training, though often used, are far less effective and should not be relied on as the sole means of mitigating errors and their consequences. The positive effects of education and training tend to dissipate over time and to erode quickly when cognitive capacity fluctuates for a number of reasons (e.g., task overload, fatigue, pain, drugs, and/or disease progression). Some types of errors will be more common in the home because the procedural and administrative safeguards that exist in formal clinical environments are not likely to be present in homes. For example, hospitals and clinics have procedural, regulatory, and administrative safeguards in place to ensure that the environment meets the operational requirements of devices in terms of cleanliness, temperature, humidity, electrical power requirements, etc. If electrical power is lost in the hospital, emergency power is available, but this is often not true in the home. Hospitals have rules that limit access to equipment by children and pets, but these are present in many homes, and their actions and unintended effects (e.g., pet hair clogging a device's air filtration system) are not always predictable or easily controlled.

It is not currently possible to estimate the magnitude of errors in medical device use in the home—or even the most common types of errors. Much of the data collected about adverse events in the home comes from home health agencies and other organizations. Although the FDA received over 19,000 reports of adverse events in the home related to device use between 1997 and 2009, it is difficult, if not impossible, to ascertain the cause of the events from the data contained in many of these reports (U.S. Food and Drug Adminisration, 2010). It is also likely that the reports reflect only the most egregious events with immediate consequences of severe injury or death that were viewed as reportable by the agencies involved. Until the FDA's recent introduction of new mechanisms for adverse event reporting (e.g., the HomeNet subnetwork of MedSun), care recipients and caregivers had limited avenues by which to report problems. Even with new reporting systems in place, however, many may not be aware of the existence or purpose of these systems or may be reluctant to report problems (National Research Council, 2010).

In an analysis of adverse events in the home reported to the FDA's MedSun database between 2002 and 2007, problems with infusion pumps topped the list; there were also notable adverse events for venous access devices, hospital beds, oxygen concentrators, ventilators, and powered wheelchairs (Marion, 2007).[2] These types of devices are among the most complex used in the home and carry the highest risks for injury, supporting the hypothesis that more serious events involving sophisticated technologies tend to be reported. This also mirrors the adverse event analyses described for hospitals in the Institute of Medicine's 2000 report, *To Err Is Human: Building a Safer Health System*, in that problems that are clearly reportable and egregious become part of the statistics, whereas other problems, which may be more common but have latent or more subtle consequences, are rarely reported.

Infusion pumps, the most problematic device according to the Marion (2007) analysis, have been a major source of problems in hospitals, as well as in home use. The concern was so great that, several years ago, an industry consortium led by AdvaMed took steps to try to prevent infusion pump

---

[2]Note that dialysis machines were not commonly used in the home during the period covered by the analysis.

use errors or at least reduce the consequences of those errors. The group considered design solutions to correct problems with IV tubing, administration of the wrong drug, administration of an incorrect drug dosage, and administration of the drug at an incorrect infusion rate. As a result, design of these devices is improving to the benefit of both formal and informal caregivers as well as care recipients caring for themselves. Problems remain, however, and this work continues (see, for example, Medical Device Consultants Inc., 2010).

Sometimes care recipients do not have the opportunity to acquire the medical device that is the best fit for them. Devices may not be appropriately or adequately prescribed by physicians when they have little knowledge of the differences among devices in a given category, of the specific capabilities and limitations of the care recipients, or of the conditions of the home environment. For some, the insurance provider determines which of several devices in a category the care recipient is eligible to receive, and the device received may not be the one that would best suit his or her needs (Vance, 2009; National Research Council, 2010).

The Role of Human Factors

In 1996, the NRC published a workshop report on the usability of home medical devices, *Safe, Comfortable, Attractive, and Easy to Use* (National Research Council, 1996). The workshop participants noted problems with device design, communications, support, training, and standards, among others. At that time the medical devices being used in the home were typically less complex and less sophisticated than they often are today, but the same problems highlighted in that workshop are still evident today. The workshop participants recognized the varied and often conflicting stakeholder interests and forces bearing on device design, but even then they noted that there were many problems that could be addressed by applying human factors knowledge and research methods.

Better understanding of the characteristics, capabilities, and limitations of care recipients and caregivers, the environment in which they must operate devices, and the tasks they must perform will enable better design of medical devices and equipment to prevent errors, or at least reduce the negative consequences of errors, and to better meet care recipient needs.

As described in Chapter 2, the users of medical devices in the home can be virtually anyone. Some device users in the home are formally trained caregivers, who have knowledge of and experience with such medical devices. But many users are untrained persons—older spouses caring for their mates, neighbors caring for neighbors, parents caring for a child, or children (sometimes fairly young children) caring for parents or grandparents. Some care recipients operate devices themselves to provide self-care, sometimes independently, sometimes with the support of others.

Regardless of their capabilities and levels of support, individuals using medical devices in the home should be able to use the devices safely, effectively, efficiently, and without making errors that could compromise the health of care recipients (Kaye and Crowley, 2000). This requirement has implications for medical device design, user training programs, and ongoing support. If the demands of the medical device exceed the capabilities of the user, the equipment burden may be too great to manage and the device may be abandoned.

As described in Chapter 6, residential environments can present a range of complexities for the introduction of medical devices. They are apt not to meet many of the environmental requirements assumed for devices used in clinical settings. For example, many homes do not meet electrical codes or maintain controlled temperature, humidity, air quality, water quality, lighting, or noise levels. Standards for cleanliness or sterile conditions may not be met. In addition, electromagnetic interference from other consumer electronic devices in the environment may interfere with device performance. Guarding against this problem may require targeted education of both device users and others who may be in the vicinity of the device. Manufacturers have started to focus on stronger shielding for these devices, but many older devices will remain in use for years.

The variety of use environments presents significant challenges for device design. It has implications for device portability (size and weight), appearance, and discreetness, as well as battery life, durability, and ruggedness. Aesthetics of a device are important to users. People generally do not want to advertise their medical condition or their need for a medical device to others; to the extent possible, devices should be unobtrusive, compatible with the lifestyles of their users.

Premarket Device Assessment

The FDA requires medical device manufacturers to demonstrate that they addressed human factors during the product's development process. The FDA requires design controls for all medical devices sold in the United States. These are explained in Title 21 of the *Code of Federal Regulations* (CFR), Part 820 of which is the Quality System Regulation (QSR). Section 820.30, Design Controls, contains key human factors requirements in its subsections c, f, and g (U.S. Food and Drug Administration, 1996):

> (c) *Design input.* Each manufacturer shall establish and maintain procedures to ensure that the design requirements relating to a device are ap-

propriate and address the intended use of the device, including the needs of the user and patient. . . .

(f) *Design verification.* Each manufacturer shall establish and maintain procedures for verifying the device design. Design verification shall confirm that the design output meets the design input requirements. . . .

(g) *Design validation.* Design validation shall ensure that devices conform to defined user needs and intended uses and shall include testing of production units under actual or simulated use conditions. Design validation shall include software validation and risk analysis, where appropriate.

In support of successful device designs, two primary human factors guidance documents have been developed by the FDA: *Do It by Design: An Introduction to Human Factors in Medical Devices* (U.S. Food and Drug Administration, 1996) and *Medical Device Use-Safety: Incorporating Human Factors Engineering into Risk Management* (Kaye and Crowley, 2000). These documents include descriptions of human factors engineering methods, such as analytical and empirical approaches to identify and understand use-related hazards, methods of assessing and prioritizing hazards, strategies for mitigating and controlling hazards, and methods of verifying and validating hazard mitigation strategies. They also discuss exploratory studies and usability testing methods.

Representative care recipients and home caregivers should be included in any user testing that is conducted in order to assess the safety of the medical device and its use in the home. By studying their use of the device and its labeling to conduct essential tasks, device manufacturers can develop medical devices to minimize any potential risks and mitigate residual risks and determine whether devices are appropriate for home use. Although it is often difficult to recruit individuals for usability tests due to travel limitations and in some cases the low prevalence of certain disabilities, appropriate user testing is essential to ensure adequate design of medical devices (Petrie et al., 2006).

Postmarket Device Surveillance

Although the application of human factors engineering processes during the design process can identify most potential problems and mitigate them through design before the device goes to market, postmarket surveillance of products is still critical to uncover unforeseen problems and to identify problems that may only appear after long-term device use. If problems are discovered, manufacturers are required to notify current users and address the problems by providing information or replacement parts or recalling the product, as appropriate to the severity of the issue.

A postmarketing study of ventricular assist devices (Geidl et al., 2009) serves to demonstrate the importance of postmarketing surveillance in further assessing the usability and safety of a home care device. Geidl found that the usability of these devices affected the success and acceptance of the treatment. Of the 16 study participants, 38 percent accidentally disconnected important components of the system at least once; 38 percent reported that parts of the system rubbed against their skin (particularly the shoulder strap against the abdomen when using a bag belt); and 56 percent reported that the noises from the pump, ventilators, and alarms were annoying; however, the alarm signals were too quiet to wake 32 percent of them. Most participants (63 percent) used a carrying case other than the one that accompanied the device, and many (44 percent) overstuffed the case with additional gear, mainly medical documents, cell phones, or eyeglasses (without which the older participants had difficulty reading the messages on the device), for which space was not provided.

Given the number of problems identified in this study and the percentage of care recipients in this small sample who experienced the same problem, it is difficult to believe that premarket human factors usability testing would not have uncovered many of these problems, especially had adequate user testing been employed. Some, however, might have been seen only in a postmarketing study, thus the importance of continuing surveillance. Data from such studies are also useful to designers as they consider the development of updated versions of the same product or new products that involve similar design aspects.

In regard to assessing use-related errors and adverse events, the FDA's postmarket surveillance process is passive, depending on people to report problems as they occur. "Postmarket issues may be identified through a variety of sources, including analysis of adverse event reports, a recall or corrective action, reports from other governmental authorities, or the scientific literature" (U.S. Food and Drug Administration, 2010). The primary mechanism for learning about problems with medical devices in the home is the FDA's adverse event reporting systems, including Maude and MedSun. Entry of incident data by health care providers and consumers, however, is not straightforward, and the system does not elicit data that could be useful to designers as they develop updated versions of products or new devices that are similar to existing ones. In addition, the reporting systems and importance of their use are not widely promoted, and many people are unaware of them. Furthermore, the FDA appears to have few resources dedicated to active surveillance or monitoring of problems as they occur in the field.

Device Labeling, Instructions for Use, and Training Issues

The adequacy of device labeling, instructions, and training can affect whether use errors occur even with well-designed medical equipment. Poor labeling increases the likelihood that users will make mistakes using a device or will be forced to seek help to answer their questions. If labels or instructions for use create too much confusion, potential users may abandon a device, which can compromise the quality of care. For this reason, the FDA has very explicit requirements for device labeling and ensuing instructions that designers must meet before a medical device is approved for placement on the market (see U.S. Food and Drug Administration, 2001).

An important limitation of this requirement is its dependence on premarket evaluation and device approval. Although it is likely that manufacturers recognize the need for specific labeling and instructions targeted toward untrained users and home environments, the current regulations present an unexpected barrier to labeling improvements as manufacturers become aware of problems with device use. Currently, in the case of many devices, changes in labeling automatically trigger a new 510(k) premarket review of the device, as well, by the FDA. Since this review presents a significant burden to manufacturers, they are unlikely to propose changes unless circumstances require them (U.S. Food and Drug Administration, 2010).

The vignette in Box 5-2 illustrates a technical support problem commonly faced by families who purchase devices over the Internet (in this case, nebulizers and replacement tubing), which sometimes come without instructions related to care and maintenance or come with instructions that are difficult to understand. The vignette also illustrates the substantial stresses and strains on caregivers, especially the burdens of complex treatment regimens and sophisticated medical devices when training and instruction have not been provided or are not readily available.

There is also the problem, for devices used both in hospitals and homes, that home use may not require many of the elements incorporated into the device. As new technologies are developed and existing technologies are enhanced, medical devices are becoming increasingly complex. Devices that were designed for hospital or clinical use by professionals often come with many features and enhancements, some of them based on marketing data from the professionals themselves. Although these features and enhancements may be useful to trained professionals, they generally increase the complexity of both the device and its operation and can overwhelm untrained users who do not need them. Burdened with requirements of care provision and busy with other aspects of their lives, untrained users need medical devices to be as simple as possible, while still achieving treatment goals. In some cases, this may suggest that manufacturers develop different models of devices for untrained and for professional users.

BOX 5-2
The Morgan Family

Lynn and Bob Morgan and their two daughters live in the southeast United States. After their 8-year-old, Amy, was diagnosed at age 4 with asthma, they used the Asthma Home Environment Checklist from the U.S. Environmental Protection Agency (EPA) (EPA402-F-03-030, Feb 2004) to check for and eliminate triggers in their home.

Lynn purchases nebulizers and replacement tubing for Amy online without a prescription. She reuses the tubing frequently but does not know the number of times she can reuse it or how to clean it. Amy has six prescription medications, one of which requires refrigeration. The family finds it difficult to read and understand all the labeling for the medication and the equipment. The local pharmacist is able to help them understand the essential information about the medications, but he is unfamiliar with the nebulizers Lynn has purchased online.

To keep Amy safe, Bob and Lynn must constantly monitor her symptoms and medication regimens. The family was part of a web-based Asthma Action Plan until it ended. The Morgans found the online plan easy to follow, and it helped them to document events and interventions and to keep Amy's school informed as well. Without the plan, they find the care regimen a greater burden.

SOURCE: Experience of committee member Mary Brady.

It is easy to see that the design of training materials for users of medical devices in the home is critical. But few care recipients and informal caregivers receive formal training on the proper use of a device. If they do, the timing of that training may well not coincide with a "teachable moment" since they may be feeling stressed, emotionally upset, and/or fatigued at the very time when a formal caregiver attempts to train them. The conditions are therefore often not optimal for training. Furthermore, one cannot expect care recipients or informal caregivers to master a new technology, especially a complex one, after a single training session, although this is often the most they can expect to receive. In addition, the training may not be delivered in a culturally appropriate manner. These challenges necessitate that users be provided with training and instructional materials that are appropriate, if not tailored, for them, to which they can refer at a time that is more conducive to learning.

Another key element in the design of labeling, including instructions for use and training materials, is limiting the burden on the user's memory. Caregivers may not use devices on a regular basis, so providing informative labeling, procedural checklists, and reminder lists can both reduce errors and increase caregiver efficiency and effectiveness. For devices that are used infrequently, it is better to have knowledge in, on, or around the device, so the user is less dependent on knowledge from memory (Norman, 1980).

For example, the failure to consider memory burden led to an unsuccessful patient education application in the vignette in Box 5-1. Martin had difficulty remembering the information that would have allowed him to interpret his blood pressure (which the system required him to do). A reminder card, an interpretative display, or an application that did the interpretation and provided feedback may have been far more effective and saved a significant amount of the formal caregiver's time. A Western Michigan University study of telehealth applications (West-Frasier, 2008; Gardner-Bonneau, 2010) showed that about one-third of chronic obstructive pulmonary disease and congestive heart failure patients in the study had difficulty taking or interpreting their blood pressure at one time or another. These difficulties resulted in many hours of training and retraining by nurses (time they could ill afford). Had the designers of the training package understood the limitations of patients, the package could have been designed to avoid the problem and to ease the training burden significantly.

It is also important to recognize that people learn differently, and training materials should reflect this. Some people learn better through pictures, others through text, and still others through the spoken word. Some people may benefit most from a video presentation dynamically demonstrating the operation of the device. It is often the case in home care that a formal home care provider (e.g., a nurse) assumes the responsibility for training members of the household and for determining the best training technique for a particular individual on a specific device because good training materials are not available. A sizable body of knowledge employed in many aspects of user interface design for home health care applications (e.g., Tufte, 2001; Association for the Advancement of Medical Instrumentation, 2009) has yet to be put to good use in the design of instruction and training. However, excellent human factors guidance is available for the design of instructional materials and user training (see, for example, Swezey and Llaneras, 1997).

Much of the FDA's guidance does not take into account many of the principles and design guidelines in the instructional systems design and training literature in the field of human factors. Swezey and Llaneras (1997), in a chapter on models of training and instruction, provide more than 100 guidelines for the design of training and instructional materials based on models of learning (acquisition), retention (memory), transfer of training, and instructional systems development. They also provide guidelines for selecting and using various types of media for instructions and training. Instructional and training materials are being provided increasingly not in paper-based manuals or instructions printed on devices but via other media, including the Internet. Valuable human factors guidance for the development of instructional and training materials using these media can be found in texts on human-computer interaction (e.g., Jacko and Sears, 2008) and instructional systems design texts, which could be used by the FDA to improve its guidance to manufacturers.

Usability testing of labeling, including the instructions for use and training, is also essential, just as usability testing is required of the device itself. This testing usually involves a representative sample of users that includes individuals with the highest risk of experiencing problems. If it is demonstrated to be difficult to produce explanatory materials for a device so that untrained users can understand them and execute tasks properly, then it is likely that the device is not suitable for home use. But as important as it is for manufacturers to produce well-designed labels, instructions, and training materials, it is equally important that they not rely on these materials to solve problems in place of modifications to the design of the device itself.

Finally, it is not obvious who should be responsible for training users of devices in the home. Health care professionals may often be in a position to provide initial instruction in the use of a device, but they are often not in the best position to address maintenance and repair issues that may occur later. In addition, because formal caregivers may not always be aware when users independently purchase devices, the manufacturers ultimately may need to provide direct support for their devices.

HEALTH INFORMATION TECHNOLOGIES IN THE HOME

The range of electronic tools, applications, and devices that individuals may use in the course of managing their health and health care is indeed broad, and several new categories of devices are emerging. The fields of biomedicine and public health are expected to become closely intertwined in the next century (Zerhouni, 2005; Gibbons, 2007). Addressing the health problems of the 21st century will require a new set of biomedical and public health resources that extend beyond historic and traditional medical devices and are built on current and emerging information technologies (Hesse, 2005). These new information technology tools will enable the future health care system to become predictive, preemptive, and personalized to the needs of individual providers, care recipients, and caregivers to an extent not previously possible (Gibbons, 2007).

Progress toward this goal began with a report by the National Committee on Vital and Health Statistics (NCVHS) (1998) entitled *Ensuring a Health Dimension for the National Information Infrastructure,* which suggested that the nation's information infrastructure could be a valuable resource to promote health (Thompson and Brailer, 2004). To achieve this vision, NCVHS experts, in a 2001 follow-up report entitled *Information for Health: A Strategy for Building a National Health Information Infrastructure,* outlined the need for a seamless network of tools, data, and people. The report further suggested that this network should focus its developments in the areas of health care providers, personal health, and population health (National Committee on Vital and Health Statistics, 2001).

Important issues of compatibility and interoperability remain in health information technology. The recent surge of activity from both public and private sectors to use and share health-related information has proceeded without a discussion concerning what the building blocks are and how they fit together. For example, myriad meanings for terms have emerged and the relationships among the terms have been inadequately defined.

To address some of these issues and to provide support for increased adoption of health information technology, in 2008 the Office of the National Coordinator for Health Information Technology requested a report entitled *Defining Key Health Information Technology Terms* (National Alliance for Health Information Technology, 2008) in which the term "health information technology" is used as an umbrella term for at least six types of technologies:

1. Electronic medical record (EMR): "an electronic record of health-related information on an individual that can be created, gathered, managed, and consulted by authorized clinicians and staff within one health care organization."
2. Electronic health record (EHR): "an electronic record of health-related information on an individual that conforms to nationally recognized interoperability standards and that can be created, managed, and consulted by authorized clinicians and staff across more than one health care organization."
3. Personal health record (PHR): "an electronic record of health-related information on an individual that conforms to nationally recognized interoperability standards and that can be drawn from multiple sources while being managed, shared, and controlled by the individual."
4. Health information exchange (HIE): "the electronic movement of health-related information among organizations according to nationally recognized standards."
5. Health information organization: "an organization that oversees and governs the exchange of health-related information among organizations according to nationally recognized standards."
6. Regional health information organization: "a health information organization that brings together health care stakeholders within a

defined geographic area and governs health information exchange among them for the purpose of improving health and care in that community."

Equally important for home health care, a growing number of experts are collectively describing tools that are designed primarily for consumers as consumer health informatics (CHI) tools, applications, and devices.

Generally speaking, with the exception of the personal health record, the health information technology tools defined above are designed for and used by medical providers (e.g., physician, nurse, allied health professional) working in a hospital, clinic, or office-based setting. Currently, health information technology tools are not in widespread public use or even generally accepted as tools for providing health care, although this may change in the future, especially with the emergence of secure web-based platforms.

There is a need for more research on how health information technologies can support collaborative home care teams. Pinelle and Gutman (2001, 2002) point out: "Home care teams have different collaboration needs than workers in inpatient settings because they are widely distributed, they are mobile, and they maintain separate care recipient records. Interviews with several home care workers identified five specific areas where team members need to collaborate with one another: scheduling visits, disseminating information, finding answers to questions, short-term treatment coordination, and longer-term treatment planning."

Impact of "Meaningful Use"

On February 17, 2009, President Obama signed the American Recovery and Reinvestment Act of 2009 (ARRA). This statute includes the Health Information Technology for Economic and Clinical Health Act (the HITECH Act) that sets forth a plan for advancing the "meaningful use" of health information technology to improve quality of care and establish a foundation for health care reform. Among its provisions, the HITECH act requires the Office of the National Coordinator for Health Information Technology, in consultation with other appropriate federal agencies, to update the Federal Health Information Technology Strategic Plan published in June 2008. This update will include specific objectives, milestones, and metrics with respect to achieving the goal of enabling the use of an electronic health record for each person in the United States by 2014.

The ARRA authorized the Centers for Medicare & Medicaid Services to provide reimbursement incentives for eligible professionals and hospitals that are successful in becoming "meaningful users" of certified EHR technology. The objective of the incentive program is to encourage use of information technology by health care providers and create a better health care delivery system. Specific to health care in the home, the objective of meaningful use of health information technologies is to improve clinical decision making and enhance care coordination among caregivers. In order to receive funds, which will become available in 2011, hospitals and eligible providers have to meet more than 20 benchmarks, including being able to write electronic prescriptions, provide care recipients with access to their own electronic medical records on request, provide clinical summaries for care recipients for each office visit, and send reminders to care recipients for follow-up or preventive care.

In response, many vendors are augmenting their EHR applications with online care recipient portals, including personal health records. These portals allow care recipients to review their records and to record significant health and medical events that their primary care physician may be unaware of. Many EHRs also contain patient discharge information or instruction modules. These instructions form an important link between what the care recipient heard during a visit or hospital stay and what he or she will be required to do at home. Given the importance of the information contained in EHRs, it is incumbent upon vendors to make this information useful and usable. If the content and form of these instructions are not clear, the care recipient is at risk. Electronic health records are expensive to implement and a challenge for health care providers to adjust to, but they have substantial promise. Therefore, while the short-term impact of EHR adoption and meaningful use remain uncertain, over the long term, digitizing health records is expected to return benefits for health care in the home relative to improved coordination of care, enhanced communications, and better guidance and support for care recipients.

Personal Health Records

Although there has been debate about public adoption of personal health records (Kahn, Aulakh, and Bosworth, 2009), some health care providers are realizing that care recipients will use online health records if they are perceived to be helpful in accessing information and/or services, such as recent lab test results, summaries of appointments, e-mail contact with their physicians, and the ability to schedule appointments (Liang, 2010). However, personal health records are becoming more than electronic repositories of care recipients' administrative and clinical data. While these data constitute the core of a PHR, in the future, care recipients will have the opportunity to have more interaction with and control over these systems, which will become aggregations of different types of data and functions that enable a range of data storage, exchange, and transactions among health care stakeholders.

Care recipients can gather and analyze their own data (so-called observations of daily living or ODLs) via PHRs to determine ways to live healthier, rather than simply to manage their illnesses. Daily living data can take many forms—from quantitative measures of sleep (e.g., sensors indicating how long the care recipient slept and how much the care recipient moved during the night) to qualitative self-reports (e.g., the care recipient reporting his or her own mood). Some PHRs are experimenting with ways to convert typically qualitative metrics into numeric values. Collection of daily living data through PHRs gives both clinicians and care recipients insights for improving health care and health outcomes that are unattainable if records contain only data captured in clinical settings.

Recording observations of daily living in a health record is not a new concept. The traditional health record contained information that was not always quantitative; it could and often did capture qualitative information obtained during a clinical encounter. But PHRs are demonstrating new ways of collecting, organizing, displaying, and using that information. The ultimate goal is to use data to understand the experience of an individual as he or she goes about daily living and how personal choices affect one's health. Human factors considerations in the design of PHRs will be critical for the development of high-quality tools and for putting care recipients in greater control of their own health care management.

Many PHRs and care recipient portals have been constructed, often based on the continuity of care record (CCR).[3] A recent study (Alkhatlan, 2010) investigated the understandability of the standard CCR terminology used in PHRs and explored users' needs and preferences for data content. The participants were 30 undergraduate and graduate students in nonhealth fields. The study found that some terms (e.g., medications, immunizations, procedures/surgeries) were "easy to understand," some terms (e.g., vital signs, health care provider information, plan of care) were "understandable with a short definition," some terms (e.g., support sources, functional status, alerts) were "understandable with a long definition," and one term (advance directives) was "difficult to understand." Of the 17 CCR terms tested, using a scale of understandability from 0 to 3.5 (low to high), all but four of the terms had a score of less than 2.0, and nearly half (8) had a score of 1.5 or lower. The study also elicited from the participants suggestions for simple terms that might be used in place of the CCR terms (see Table 5-2). The author commented that vendors design PHRs primarily on the basis

---

[3]The CCR is a health record standard specification developed jointly by ASTM International, the Massachusetts Medical Society, the Healthcare Information and Management Systems Society, the American Academy of Family Physicians, the American Academy of Pediatrics, and other vendors of health information technologies. For more information, see http://www.astm.org/Standards/E2369.htm [February, 8, 2011].

TABLE 5-2 Continuity of Care Record (CCR) Terms Versus Participants' Suggested Simple Terms, in Order of Increasing Difficulty to Understand

Continuity of Care Record Term	Term Suggested by Participants
Payers/payment	Insurance information
Encounters/consultations	Appointments Doctor visits Health care professional visits
Health care provider information	Health care practitioners Health care professionals Health care personnel
Plan of care	Treatment plan
Social history	Lifestyle Social habits
Health status	Description of current health
Problems	Major medical problems Health problems Health problem history Current/past medical problems
Medical equipment	Personalized medical devices Internal or external medical devices used
Support sources	Emergency contact information
Functional status	Functional ability
Alerts	Allergies
Advance directives	Legal documents Living will Power of attorney

SOURCE: Alkhatlan (2010, p. 108).

of data needed from the perspective of health care providers, which results in interfaces that may be neither suitable nor desirable for care recipients (Alkhatlan, 2010).

Consumer Health Informatics

Increasingly, health information technology tools, applications, and devices are being produced for and used by healthy consumers, not just for individuals with suspected or diagnosed illness. They are also being used by informal caregivers to provide health information or obtain health management support, often without the involvement of formal caregivers. This new genre of health applications, known as consumer health informatics tools, was defined in 2000 by Eysenbach, and more recently revised by the Agency for Healthcare Research and Quality, to include any electronic tool, technology, or system that (Gibbons et al., 2009)

1. Is primarily designed to interact with health information users or consumers;
2. Both uses and provides personal health information; and
3. Is used for the purpose of helping consumers manage their health or health care maybe with, but is not dependent on, a health care professional and is not considered a tool within the context of routine clinical care.

Popular consumer health informatics devices include interactive, personal monitoring devices and decision support aids loaded onto cell phones, personal digital assistants, laptop computers, wireless-enabled devices (e.g., weight scales), personal health records, text messaging, discussion/chat groups, and online websites.

Because consumers often cite cost, convenience, and anonymity among the most important benefits of using the Internet to obtain health information and support, growth in societal interest in these tools and applications is likely to continue. In addition, because approximately 30 million newly insured Americans will enter the health care system over the next few years, the need, interest, and demand for ever more powerful consumer health informatics tools are expected to continue to grow well into the future.

Importantly, interactions between the consumer health informatics tools available to care recipients and the electronic health records that primary care providers and hospitals use raise issues that have a direct impact on health care in the home. Two of these issues are data ownership and data reliability. There is controversy about who should own the data in an EHR, whether the care recipient can simply annotate the data or should have the right to demand that items be expunged. The reliability of data that a care recipient enters into a PHR or care recipient portal is unknown, since data input can be affected by interface design, guidance, instructions, definitions, etc. This in turn will affect how much weight primary care providers should give to the data. These practical issues will have to be addressed as adoption of new technologies increases.

Health Information-Seeking Behaviors

Much has been written about health information-seeking behavior, although the term is used in various ways, and clear definitions, theoretical frameworks, and consensus on the meaning of the term are all lacking.

Lambert and Loiselle (2007) conducted a review of approximately 100 articles and five books and studied the topic as related to three issues: (1) coping with a health-threatening situation, (2) participation and involvement in medical decision making, and (3) behavior change and prevention behavior. They found that patterns of health information-seeking behavior reflected individuals' selectivity in the type and amount of information needed and the sources and actions used.

Estimates of the use of the Internet for finding medical information vary significantly. One reason for this seems to be the time frame referents used in different studies. Those that asked if respondents had "ever" used the Internet to find health information found prevalence rates of 70 percent to more than 80 percent. Studies that asked about a narrower time frame (e.g., in the past year) found rates of 40 to 60 percent. One large study (n = 6,119) that asked about searching in the previous 30 days found rates of 13 percent among all respondents and 21 percent among respondents with Internet access (n = 3,829) (Weaver et al., 2009).

Use of the Internet is limited if the content is not retrievable by the user. This can be the case for individuals with disabilities who have to rely on special devices or technologies to process online information due to their sensory, mobile, or mental limitations. One study (Zeng and Parmanto, 2003) found that none of the 108 consumer health information websites examined satisfied all of the web accessibility requirements. In determining web accessibility, the authors constructed a measurement framework and scoring system based on specifications[4] that offer checkpoints to determine content access for people with disabilities. In a 2009 examination of health care websites (Parmanto, 2010), the author determined there was still a long way to go to remove barriers to accessibility for people with disabilities.

The preferred medium for receiving health information varies significantly by age, gender, and ethnicity. For example, when seeking information specifically about cancer, Americans ages 65 and older are almost 10 times more likely to say they prefer going to health care providers first, before looking on the Internet, than people ages 18-64. Women are more likely than men to seek cancer information from sources other than the Internet. Compared with all other racial/ethnic groups, a higher percentage of Hispanics seek cancer information from health care providers and friends or family, and more blacks seek information from printed materials; more

---

[4]The widely referenced specifications included the World Wide Web Consortium (W3C) Web Content Accessibility Guideline 1.0 (WCAG), a stable international specification developed through a voluntary industry consensus, and the Electronic and Information Technology Accessibility Standards, published by the U.S. Access Board in December 2000 as required by Section 508 of the Rehabilitation Act Amendments of 1998.

whites and non-Hispanic others seek information on the Internet (National Cancer Institute, 2005).

Consumers are increasingly comfortable using the Internet as a research tool to obtain information on medical conditions, treatments, and wellness (Fox and Jones, 2009). This may be fueled in part by health care providers. Recent evidence suggests that nurses are very savvy when it comes to using information technology for health, and approximately three out of four U.S. nurses recommend health websites to care recipients. The average nurse spends eight hours per week online for professional purposes, the same amount as physicians, and almost all of them use the Internet between care recipient consultations. Nurses are also proactive in researching medical product information specifically online—over 80 percent have visited a pharmaceutical, biotechnology, or medical device company website in the past year (Manhattan Research, 2009).

User-Centered Design

User-centered design methods incorporate the needs of care recipients and caregivers, who are the intended users of a technology, into product design and evaluation. For example, these methods may be used by designers to address the needs of racial/ethnic minorities related to experiences with the mismatch of power between care recipient and health care provider, varying mental models of illness, and language barriers. Input and feedback obtained from users about these issues may be used to inform the design of care recipient–focused technologies.

The user-centered process has been effectively applied in the design of the Comprehensive Health Enhancement Support System (CHESS). CHESS was developed by a team of decision, information, education, and communication scientists at the University of Wisconsin–Madison's Center for Health Enhancement Systems Studies, who used user-centered approaches in the design and evaluation of the system (Shaw et al., 2006). Through needs assessment surveys, users were asked to evaluate both the relevance and feedback provided by content that was created by clinical experts. Use of CHESS has been shown to improve care recipients' quality of life, reduce demands on physician time, and in some cases even reduce the cost of care. Although the impact of user-centered design was not tested directly, the high levels of CHESS usage reported across racial, socioeconomic, gender, and age lines suggest that these methods had a positive effect on the design of this care recipient–focused information technology (Gustafson et al., 2002).

STANDARDS AFFECTING MEDICAL DEVICES AND HEALTH INFORMATION TECHNOLOGIES

A number of design standards and guidelines have been developed to guide the medical device and system design process (see Table 5-3). The Association for the Advancement of Medical Instrumentation (AAMI) developed many of the existing U.S. medical device standards, and, in response to the emergence of home health care as an important standardization area, recently established a new committee to focus on home health care. This group, called Medical Devices and Systems in Home Care Applications, will focus on health care devices specifically intended for use in the home environment. The efforts of this AAMI committee are intended to complement the FDA's recent Medical Device Home Use Initiative (U.S. Food and Drug Administration, 2010), designed to support the safe use of medical devices in a residential setting, and, in turn, AAMI anticipates that the FDA initiative will augment the committee's efforts (Association for the Advancement of Medical Instrumentation, 2010).

A number of user-interface standards and guidelines focus on various types of information technologies that play a role in health care in the home. Some standards and guidelines cover websites, some cover web and software applications, and some provide guidance for the design of hardware, including medical devices (see Table 5-4). However, standards and guidelines specific to health information technology applications are few.

Medical devices are migrating into the home with increasing frequency, and health information technologies are playing an ever-growing role in home-based health care, but useful guidance and regulatory oversight are not keeping pace. There is insufficient guidance regarding labeling for medical devices and regarding the content, structure, accessibility, and usability of health information technologies. The FDA's postmarket surveillance system is insufficient to capture data to assist in the understanding of problems with medical devices in the home. Despite the proliferation of health information and integrated technologies for health care in the home, guidance and standardization are lacking for these new products regarding their content, format, structure, and usability, especially for untrained users (Karsh et al., 2011).

INTEGRATED TECHNOLOGIES IN THE HOME

A variety of health care applications and systems that integrate medical devices and health information technologies promise to facilitate practice of health care in the home in the future. Integrated technologies include context-aware medication dispensing systems, infusion pumps, mobility assistive devices, wearable monitoring and reminding devices, stationary

TABLE 5-3 Key Standards for Medical Device Design

ANSI/AAMI HE74:2001 *Human Factors Design Process for Medical Devices*	The document describes "a recommended human factors engineering process for use in fulfilling user interface design requirements in the development of medical devices and systems, including hardware, software, and documentation." The standard includes an overview and a discussion of the benefits of human factors engineering, a review of the human factors engineering process and its analysis and design techniques, and a discussion of implementation issues. The information about humans comes from a variety of sources, such as review of existing literature, databases, and information from laboratory and observational studies, surveys, and questionnaires.
ANSI/AAMI HE75:2009 *Human Factors Engineering—Design of Medical Devices*	This document's 25 sections provide requirements and recommendations for nearly all human factors aspects of medical device design, including visual display, controls, alarms, connectors and connections, device software, documentation and labeling, packaging, and testing and evaluation. Special topics with particular relevance for health care in the home are covered in sections on home health care, medical device accessibility, mobile devices, and cross-cultural and cross-national design.
IEC 62366:2007 *Medical Devices— Application of Usability Engineering to Medical Devices*	This standard: "Specifies a process for a manufacturer to analyse [sic], specify, design, verify and validate usability, as it relates to safety of a medical device. This usability engineering process assesses and mitigates risks caused by usability problems associated with correct use and use errors, i.e. normal use. It can be used to identify but does not assess or mitigate risks associated with abnormal use."
IEC 60601-1-11:2010 *Requirements for Medical Electrical Equipment and Medical Electrical Systems Used in the Home Healthcare Environment*	This standard addresses some of the issues related to electrical medical devices used in the home. Although it offers significant guidance with respect to electrical power considerations for home use devices, as well as some guidance on instructions for use, remotely audible alarms (since untrained caregivers may not always be in close proximity to the equipment or the care recipient in the home), and other issues, it is by no means complete. Its guidance is limited, for example, to electrically powered devices and does not address other devices. Furthermore, its guidance on the design of instructions for use is quite limited, and it has little to say with regard to user training and instructional materials that are critical for home users.

TABLE 5-4 Standards and Guidelines for User Interfaces

Microsoft Common Health User Interface	By far the most developed and rich set of standards for health information technology applications are those developed by Microsoft under the Microsoft Common Health User Interface (MCHUI) initiative. Together with the United Kingdom's National Health Service, Microsoft has developed an impressive evidence-based set of standards, guidelines, and design patterns to help developers quickly and easily generate user interfaces related to health. MSHUI, in over 1,000 pages, provides detailed guidance to developers on content-specific areas, along with required and recommended elements and any research studies they did to substantiate the findings.
Usability.Gov	The research-based web design and usability guidelines at usability.gov are among the best set of guidelines available for web-based user interfaces. It was developed under the aegis of the National Cancer Institute and U.S. Department of Health and Human Services. Usability.gov guidelines cover a broad range of usability and user experience issues with extensive references and "strength of evidence" ratings. While these guidelines are not specific to health care, designers and developers will find them very usable.
User Interface Requirements for the Presentation of Health Data—Australia HB 306-2007	This document provides guidelines for the design of effective user interfaces for health information technology systems. It focuses on improving how the system meets the needs of users in their workflows, learning, information architecture in design of the user interface, error/warning messaging, and user acceptance. It identifies the specific requirements for designing user interfaces for health care information systems in order to ensure care recipient safety and consistent use of graphical elements and interface components in health information systems.
Web Content Accessibility Guidelines-W3C	Primarily intended for people who develop web content, the intent of these guidelines is to make web content accessible to people with disabilities. By adhering to these standards, designers and developers do make web content more available and usable to anyone who uses a compliant site.

or mobile robots, and environmental sensors. Devices and systems will be capable of sensing the environment, detecting resident movements or lack of movement, inferring what people are doing, and determining when they might need or want assistance. Medical devices or other devices in the environment, such as mobile telephones, televisions, or other information appliances, may generate alerts or other "just-in-time" information (i.e., presented at the moment at which it may be needed). It will be possible for devices or systems to provide instructions for use, to alert and inform users to modify or correct their behaviors, and, in some cases, to provide physical, cognitive, or emotional support. Instructions for use may appear on paper, but in addition or instead they may reside in the device or appear in a dedicated information product or within an existing home technology (such as a television); electronic instructions may be updatable over time, and their formats may be customizable to the needs and preferences of the individual user. Robotic systems may augment their users' functional abilities, such as their strength, balance, and sensory and cognitive capabilities, while conducting daily activities. Some components of these systems may interact with one another and may transmit information to health care providers in another location. In applications such as these, the challenges of interoperability among devices, systems, and information sources will be especially important. If there is no way to ensure that the components, whatever their origins or providers, are designed from the beginning to work together, it may be very difficult to implement effective systems.

Information technologies will play an increasing role in supporting health and wellness in the home. Some current remote telemonitoring devices in home care, such as the Health Buddy (Bosch Healthcare), are being leapfrogged by technical advances and, in fact, the definition of a medical device is growing fuzzier. For example, smart phone applications are available that can perform functions that were once relegated to single-purpose medical devices, such as glucose monitoring. Emerging technologies will not necessarily originate from traditional health care companies; many high-tech firms recognize the opportunities that exist in health care and are responding with creative solutions. In these technologies, both the medium and the message are important. As enabling technologies proliferate, they are becoming wireless, more specialized, and highly embedded, and the user interface of tomorrow will not necessarily involve a display. The user interface could be a surface that recognizes human gestures, a biometric device that detects sleep patterns, or even advanced robotic prosthetics (Bogue, 2009).

Future technological advances will bring new devices, such as improved pacemakers, cochlear implants, and medicine delivery systems. Miniaturization of various components, including microprocessors and nanotechnology, will make possible advances in many types of medical devices used inside and outside formal health care settings. Some of the devices envisioned will be embedded in common household objects, such as a biosensing chip in a toothbrush that will check blood sugar and bacteria levels; "smart" bandages made of fiber that will detect bacteria or a virus in a wound and then recommend appropriate treatment; "smart" t-shirts that will monitor the wearer's vital signs in real time; or "heads-up" displays for glasses that use pattern recognition software to help people remember human faces, inanimate objects, or other data. Novel handheld devices may provide new capabilities for home health care, such as skin surface mapping, an imaging technology that will track changes in moles to detect malignancies; biosensors that will perform as portable laboratories; or alternative input devices, such as eye blinks (electromyography) or brain activity (electroencephalography), that will facilitate hands-free device control, which will be especially useful for people with limited use of their upper extremities (e.g., people with paralysis or arthritis) (Lewis, 2001).

A few technologies that have a lot of promise are available now. For example, there is evidence that text messaging can be effective in disease monitoring and care recipient self-management, improving adherence to medication, and preparing for certain procedures (Miloh et al., 2009). The smart phone (e.g., iPhone, BlackBerry) is a multifunctional tool that enables users to download applications that assist them in tracking important measures, such as sleep, exercise, nutrition, blood sugar, and overall wellness. Several applications currently available allow care recipients to update and view their personal health record, understand and track medication usage, communicate with their physicians, and even participate in clinical trials. Internet-based information resources have great potential to assist people to make well-informed health care choices and navigate health care systems.

One of the most innovative areas of new digital technologies is the use of game systems to support rehabilitation regimens. Recent advances in accelerometers have propelled the development of small digital devices that monitor movement (personal motion technologies) and are highly adaptable. Game systems like the Nintendo Wii that use unique input and feedback measures can be used to support aerobic activity, flexibility, and even physical therapy (Halton, 2008). These systems are increasingly being used in nursing homes and rehabilitation centers, but the affordability and creativity of the software make the technology appropriate for use in the home.

Technologies like exercise game systems support health and wellness goals by providing real-time feedback on progress, such as toward a daily goal of calories burned. The theory behind these devices is that knowledge will motivate the user, although many of these applications go beyond the individual and provide opportunities to create a social network. Some studies suggest that participation in a group provides greater motivation to reach a goal than does individual participation. But the application of personal motion technologies extends far beyond measuring and reporting calories; these devices can also be important in care recipient safety by monitoring for falls or ensuring that care recipients get sufficient exercise (National Research Council, 2010). Most of the technologies come with an online component that may make them more useful for monitoring daily behaviors and detecting patterns that occur over time.

New "smart home" technologies, which include automatic sensors, collect data that gets stored or transmitted to off-site caregivers (Demiris, 2010). Increasing numbers of wireless-enabled devices, like pulse oximeters, blood pressure cuffs, and scales, automatically log and transmit their values to personal health records and care providers. Some initiatives, such as Dossia (personal health platforms) and Continua Health Alliance (hardware), provide tightly coupled health "eco-systems" of applications and devices to manage disease, track wellness, and provide for healthier living. Even in the area of medication management, medication-dispensing machines for the home can be remotely managed over an Internet connection. Recent advances in digital TV will soon enable care recipients to have access to rich Internet applications on their television sets. These can include using video content sites to deliver training or instructional material and perhaps full two-way communications between individuals and their caregivers in different locations.

Technologies that provide remote access to monitor care recipient status have become important aids to caregivers and clinicians. Although episodic monitoring is currently used in some telehealth systems that enable a care recipient–caregiver dyad to check in remotely with a health care professional, more continuous monitoring of caregiver performance and providing real-time instruction or guidance have not been implemented (Schulz and Tompkins, 2010). Many of these technologies raise privacy concerns that may make them difficult to implement, but recent research in this area suggests that with increasing levels of disability, individuals become more willing to relinquish privacy for increased functioning and independence (Beach et al., 2009). However, little is known about caregivers' willingness to be monitored and remotely guided by health care professionals.

Issues of cost, usability, and privacy will prevent some of these advanced technologies from realizing widespread adoption, creating a penetration gap that has been called the "digital divide." Many of these technologies are not particularly expensive relative to health care costs in general, yet they pose a cost burden that must be recognized. For example, although adoption of technologies such as the Internet is generally high among adults in the United States, rates of computer technology use and broadband access are lower among minority populations and people of lower socioeconomic status, people who have a physical disability, and older adults. This is problematic, given the increased use of the Internet as a vehicle for the delivery of health information and services. Health care solutions that can be delivered on ubiquitous technologies, such as smart phones, may help bridge this divide.

At the same time, cost may not be as imposing an issue as usability. Although these products may be promising, many of them, from a usability point of view, still display the rough edges of nascent technology. Applications that rely on care recipient behavior to generate accurate data will always be prone to human error (e.g., a blood pressure cuff wrapped around the wrong location). For optimal health outcomes, it is important that these technologies be developed by applying a user-centered design approach that takes into consideration the needs, characteristics, abilities, and preferences of all potential user populations. For example, it is important to consider the full range of users' functional abilities, health literacy, self-efficacy, readiness to change, and motivations for and barriers to changing health behaviors. It is also important to honor the users' cultural norms and their preferences for how and with whom to share data, action recommendations, or options and key decisions. For example, an older adult may be willing to share home monitoring or health data with one adult child but not another, requiring simple but effective system authentication and access control protocols.

Technology developments have the potential to increase the amounts of health care information transmitted to and from the home. There is general agreement regarding the protection of individuals' privacy and the need to reach an appropriate balance between keeping health information confidential and sharing essential information among caregivers to assure proper treatment as well as among researchers to advance knowledge about health care (Institute of Medicine, 2001, 2009). In a recent workshop on the role of human factors in home health care, participants noted that "the Health Insurance Portability and Accountability Act (HIPAA) plays a major role in telehealth applications and web-based applications in which individuals transmit personal health information over the Internet. However, HIPAA cannot address some of the new and emerging trends in health information technology" (National Research Council, 2010, p. 42). Adding to the complexity of privacy concerns, emerging tools aren't necessarily regulated by HIPAA because developers of the PHR and other applications are not considered "covered entities" as defined by HIPAA. There have been calls to address this gap in current HIPAA regulations (Kahn et al., 2009; Demiris et al., 2010; Geiger, 2010).

REFERENCES

Alkhatlan, H. (2010). *Doctoral dissertation: Evaluation of young adults' preferences, needs, and the understandability of the personal health record data contents.* University of Pittsburgh, School of Health and Rehabilitation Sciences, PA.

Association for the Advancement of Medical Instrumentation. (2009). *Human factors engineering—Design of medical devices.* American National Standard, ANSI/AAMI HE75:2009. Available: http://marketplace.aami.org/eseries/scriptcontent/docs/Preview%20Files/HE750910_preview.pdf [May 12, 2010].

Association for the Advancement of Medical Instrumentation. (2010). New AAMI committee tackles home use device challenges. *Home Healthcare Horizons,* p. 7. Available: http://www.aami.org/publications/HomeHealthcare/articles/7_News_Committee.pdf [March 31, 2011].

Beach, S., Schulz, R., Downs, J., Matthews, J., Barron, B., and Seelman, K. (2009). Disability, age, and informational privacy attitudes in quality of life technology applications: Results from a national web survey. *ACM Transactions on Accessible Computing, 2*(1), 1-21.

Bogue, R. (2009). Nanosensors: A review of recent research. *Sensor Review, 29*(4), 310-315.

Demiris, G. (2010). Information technology and systems in home health care. In National Research Council, *The role of human factors in home health care: Workshop summary* (pp. 173-200). S. Olson, Rapporteur. Committee on the Role of Human Factors in Home Health Care. Committee on Human-Systems Integration, Division of Behavioral and Social Sciences and Education. Washington, DC: The National Academies Press.

Demiris, G., Charness, N., Krupinski, E., et al. (2010). The role of human factors in telehealth. *Telemedicine and e-Health, 16*(4), 446-453.

Eysenbach, G. (2000). Consumer health informatics. *British Medical Journal, 320*(7251), 1713-1716.

Federal Telemedicine News. (2010, April 25). *Telehealth vital in home care.* Available: http://telemedicinenews.blogspot.com/2010/04/telehealth-vital-in-home-care.html [March 31, 2011].

Fox, S., and Jones, S. (2009). *The social life of health information. Summary of findings.* Available: http://www.pewinternet.org/Reports/2009/8-The-Social-Life-of-Health-Information/01-Summary-of-Findings.aspx [April 2011].

Gardner-Bonneau, D. (2010, April 14, 2010). *Device use outside the clinic and hospital: Human factors implications for home use medical device design.* Presentation to the Design of Medical Devices Conference, University of Minnesota, Minneapolis.

Geidl, L., Zrunek, P., Deckert, Z., et al. (2009). Usability and safety of ventricular assist devices: Human factors and design aspects. *Artificial Organs, 33*(9), 691-695.

Geiger, H. (2010, July 9). *HHS issues proposed updates to HIPAA privacy regulations.* Center for Democracy and Technology. Available: http://www.cdt.org/blogs/harley-geiger/hhs-issues-proposed-updates-hipaa-privacy-regulations [March 31, 2011].

Gibbons, C.M., Wilson, R.F., Samal, L., et al. (2009). Impact of consumer health informatics applications. *Evidence Report/Technology Assessment.* Baltimore, MD: Johns Hopkins University Evidence-Based Practice Center.

Gibbons, M.C. (2007). *Ehealth solutions for healthcare disparities.* New York: Springer.

Gustafson, D.H., Hawkins, R.P., Boberg, E.W., et al. (2002). CHESS: 10 years of research and development in consumer health informatics for broad populations, including the underserved. *International Journal of Medical Informatics, 65*(3), 169-177.

Halton, J. (2008). Rehabilitation with video games. *Occupational Therapy Now, 10*(1), 12-14.

Hesse, B.W. (2005). Harnessing the power of an intelligent health environment in cancer control. *Studies in Health Technology and Informatics, 118,* 159-176.

Institute of Medicine. (2000). *To err is human: Building a safer health system.* L.T. Kohn, J.M. Corrigan, and M.S. Donaldson, Eds. Committee on Quality of Health Care in America. Washington, DC: National Academy Press.

Institute of Medicine. (2001). *Crossing the quality chasm: A new health system for the 21st century.* Committee on the Quality of Health Care in America. Washington, DC: National Academy Press.

Institute of Medicine. (2009). *Beyond the HIPAA privacy rule: Enhancing privacy, improving health through research.* S.J. Nass, L.A. Levit, and L.O. Gostin, Eds. Committee on Health Research and the Privacy of Health Information: The HIPAA Privacy Rule. Washington, DC: The National Academies Press.

Jacko, J.A., and Sears, A. (2008). *The human-computer interaction handbook: Fundamentals, evolving technologies and emerging applications* (2nd ed.). Mahwah, NJ: Lawrence Erlbaum Associates.

Kahn, J.S., Aulakh, V., and Bosworth, A. (2009). What it takes: Characteristics of the ideal personal health record. *Health Affairs, 28,* 369-376.

Karsh, B.-T., Weinger, M.B., Abbott, P.A., and Wears, R.L. (2011). Health information technology: Fallacies and sober realities. *Journal of American Medical Information Association, 17,* 617-623.

Kaye, R., and Crowley, J. (2000). *Guidance for industry and FDA premarket and design control reviewers. Medical device use-safety: Incorporating human factors engineering into risk management.* Washington, DC: U.S. Food and Drug Administration. Available: http://www.fda.gov/downloads/MedicalDevices/DeviceRegulationandGuidance/GuidanceDocuments/ucm094461.pdf [April 2011].

Lambert, S.D., and Loiselle, C.G. (2007). Health information-seeking behavior. *Qualitative Health Research, 17*(8), 1006-1019.

Lewis, C. (2001). *Emerging trends in medical device technology: Home is where the heart monitor is* (vol. 35). Rockville, MD: U.S. Department of Health and Human Services, Food and Drug Administration.

Liang, L. (2010). *Connected for health: Transforming care delivery at Kaiser Permanente.* San Francisco, CA: Jossey-Bass.

Manhattan Research. (2009). *Taking the Pulse® Nurses: Nurses and emerging information technologies.* New York: Author. Available: http://products.manhattanresea rch.com/files/PRESS/Taking_the_Pulse_US_Nurses_Brochure.pdf [April 2011].

Marion, J. (2007). *MedSun adverse event reports related to home healthcare devices. MedSun: Newsletter 17.* Available: http://www.accessdata.fda.gov/scripts/cdrh/cfdocs/medsun/news/newsletter.cfm?news=17 [April 2011].

Medical Device Consultants, Inc. (2010). Notes from general hospital and personal use devices panel meeting of March 5, 2010. *Medical Device News and Insights.* Available: http://www.mdci.com/blog/?tag=insulin-infusion-pumps [April 2011].

Miloh, T., Annunziato, R., Arnon, R., et al. (2009). Improved adherence and outcomes for pediatric liver transplant recipients by using text messaging. *Pediatrics, 124*(5), e844-e850.

National Alliance for Health Information Technology. (2008). *Defining key health information technology terms.* Report to the Office of the National Coordinator for Health Information Technology. Washington, DC: U.S. Department of Health and Human Services.

National Cancer Institute. (2005). *Health information national trends survey: How Americans find and use cancer information. Brief 1: Cancer seeking information behaviors.* Washington, DC: Author. Available: http://hints.cancer.gov/brief_1.jsp [April 2011].

National Committee on Vital and Health Statistics. (1998). *Ensuring a health dimension for the national information infrastructure: A concept paper from the National Committee on Vital and Health Statistics.* Available: http://www.ncvhs.hhs.gov/hii-nii.htm [April 2011].

National Committee on Vital and Health Statistics. (2001). *Information for health: A strategy for building a national health information infrastructure: Report and recommendations from the National Committee on Vital and Health Statistics.* Available: http://aspe.hhs. gov/sp/nhii/documents/NHIIReport2001/default.htm [April 2011].

National Research Council. (1996). *Safe, comfortable, attractive, and easy to use: Improving the usability of home medical devices.* Committee on Human Factors. Commission on Behavioral and Social Sciences and Education. Washington, DC: National Academy Press.

National Research Council. (2010). *The role of human factors in home health care: Workshop summary.* S. Olson, Rapporteur. Committee on the Role of Human Factors in Home Health Care, Committee on Human-Systems Integration, Division of Behavioral and Social Sciences and Education. Washington, DC: The National Academies Press.

Norman, D.A. (1980). *The psychology of everyday things.* New York: Basic Books.

Parmanto, B. (2010). *A model for accessibility of health records: From EHR to PHR (presentation).* Paper presented at the Interagency Committee on Disability Research Health, Disability and Technology Conference, May 13-14.

Petrie, H., Hamilton, F., King, N., and Pavan, P. (2006). Remote usability evaluations with disabled people. *Proceedings of the ACM Conference on Human Factors in Computing Systems,* April 22-27, Montreal, Quebec, Canada. Available: http://www-course.cs.york. ac.uk/rmh/p1133-petrie.pdf [April 2011].

Pinelle, D., and Gutman, C. (2001). *Collaboration requirements for home care.* Technical Report HCI-01-01, Department of Computer Science, University of Saskatchewan. Available: http://hci.usask.ca/publications/2001/homecare.pdf [April 2011].

Pinelle, D., and Gutwin, C. (2002). Supporting collaboration in multidisciplinary home care teams. *Proceedings of the American Medical Informatics Association (AMIA): Annual AMIA Symposium.* Available: http://www.ncbi.nlm.nih.gov/pmc/articles/PMC2244174/ pdf/procamiasymp00001-0658.pdf [April 2011].

Schulz, R., and Tompkins, C.A. (2010). Informal caregivers in the United States: Prevalence, caregiver characteristics, and ability to provide care. In National Research Council, *The role of human factors in home health care: Workshop summary* (pp. 118-144). S. Olson, Rapporteur. Committee on the Role of Human Factors in Home Health Care. Committee on Human-Systems Integration, Division of Behavioral and Social Sciences and Education. Washington, DC: The National Academies Press.

Senders, J.W. (1994). Medical devices, medical errors, and medical accidents. In M.S. Bogner (Ed.), *Human error in medicine* (pp. 159-177). Hillsdale, NJ: Lawrence Erlbaum Associates.

Shaw, B., Gustafson, D.H., Hawkins, R., et al. (2006). How underserved breast cancer patients use and benefit from ehealth programs: Implications for closing the digital divide. *American Behavioral Scientist, 49*(6), 823-834.

Story, M. (2010). Medical devices in home health care. In National Research Council, *The role of human factors in home health care: Workshop summary* (pp. 145-172). S. Olson, Rapporteur. Committee on the Role of Human Factors in Home Health Care. Committee on Human-Systems Integration, Division of Behavioral and Social Sciences and Education. Washington, DC: The National Academies Press.

Swezey, R.W., and Llaneras, R.E. (1997). Models in training and instruction. In G. Salvendy (Ed.), *Handbook of human factors and ergonomics* (2nd ed.). New York: John Wiley and Sons.

Thompson, T., and Brailer, D. (2004). *The decade of health information technology: Delivering consumer-centric and information-rich health care: Framework for strategic action.* Washington, DC: U.S. Department of Health and Human Services. Available: http://www.providersedge.com/ehdocs/ehr_articles/The_Decade_of_HIT-zDelivering_ Customer-centric_and_Info-rich_HC.pdf.

Tufte, E.R. (2001). *The visual display of quantitative information* (2nd ed.). Cheshire, CT: Graphics Press.

U.S. Environmental Protection Agency. (2004). *Asthma home environment checklist: EPA 402-F-03-030.* Washington, DC: Author.

U.S. Food and Drug Administration. (1996). *Do it by design: An introduction to human factors in medical devices.* Available: http://www.fda.gov/MedicalDevices/DeviceRegulationandGuidance/GuidanceDocuments/ucm094957.htm [April 28, 2010].

U.S. Food and Drug Administration. (2001). *Guidance on medical device patient labeling.* Washington, DC: Health and Human Services, U.S. Food and Drug Administration. Available: http://www.fda.gov/MedicalDevices/DeviceRegulationandGuidance/GuidanceDocuments/ucm070782.htm [April 2011].

U.S. Food and Drug Administration. (2010). *Medical device home use initiative.* Washington, DC: Author.

Vance, A. (2009). Insurers fight speech-impairment remedy. *The New York Times.* Available: http://www.nytimes.com/2009/09/15/technology/15speech.html?scp=3&sq=September%2015,%202009&st=cse [March 31, 2011].

Weaver, J.B., Mays, D., Lindner, G., et al. (2009). Profiling characteristics of internet medical information users. *Journal of the American Medical Informatics Association, 16,* 714-722.

West-Frasier, J. (2008). *The impact of telemonitoring on self-efficacy, emotional well-being and clinical outcomes in patients with chronic obstructive pulmonary disease of heart failure.* Kalamazoo, MI: Western Michigan University, College of Health and Human Services.

Zeng, X., and Parmanto, B. (2003). Evaluation of web accessibility of consumer health information websites. *AMIA Annual Symposium Proceedings,* pp. 743-747. Available: http://www.ncbi.nlm.nih.gov/pmc/articles/PMC1480305/ [April 2011].

Zerhouni, E.A. (2005). U.S. biomedical research: Basic, translational, and clinical sciences. *Journal of the American Medical Association, 294*(11), 1352-1358.

6

The Home Environment

As homes increasingly become the places for health care delivery and self-management, the intertwined effects of multiple environments (physical, social/cultural, community, and policy) on the well-being of care recipients and caregivers are more visible (Wahl et al., 2009). Managing health care at home is a challenge confronted by many people, including older persons, children, and younger adults with disabilities, who are especially vulnerable to their environments. This is also true for people with low incomes, multiple chronic illnesses, limited social supports, and health disparities as well as those who live in unsafe neighborhoods or poor-quality housing. A majority of vulnerable individuals do not receive effective health care for their chronic illnesses and live in housing that does not support their independence or functioning.

Without accessible and supportive housing, the options for delivery of health care in the home are limited. This chapter discusses the environmental factors that impact health care at home, with the intent of exploring how residents, health professionals, and policy makers can work together to improve environments that support better health. The lens of human factors considers the relationships among individuals, the tasks they perform, and the environment, offering a systems perspective to understand how the home environment can better support health care.

The environment for home-based health care is multilayered (see Figure 3-1). It includes the physical attributes of the home; social and cultural influences, such as social activity and personal values; community and municipality characteristics; and health/social service policy and governmental regulations. This chapter discusses the attributes of different environments as they apply to health care in the home. The family vignettes in Boxes 6-1 and 6-2 serve to illustrate many of the points made.

PHYSICAL ENVIRONMENTS

In contrast to more structured settings, such as hospitals, nursing homes, or doctors' offices, the physical environments of homes are more uncontrolled, dynamic, personal, and diverse (Gitlin, 2003; Siebert, 2009). These locations therefore pose novel challenges to providing direct health care and using health technology and equipment. Homes vary widely in their location, size, condition, and physical characteristics (see Table 6-1). Each of these factors affects provision of care and how health technologies are used. Home environments can either help or hinder the ability of individuals to perform physical functions, carry out personal care tasks, or use health technologies. Individuals and families also differ in their willingness to change the home environment to facilitate health care, their preferences for where they perform basic activities of daily living, and their willingness to use health technologies (Albert, 2010). As each home is unique, solutions that may be suitable for one individual, family caregiver, and home may not be appropriate or effective for others.

Housing in the United States

The United States is characterized by great diversity of residential locations, housing types and conditions, and cultural, neighborhood, and health policy influences. These variations have important implications for the provision of health care in the home.

According to 2010 U.S. census data, approximately 244 million persons in the United States live in urban and suburban areas, and 65 million live in rural areas (U.S. Census Bureau, 2010). These locations have different capacities to support the health needs of individuals due to the varying availability of public transit, housing options, and health care services. Moreover, the types of housing vary considerably: nearly 79 million are detached single-family homes, 5 million are duplexes, 28 million are multifamily units, and 9 million are mobile homes (American Community Survey, 2008).

In these different settings, older adults make up a large proportion of the 133 million U.S. residents with one or more chronic illnesses (Wu and Green, 2000). Nearly 86 percent of the more than 37 million people over age 65 have chronic illness (Centers for Disease Control and Prevention, 2008), but many older adults reside in older homes that are not well suited to their changing needs (Gill et al., 1999; Commission on Affordable

TABLE 6-1 Environmental Factors That Affect Medical Care and Life at Home

Physical Environment	Types of homes (detached single-family house, duplex, townhouse, apartment, mobile home)
	Age and condition
	Layout including location of bathrooms and bedrooms
	Accessibility in, out, and around the home
	Supportive features
	Communications/Internet access
	Adequacy of utilities
	Presence of children and animals
Social Environment	Immediate family
	Extended family
	Friends
	Religious affiliates
	Colleagues
	Cultural community
	Neighborhood community
	Clubs/associations
	Charitable activities
	Leisure activities
Community Environment	Safety conditions
	Weather conditions
	Presence and condition of streets and sidewalks
	Presence and condition of parks and recreation opportunities
	Presence and condition of meeting centers/locations
	Availability of goods and services
	Availability of public transportation
Health Policy Environment	Housing policies
	Zoning policies
	Building codes
	Social services policies
	Medical insurance company policies
	Medicare policies
	Medicaid policies
	Health care and long-term care reimbursement policies

Housing and Health Facility Needs for Seniors in the 21st Century, 2002; Donald, 2009).

Housing Conditions

Too many individuals live in housing that may adversely affect their health and the delivery of care. For example, over 6 million households (about 5 percent of the total) live in housing that has moderate or severe physical problems related to heating, plumbing, and electrical deficiencies (U.S. Department of Housing and Urban Development, 2009, p. 389). Such problems are more prevalent in homes of low-income persons who are also at risk of exposure to lead paint, vermin and pest infestations, water leakage, and lack of air conditioning. These issues pose an especially serious risk to vulnerable populations, such as children with asthma, older adults with cognitive or physical impairments, and individuals with chronic diseases or disabilities, who are more susceptible to toxic exposures, respiratory problems, infections, and dehydration or hypothermia (U.S. Department of Housing and Urban Development, 2009). Moreover, such physical hazards impact the ability to install and use life-sustaining health devices.

Housing Barriers

The physical layout of homes can put individuals at greater risk of accidents, make daily living activities more difficult to perform, and even necessitate moving to a different home, assisted living, or nursing home (Fänge and Iwarsson, 2003; Iwarsson, 2005; Lau et al., 2007; Stark, 2008). For example, an older adult with mobility difficulties living in a three-story home may begin to experience difficulty navigating its stairs. An older adult who uses a diuretic living in a home with a bathroom only on the second floor may become nonadherent due to lack of easy access to the bathroom.

The role of the physical environment in accidents such as falls is of significant concern for persons with disabilities and those who are frail. One study of outpatients with lower limb amputations found that 58 percent of individuals with unilateral amputations and 27 percent of those with bilateral amputations reported at least 1 fall in the previous 12 months. Among people with unilateral amputations, 12 percent of falls were related to the prosthesis alone, 22 percent were related to the environment alone, and 48 percent were a result of intrinsic patient-related factors (Kulkarni et al., 1996). Older adults are also at increased risk for falls. Environmental factors, implicated in 40 to 50 percent of falls of older persons, include slippery surfaces, inadequate lighting, loose or deep pile or worn carpet, staircases without an appropriate railing, badly arranged furniture, and poorly designed bathrooms (Clemson, Cumming, and Roland, 1996; Pynoos et al., 2006).

The spatial layout of a home can even hinder performance of activities of daily living. Insufficient space can make it difficult for caregivers to provide assistance and can hinder placement of medical devices (Sanford, 2010). Narrow staircases and small rooms illustrated in the vignette (see Box 6-1) are typical in that they were not designed for persons with disabilities, let alone for the delivery of health care or use of health technologies.

Home Modifications

The way in which individuals adapt to changing functional ability at home tends to follow a hierarchy of choices (see Figure 6-1). Individuals, particularly older adults, initially respond to functional difficulties by modifying their behaviors in the home, often reducing the frequency of an activity or taking more time to accomplish a particular task. If this does not work, they then adopt the use of an assistive device. When these strategies are no longer effective, individuals may choose to modify their home or use a combination of behavioral and environmental modifications along with personal care assistance when other strategies no longer are effective (Norburn et al., 1995).

At any of these stages, telehealth technologies can be employed. Telehealth is the delivery of health care services or information via telecommunications technologies. Often is it used to link care recipients and caregivers to external health care providers, but it can also be used for communications between care recipients and caregivers. Today, telehealth can include a telephone call, an e-mail, an online course, remote monitoring, and an online portal to store and send information. In the future, the presence of telehealth technologies will rise dramatically as they become more affordable and readily integrated into users' lifestyles. More devices will be smaller, wireless, and embedded and/or integrated with other devices and systems. More robotic tools and sophisticated software will be available to enable automatic surveillance and decision support.

When behavioral modifications include reducing the frequency of self-care, individuals are at risk for negative health effects, including depression, health problems, and functional decline (Wrosch, Schulz, and Heckhausen, 2002). A supportive home environment can compensate for a person's impaired functional capacity. Home modifications can enhance accessibility and minimize barriers of conventional housing, particularly for persons with impaired ambulation (Schaie et al., 2003; Gitlin, 2007). In addition, it appears that home modifications, when used in conjunction with exercise and medical risk assessment, can reduce the risk of falls among older adults (Pynoos, Steinman, and Nguyen, 2010).

BOX 6-1
The Johnson Family

Sam Johnson is a 38-year-old veteran who lost his hearing and both legs after stepping on a land mine in Iraq. He arrived home recently to the small two-story rowhouse he shares with his wife, Barbara, and their 8-year-old son, Aaron. Barbara assists her husband with activities of daily living in the evenings and on weekends when she is home from her job and Sam's home health aide is unavailable. Sam spends the majority of his time in their second-floor bedroom because he doesn't like going up and down the stairs on his artificial limbs. At times, he uses a wheelchair for mobility, but he keeps it on the first floor. He's glad that he cannot hear the doorbell, because it gives him an excuse not to struggle with the stairs.

Sam's rowhouse was built in 1946. It has 4 steps up to the front door and 12 more on a narrow stairway with handrails leading to a second floor with two bedrooms and a small bathroom with a toilet, bathtub, and sink. The house is dimly lit, and the staircase has a light switch only at the bottom. Sam has fallen on his way to the bathroom at night a couple of times since he came home.

Barbara, tired from her caregiving duties, has little time to herself as she tries to manage her own anxiety, hypertension, and chronic back pain, along with her husband's needs. She is concerned about keeping everything straight, especially regarding their different medication schedules, and fears making errors. She struggles to communicate with Sam due to his hearing loss and often writes notes to make sure he understands what she's saying to him.

Modifications to their home, adoption of available technologies, and some training could make this family's life easier. It could be advantageous to set up a room on the first floor as Sam's bedroom and add a small first-floor bathroom. Installing a light in the bedroom that flashes when someone rings the doorbell (which he cannot hear) would alert him that he has a visitor. A lift chair to help him transfer from sitting to standing would also be helpful. Although it would help to install a walk-in (i.e., curbless) shower so caregivers could safely help Sam bathe, such a change would depend on available space and funds.

Sam receives an array of support through the U.S. Department of Veterans Affairs (VA), such as monthly disability compensation for him and his dependents (averaging $2,932 per month), health care through the VA hospitals and health care system, and funds for home modifications.

SOURCE: Research experience of committee member Sara J. Czaja.

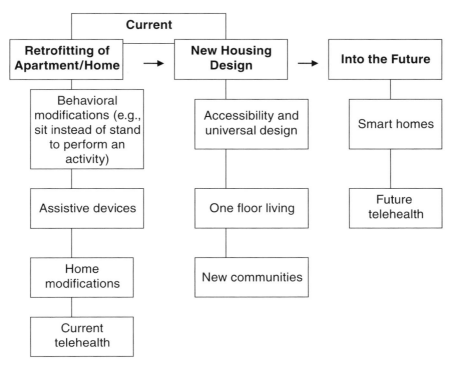

FIGURE 6-1 Continuum of housing modification options.
SOURCE: Adapted from Gitlin (2007).

Home modifications may include removing hazards; adding special features, such as grab bars, stair lifts, and ramps; and rearranging furnishings to create clear pathways. In addition, spaces can be renovated and the purpose of a room may be modified to accommodate a person with mobility limitations who cannot climb stairs or needs constant supervision (Pynoos et al., 1987). Many care recipients benefit from both low-cost home modifications and training in their use to enable them to engage in their daily activities more safely and efficiently (Gitlin and Corcoran, 2000; Gitlin et al., 2009).

Cognitive deficits affect over 5.3 million older persons, adding a layer of complexity to health care in the home (Hebert et al., 2003; Alzheimer's Association, 2010). Because persons with cognitive impairments have diminished capacity in problem solving, decision making, and recognizing environmental cues, they have special environmental needs (Olsen, Ehrenkrantz, and Hutchings, 1993) and interventions. For example, as dementia can affect depth perception, it is important to keep objects out of pathways to prevent people from falling. Night lights that automatically turn on at dusk could make it easier and safer to navigate the home during the evening. Likewise, large labels can help compensate for limited vision to help identify objects and use them appropriately. Devices that monitor people's movements or detect a fall, alarms that indicate a door has opened, and safety alert bracelets may improve the safety of persons with dementia and provide reassurance to caregivers.

A survey by the American Association of Retired Persons (2000) of people over age 45 found that a substantial percentage of respondents had made the following home modifications:

- Installing light switches at the top and bottom of stairs (24 percent),
- Adding handrails on stairs (17 percent),
- Making changes to live on a first floor (14 percent),
- Widening doorways (9 percent),
- Adding a ramp or stair lift (4 percent).

Bathroom modifications were more likely to be made in the homes of older persons (ages 75 and over), the population with the greatest need (Freedman, 2011).

Although there is an array of home modification products on the market, there is no single place to purchase them all. Building supply stores carry a limited range of products, such as single-lever handles, "comfort" height toilets, handheld showers, grab bars, and hand rails. Medical supply and drug stores tend to focus on assistive devices (e.g., reachers, raised toilet seats) rather than home modifications. A growing number of specialized home modification firms have evolved that offer a variety of products (e.g., grab bars in different materials, stair lifts, curbless showers, easy access bathtubs) and a number of websites provide access to a range of products. For example, AbleData, a website maintained by the National Institute on Disability and Rehabilitation Research (NIDRR), features a product listing to help locate product manufacturers or distributors.[1] Occupational therapists who specialize in home assessments are particularly skilled at helping to identify what will work for a particular individual and how to install home modifications to maximize an individual's abilities.

A systematic home assessment by a trained occupational or physical therapist can help identify potential problems and solutions in the home

---

[1] The AbleData database of assistive technology contains objective information on almost 40,000 assistive products. For each product, the database includes a detailed description of the product's functions and features, price information (when available), and contact information for the product's manufacturer and/or distributors.

environment. A home assessment can also help caregivers provide better care, simplify tasks, and effectively use such assistive devices as a tub bench or lift chair (Pynoos et al., 1997). A home assessment prior to a person's discharge from the hospital can also facilitate the transition to home and possibly minimize functional decline that can have a role in hospital readmissions (van Haastregt et al., 2000; Stuck et al., 2002).

There is a large unmet need for home modifications. About 1 million older persons have unmet needs for home modifications due to such factors as costs, their own inability to make changes, and lack of skilled installers. People are also reluctant to make some changes because they do not like their appearance (American Association of Retired Persons, 2000). Renters in particular may hesitate to make modifications because, even though the Fair Housing Amendments Act of 1998 gives them the right, they fear objections from their landlords or that they may have to take them out when they move (Newman and Mezrich, 1997; Pynoos et al., 2008).

Health-Related Technologies in the Home

A wide range of technology solutions is available to assist care recipients and caregivers in the home in order to make the environment more assistive and inclusive. Solutions that facilitate bedside care include adjustable beds that change position and height, pressure-relieving bed surfaces (e.g., gel mattress, low-air-loss mattress), lift devices (to facilitate transferring from one surface to another and reduce risk of caregiver injury), and seating devices to relieve pressure and prevent contractures.

Other low-tech assistive devices include grab bars, raised toilet seats, and clocks or telephones with large numerals (Gitlin et al., 2005, 2009, 2010). In addition, simple monitoring devices, such as intercoms or cell phones, can facilitate communication. There are also innovations in remote health monitoring that may help caregivers by providing mechanisms for monitoring safety and well-being. In cases involving persons with early-stage dementia, the technologies that are likely to be most useful are passive and do not require learning new procedures or practices. These include motion monitors that send alerts for people at risk of falling, video monitoring for activities and well-being, and interactive telehealth systems that encourage communication among care recipients, informal caregivers and formal caregivers. Although these technologies are promising, strong evidence is not yet available for the effectiveness of any particular remote monitoring technologies in achieving specific health outcomes. These approaches warrant further development and testing.

Although telehealth technologies and assistive devices may alleviate the burden of care (Gitlin, Winter, and Dennis, 2010), there are significant environmental challenges to their effective use. These include physical aspects of the home (e.g., narrow hallways and staircases) that may hinder installation of assistive devices, lack of reliable electricity, and absence of Internet connections. Some technologies may be too costly, and the lack of reimbursement could require families to pay for them out of pocket. Any personal discomfort with technologies or devices in general could also reduce their use.

The Home as a Work Environment

The home can be a challenging environment for both residents and their formal caregivers, such as registered nurses, physical therapists, occupational therapists, physicians, or personal care aides (Piersol and Ehrlich, 2009).

Environmental conditions that can affect self-management and provision of health care in the home include lighting conditions; noise levels and room acoustics; temperature and humidity levels; air and water quality; electrical capacity and outlets; spatial layout and privacy; sanitation; the overall condition of the home (e.g., windows or doors that do not open or shut, falling ceilings, inadequate plumbing); and accessibility. Poor heating and air conditioning can place individuals at risk of heatstroke or hypothermia. Finally, a home may have broken windows or locks or unsafe walls and leaky roofs (Gershon et al., 2008). Rooms may be physically crowded or cluttered, making it difficult for the person providing or receiving care to maneuver within the space. Injuries to one or both parties may occur during transfers in confined spaces with few physical supports and no room for a lift device. Carpeting or stairs may hinder medical device or mobility aid maneuverability. The home may not be clean, increasing the risk of infection or disease. The household may be busy with other residents and activities, providing distractions that may confuse people while they engage in health-related activities.

Conditions may especially make it difficult to use electronic devices. For example, the lighting level may be low, making it hard to see people or device displays and controls. The noise levels may be high, making it difficult to hear people or device prompts and alarms. The temperature may be very high (e.g., in Florida) or very low (e.g., in Alaska), which can affect people or equipment. The humidity may be very high (e.g., in Louisiana), which can cause condensation, or very low (e.g., in Arizona), which can produce static electricity. Children, unauthorized users, pets, or vermin in the home can also put them at risk (e.g., playing with syringes), cause damage to devices (e.g., chewing on tubing), or change device settings, which may not be noticed before the unit is used again.

SOCIAL AND CULTURAL ENVIRONMENTS

Table 6-1 provides examples of social and cultural networks and activities. These networks provide support as well as prevailing attitudes about health care, and activities provide a sense of well-being and self-worth.

Care recipients' mental outlook and physical health benefit from outdoor activity (National Institute on Aging, 2001; World Health Organization, 2002; Kai, Anderson, and Lau, 2003; Li et al., 2006). Enabling care recipients to participate in meaningful activities may reduce their apathy, boredom, and risk of depression (Gitlin et al., 2008, 2009). In addition, enabling family members who find themselves as informal caregivers to engage in meaningful activities and to take care of their own health can help them provide care for a longer period of time. For example, the ability to obtain formal daily supportive services for care recipients would also allow informal caregivers time to attend to their own needs. The availability of instruction on proper care techniques, such as how to assist with transfer in and out of the bed, would help informal caregivers reduce their own risk of injury (Sörensen et al., 2002; Pinquart and Sörensen, 2006).

Health care in the home is not only influenced by the availability and capability of social networks. It is also influenced by varying attitudes toward health care by different cultural and ethnic groups. Cultural beliefs about health affect how people cope with illness and maintain home care regimens. In a broad sense, the kind of health care a person receives at home depends on the meaning of "home" to them. This includes whether they are motivated to adapt their home and manage serious illness or disability in the community. Families differ in their willingness to reorganize living spaces to accommodate an ill family member (Albert, 1990) and in their tolerance for disorder and strategies for managing it (Rubinstein, 1990). People also differ in their attitudes about using medical technology, such as home infusion therapy or lift devices. For example, some people do not want their homes turned into what they perceive as a hospital, while others are willing to accept various devices and technology that would help them to function better and socialize.

Personal values also play a role in end-of-life care at home. For example, some people consider a peaceful death at home as the preferred outcome. For others, experiencing a loved one's death in the home is stressful or uncomfortable. These beliefs determine the nature of care delivered in the final days of life (Kagawa-Singer, 2001).

COMMUNITY ENVIRONMENTS

Table 6-1 illustrates community environmental factors that can play an important role in whether care recipients can live independently and manage their health care at home (Golant, 2006, 2007). Poor neighborhood conditions are linked to higher rates of depression, worse chronic illness, and poor access to formal care staff (Bowling and Stafford, 2007; Beard et al., 2009). The local community can influence whether care recipients can carry out daily living tasks, participate in social activities, and engage in healthy behaviors, such as walking safely in their neighborhood and shopping for healthy foods. Neighborhoods can be ill suited to outdoor activity when, for example, sidewalks and intersections are lined with hazards and debris and the traffic signals are too short to allow time for care recipients to cross the street safely (Li et al., 2006). Many communities lack adequate public transit or pay only limited attention to sidewalk and street crossing maintenance. Many neighborhoods in suburban areas do not have sidewalks at all.

Community features vary widely, including land use patterns/development density, road conditions, street and pedestrian connection systems, street safety (e.g., separation from traffic, crossings), street design (e.g., furniture, trees, lighting), sidewalk maintenance and amenities (e.g., benches, street lights, width, snow, cracks), and accessibility features (e.g., curb cuts) to promote mobility, activity, and health (Sallis and Owen, 1999; Ewing, Schieber, and Zegger, 2003; Frank, Engelke, and Schmid, 2003; Frumkin, 2003; Roper et al., 2003; Saelens, Sallis, and Frank, 2003; Boslaugh et al., 2004; Fisher, Tzamaras, and Scherer, 2004; Frank et al., 2005; Suminski et al., 2005).

Access to reliable utilities and phone service also varies by community. Intermittent access to electrical power, telephone service, or cell-phone reception can make it challenging for formal caregivers to contact individuals, make appointments, and help them properly manage their own health. Neighborhoods can also influence whether caregivers feel safe (Gershon et al., 2008).

These concerns have led some localities to focus on developing more livable communities for persons of all ages and abilities (Alley et al., 2007). The Indiana AdvantAge Initiative has created a list of components of an elder-friendly community and a set of 33 indicators of elder-friendliness (Oberlink and Stafford, 2009). The Atlanta Regional Commission has undertaken a broad approach through its Lifelong Communities planning process, intended to promote housing and transportation options, encourage healthy lifestyles, and expand information and access (Lawler and Berger, 2009).

HEALTH POLICY ENVIRONMENTS

Table 6-1 identifies policies that can influence the state and quality of health care services and technologies in the home. Inadequate incentives contribute to shortages of primary care physicians, nurses, occupational and physical therapists, and personal care aides in general and in home care in particular (Institute of Medicine, 2008). Though new mobile diagnostic devices and health information technologies are emerging, currently little reimbursement is provided for these tools.

Medicare was created in 1965, and at that time care recipients predominantly experienced time-limited acute illness; over the years, hospital stays have shortened and care recipients are returning home in need of more complex care, including a wide range of medical and nursing services. There is a mismatch, however, between current reimbursement policy, which rewards volume of services in the inpatient and subspecialty environment, and the need for home-based care of those with multiple chronic illnesses and disabilities. For example, some care recipients must choose between paying $150 for a round-trip wheelchair van ride to a doctor's office or not seeing the doctor at all.

At home, care recipients are in need of primary care teams trained to evaluate their homes and coordinate all needed medical, social, and housing services. This would require payment incentives to fund providers who coordinate care across settings and time.[2] Also, informal caregivers would benefit from services that increase their skills in managing the complex health conditions and functional disabilities of their care recipients. These services require payment mechanisms to support their delivery (Gitlin, Jacobs, and Vause-Earland, 2010).

Growing populations of frail elders, younger adults with disabilities, disabled veterans, and children with special health care needs require care coordination in the home and community (Bodenheimer, 2008; Administration on Aging, 2009; Vincent and Velkoff, 2010). A wide range of experts has concluded that care coordination for high-need individuals has a positive effect on health care outcomes and costs of care (Chen et al., 2000; Brown et al., 2007; Administration on Aging, 2009; National Advisory Board, 2009; Vincent and Velkoff, 2010). Their research has shown that the key elements to improve care and reduce costs are (a) involvement of primary care physicians, (b) a focus on high-risk beneficiaries, (c) well-trained teams that execute customized plans of care, (d) frequent in-person contact in the home, and (e) specific incentives for good results and savings. Other

---

[2]The Patient Centered Medical Home (PCMH) is one model for providing comprehensive primary care and is generally institutionalized in a health care setting that facilitates partnerships between individual care recipients and their personal physicians and, when appropriate, formal caregivers in the home and the care recipient's family.

studies have shown benefits of home-based primary care that includes these elements for high-need populations (Counsell et al., 2007; Edes, 2010).

Current fee-for-service payments from Medicare and Medicaid, however, discourage coordination of care (Davis, 2007; Bodenheimer, 2008). This payment policy has led to fragmented care, increasing costs per beneficiary, and a projection that the Medicare Trust Fund will be empty by 2029 (Social Security and Medicare Board of Trustees, 2010). Recent research has shown that fee-for-service methods lead to "supply-sensitive" care, wherein the density of hospital beds and subspecialists drive costs of care (Dartmouth Atlas of Health Care, 2008).

To support comprehensive home-based health care, policy makers need to promote innovations that challenge the status quo, such as mobile primary care teams (Christensen, Bohmer, and Kenagy, 2000). This would have the benefits of better coordinated care in the home, improved access for care recipients and families, and lower overall costs. The Patient Protection and Affordable Care Act (PPACA) includes elements that could promote care coordination at home for high-need populations. These include the Medicare Center for Innovation, the Medicare Shared Savings Program, and the Independence at Home Act.

Several related ongoing innovative programs in Medicaid, such as 1915(c) Home and Community-Based Waivers and 1915(j) Cash and Counseling (Doty, Mahoney, and Sciegaj, 2010), are intended to keep people in the community and out of institutional settings. Cash and Counseling allows participants to manage a fixed monetary allowance that can be used for employing outside service providers, friends, or family members to provide care. In addition, it can be used for services not generally covered by Medicaid such as transportation, rehabilitation, procurement of assistive technology, and installation of home modifications.

Although no federal program covers the cost of or finances home modifications, a range of public and private financing sources are available, including loans available to individuals as well as programs supported by housing, health, and social service sectors. Resources vary considerably and may depend on such factors as where a person lives, income/assets, type of housing (e.g., rented/owned), and specific problems or health conditions. The U.S. Department of Veterans Affairs has several programs to assist disabled veterans and service members with home modifications. For example, the Specially Adapted Housing (SAH) Grant Program is designed to provide barrier-free living environments that support independent living in a newly constructed home or one that is modified to meet their adaptive needs. The program provides up to $63,000 and serves permanently disabled veterans with such problems as loss or loss of use of both lower extremities and blindness (U.S. Department of Veterans Affairs, 2010). A separate program, the Special Home Adaptation (SHA) Grant Program, targets veterans and service members with permanent disabilities, such as blindness in both eyes or loss of use of both hands and extremities below the elbows. This program provides up to $12,756 to modify an existing home to meet adaptive needs, such as assistance with mobility (U.S. Department of Veterans Affairs, 2010).

Other care recipients, like Mrs. Harper in Box 6-2, have fewer support options and might have to piece together resources to implement home modifications. The U.S. Department of Housing and Urban Development Community Development Block Grant funds and Administration on Aging Title III funds have often been used by local communities for home modification programs for low-income persons. In addition, Medicaid waiver programs intended to keep low-income persons in the community often cover environmental modifications. Many such programs, however, operate with

---

BOX 6-2
The Harper Family

Mrs. Harper, an 86-year-old woman with multiple chronic conditions, including early-stage dementia, depression, low vision, and severe rheumatoid arthritis, depends on her granddaughter Susan for some of her care. Susan lives in the suburbs 24 miles away from her grandmother, who lives alone in a mobile home. The mobile home has six steps up to the front door, which prevent her from getting out of the house. The home's hallways are narrow and the bathroom, typical of such homes, is very small.

Mrs. Harper needs assistance getting into and out of the bathtub, but limited space makes it hard for someone to assist her. Previously active and socially engaged, she now spends most of her time sitting in a recliner in her living room. With little to occupy her, she has become depressed and lost muscle strength due to inactivity.

The addition of an outside stair lift would give her better access into and out of the house, and her bathroom needs modification. At a minimum, grab bars should be added, taking into account that they need to be specially secured because her bathing area has fiberglass surfacing. Until she can modify the bathroom or obtain outside help, she might take a sponge bath instead of using the bathtub. Mrs. Harper could also benefit from single-lever or motion sensor–activated faucets, anti-scald devices on plumbing fixtures, and nonslip flooring to reduce fall risk.

SOURCE: Clinical experience of committee member Eric DeJonge.

caps on expenditures (often less than $1,000), serve defined geographic areas, pay for a limited range of modifications, and require eligibility related to income and need. Existing private long-term care insurance policies often have allowances for home modifications, but they also may have caps and eligibility requirements. Medicare is not a viable option for home modification funding, as it pays for only medically necessary durable medical equipment and supplies, not for changes to the physical environment (Pynoos and Nishita, 2003). It is possible for a person to count medically related home modifications as a medical deduction if their total expenditures for health care reach at least 7.5 percent of their income. Finally, although the recently adopted long-term care insurance program (the Community Living Assistance Services and Supports Act, known as the CLASS Act) included in the Patient Protection and Affordable Care Act will pay eligible persons a daily amount that they can use for care and home adaptations, it is not yet clear how payment for expensive modifications will be covered.

Under Medicare, in order to obtain the services of an occupational therapist for a home assessment and treatment, a referral is needed from a physician, and coverage for a limited number of visits is restricted to individuals with functional decline or safety concerns (Pynoos et al., 1987, 1997, 1998; Pynoos, 1993; Gitlin et al., 2010). A home assessment for home modifications by occupational therapists is also available through some state programs, but they, too, are highly restricted. Consequently, given the patchwork of resources, it is estimated that three-quarters of older persons pay for home modifications out of pocket (LaPlante et al., 1992).

FUTURE ENVIRONMENTAL TRENDS

Physical Housing Modifications

Home modification interventions occur along a continuum. As shown in Figure 6-1, the current approach involves introducing modifications into conventional homes and developing products that fit preexisting specifications. The main barriers for retrofitting conventional homes are insufficient resources for paying for modifications and installing assistive products. Future trends include building new homes with accessibility features, creating healthy communities, and developing smart homes.

Accessibility and Universal Design

New homes and housing developments can be built to contain a minimum set of accessibility features. The Fair Housing Amendments Act of 1998 (FHAA) has a set of standards and guidelines that require such features in multiunit and townhouses with four or more units. However, single-family housing and smaller townhouses—in which the majority of U.S. residents live—are exempt from the FHAA. In order to provide a minimum level of accessibility in housing not subject to FHAA, 17 states and 30 cities in the United States have passed what are called "visitability" codes, which currently apply to 30,000 homes (Nishita et al., 2007; Maisel, Smith, and Steinfeld, 2008). These codes add very little to costs but result in housing that accommodates visitors with disabilities (for example, ensuring no-step entrances) and also allows "aging in place" for individuals who experience mobility impairments. The International Code Council (ICC) and the American National Standards Institute (ANSI), which respectively focus on building codes and accessibility, have both endorsed voluntary accessibility standards (i.e. ICC/ANSI A117.1, *Accessible and Usable Buildings and Facilities*). These standards could facilitate more jurisdictions to pass such visitability codes and encourage legislative consistency throughout the country.

Universal design is a broader concept than visitability or accessibility, as it is intended to create residential settings that work for everyone regardless of size, age, or ability. The "universal" in universal design signifies that design features of a home should enhance the lives of young families with children, persons who are middle aged, and older persons who want to age in place. Instead of a special approach to accommodate disabilities, universal design is based on a set of seven principles: (1) equitable use, (2) flexible use, (3) simple and intuitive use, (4) perceptible information, (5) tolerance for error, (6) low physical effort, and (7) size and space for approach and use (Steinfeld and Shea, 2001; Story, 2001; Young and Pace, 2001). Homes based on these principles, sometimes also referred to as inclusive or lifetime housing, are intended to be residential in appearance and the design features integrated and virtually invisible (Center for Inclusive Design and Environmental Access, 2010). For example, fully realized homes with universal design could include such features as a no-step path to a no-step entry, doorways that are at least 34-inches wide, at least one accessible full bathroom on the main floor, kitchen countertops and cabinetry that allow a person to work in the kitchen in a seated position, nonglare surfaces, a curbless shower in the bathroom, anti-scald faucet devices to avoid burns, nonslip flooring, variable height counters, doors and faucets with single-lever handles, and a bedroom on the main floor. Such features can help persons and their caregivers carry out everyday tasks and prevent serious and costly accidents (e.g., falls, burns). Moreover, because it avoids the costs and inconveniences of home modifications (e.g., ramps, lifts, bathroom remodels), universal design is aligned with the overall goal of sustainability. In the long run, implementing universal design in more homes will result in housing that suits the long-term needs of more residents, provides more housing choices for persons with chronic conditions and disabilities, and causes less forced relocation of residents to more costly settings, such as nursing homes.

Currently, few housing codes require universal design, and builders and architects are not designing most homes according to its principles. This is due to lack of knowledge about the concept, perceived low demand, and concern about costs. However, surveys indicate that there is an increasing demand for such features (American Association of Retired Persons, 2003), and they are considered beneficial.

A third approach is to develop new housing options that can be created within an existing unit (e.g., by converting a garage into a living space), constructed as a temporary or permanent extension of a house or built as a free-standing unit in the backyard (Kunkle, 2010) to accommodate a person with a chronic condition or disabilities. Although impractical in some cases, such solutions could work in communities in which the zoning codes allow for such changes and lots are large enough to accommodate them. New homes could also be designed to include "mother-in-law suites" or first-floor master or guest bedrooms.

New Communities

Complementary efforts are focusing on creating healthy neighborhoods and communities. For example, planned communities with restricted access are increasing in number. Almost 9 million residents lived in this type of setting in 1997 (Cannuscio, Block, and Kawachi, 2003); this trend began in Florida and California and is likely to increase in coming years in major metropolitan areas, with more people living in communities that have community centers (e.g., exercise facilities, convenience stores), social networking opportunities, and basic services, such as home repair and gardening. There is no guarantee, however, that they will include an array of housing options (including those that are affordable) nor homes that allow for aging in place or that meet the needs of persons with disabilities. However, it is encouraging that some builders, such as those in the planned community of Irvine, California, have provided prospective buyers with brochures and information about universal design features that can be included in homes to be constructed.

Another housing trend is the rise of naturally occurring retirement communities (NORCs) throughout the United States. These communities may be vertical (typically apartment buildings or condominiums) or horizontal and have large concentrations of older persons. Although not initially planned for older persons, over time the residents of these communities have aged and now need supportive services and home modifications to remain in their homes. Because of economies of scale, such neighborhoods present a natural setting for developing comprehensive home-based services

(Vladeck, 2004; Enguidanos et al., 2010) to provide a social supportive safety net for vulnerable populations.

Smart Homes

Although not necessarily an essential feature of universal design, the "smart house" concept involves a home that is outfitted for telehealth services and other computer-based technologies to support people, including those with cognitive impairments (Sanford, 2010). As described in Chapter 5, existing technologies include motion detectors for tracking an individual's movement through key areas of the home (i.e., kitchen, bathroom, bedroom) and alerting designated responders about a fall, sensors that detect if a person has left the house, and health monitoring systems that operate in conjunction with each other and allow information to be transmitted to health care providers, caregivers, or selected family members.

Sophisticated technologies are increasingly being constructed into homes worldwide (Chan et al., 2009). Over the last decade and a half, a number of demonstration smart homes have been built by universities (e.g., Georgia Institute of Technology, University of Florida) to test such new technologies. In addition, several homes have been developed, such as the Eskaton National Demonstration Home just outside Sacramento, California, that integrate smart home technology, health monitoring, and "green" house features. Researchers from five countries (Finland, Ireland, Lithuania, Norway, and the United Kingdom) joined their efforts for the ENABLE project (Cash, 2003), which promotes the well-being of people with early dementia with several features, such as a locator for lost objects, a temperature monitor, and an automatic bedroom light. In Toulouse, France, the PROSAFE project is using a set of infrared motion sensors to support automatic recognition of resident activity and of possible falls (Chan et al., 1999).

Advances in robotics, artificial intelligence, and machine learning are enabling development of automated systems capable of inferring (through motion detectors, camera vision, and infrared, sonar, and laser sensors) what a person is doing at home and providing physical or cognitive assistance when needed or desired (Nugent et al., 2008; Chan et al., 2009). Examples include wearable, installed, or mobile robotic systems that work cooperatively with people who are otherwise unable to function safely and independently without help from others. Many of these emerging quality-of-life technologies are still in the proof-of-concept stage or undergoing usability testing of prototypes in small-sample laboratory or field trials and are far from having demonstrated efficacy or being commercially available. Despite concerns about cost, privacy, and the potential for reducing human contact that have been expressed by older adults and persons with disabilities (Matthews et al., 2010), many potential users indicate that they would be willing to use these types of context-aware and responsive technologies (Beach et al., 2009), especially if doing so would enable them to live in the residential environment of their choosing (Beach et al., 2009, 2010).

Changes in Health Policy

Federal and state health policy reforms are moving from volume-based reimbursement to paying more for clinical and financial results. In the 2010 Patient Protection and Affordable Care Act (PPACA), there are several elements, such as the Medicare Center for Innovation, Accountable Care Organizations (ACOs), the Independence at Home (IAH) Demonstration Program, and the Transitional Care Program, that change reimbursement to promote better care in lower cost settings. Several of these initiatives propose to "share savings" with the most effective providers. The Medicaid Health Home Program (Section 2703, PPACA) also seeks to build better community-based care and lessen the state and federal costs of dual-eligible persons. The budgetary imperative of unsustainable Medicare and Medicaid costs is driving such reimbursement incentives to monitor and deliver care in the home. This includes more human services (such as home health aides, nursing, and medical staff), better mobile technology, and more intensive coordination of care. These efforts will be buttressed by the CLASS Act, as noted earlier also part of the PPACA, that will build a reserve of funds for long-term care services to assist younger persons with disabilities and older persons who are frail. Delivery of daily supportive services, complex medical care, and mobile technology can lower costs and improve the experience of people who are living at home. In order for such policy efforts to succeed, however, home-based health care needs to overcome the challenges noted in this and other chapters and demonstrate practical and safe care in a lower-cost setting.

REFERENCES

Administration on Aging. (2009). *A profile of older Americans.* Available: http://www.aoa.gov/AoARoot/Aging_Statistics/Profile/2009/2.aspx [July 2010].

Albert, S.M. (1990). The dependent elderly, home health care, and strategies of household adaptation In J.F. Gubrium and A. Sankar (Eds.), *The home care experience: Ethnography and policy.* Thousand Oaks, CA: Sage.

Albert, S.M. (2010). Impact of cultural, social, and community environments on home care. In National Research Council, *The role of human factors in home health care: Workshop summary* (pp. 247-274). S. Olson, Rapporteur. Committee on the Role of Human Factors in Home Health Care. Committee on Human-Systems Integration, Division of Behavioral and Social Sciences and Education. Washington, DC: The National Academies Press.

Alley, D., Liebig, P., Pynoos, J., Banerjee, T. and Choi, I.H. (2007). Creating elder-friendly communities. *Journal of Gerontological Social Work, 49*(1), 1-18.

Alzheimer's Association. (2010). *Alzheimer's disease facts and figures.* Available: http://www.alz.org/documents_custom/report_alzfactsfigures2010.pdf [March 31, 2011].

American Association of Retired Persons. (2000). *Fixing to stay: A national survey of housing and home modification issues.* Washington, DC: Author.

American Association of Retired Persons. (2003). *These four walls: Americans 45+ talk about home and community.* Washington, DC: Author.

American Community Survey. (2008). *Physical housing characteristics for occupied housing units data set: 2005-2007 American Community Survey 3-year estimates.* Washington DC: U.S. Census Bureau.

Beach, S., Schulz, R., Downs, J., Matthews, J., Barron, B., and Seelman, K.. (2009). Disability, age, and informational privacy attitudes in quality of life technology applications: Results from a national web survey. *ACM Transactions on Accessible Computing, 2*(1), 1-21.

Beach, S., Shultz, R., Seelman, K., Cooper, R.A., and Teodorski, E. (2010). *Trade-offs and tipping points in the acceptance of quality of life technology: Results from a survey of manual and power wheelchair users.* Paper presented at the International Symposium on Quality of Life Technology, June 28-29, Las Vegas, NV.

Beard, J.R., Cerda, M., Blaney, S., Ahern, J., Vlahov, D., and Galea, S. (2009). Neighborhood characteristics and change in depressive symptoms among older residents of New York City. *American Journal of Public Health, 99,* 1-7.

Bodenheimer, T. (2008). Coordinating care: A perilous journey through the health care system. *New England Journal of Medicine, 358,* 1064-1071.

Boslaugh, S.E., Luke, D.A., Brownson, R.C., Naleid K.S., and Kreuter M.W. (2004). Perceptions of neighborhood environment for physical activity: Is it "who you are" or "where you live"? *Journal of Urban Health, 81*(4), 671-681.

Bowling, A., and Stafford, M. (2007). How do objective and subjective assessments of neighborhood influence social and physical functioning in older age? Findings from a British survey of aging. *Social Sciences and Medicine, 64,* 2533-2549.

Brown, R., Peikes, D., Chen, A., Ng, J., Schore, J., and Soh, C. (2007). *Evaluation of the Medicare coordinated care demonstration: Findings for the first two years.* Princeton, NJ: Mathematica Policy Research. Available: http://www.mathematica-mpr.com/publications/pdfs/mccdfirsttwoyrs.pdf [March 31, 2011].

Cannuscio, C., Block, J., and Kawachi, I. (2003). Social capital and successful aging: The role of senior housing. *Annals of Internal Medicine, 139*(5 II), 395-399.

Cash, M. (2003). Assistive technology and people with dementia. *Reviews in Clinical Gerontology, 13,* 313-319.

Center for Inclusive Design and Environmental Access. (2010). *Inclusive housing: A pattern book.* New York: W.W. Norton.

Centers for Disease Control and Prevention. (2008). *Percent of U.S. adults 55 and over with chronic conditions.* Available: http://www.cdc.gov/nccdphp/overview.htm [July 2010].

Chan, M., Bocquet, H., Campo, E., Val, T., and Pous, J. (1999). Alarm communication network to help carers of the elderly for safety purposes: A survey of a project. *International Journal of Rehabilitation Research, 22,* 131-136.

Chan, M., Campo, E., Estève, D., and Fourniols, J.Y. (2009). Smart homes: Current features and future perspectives. *Maturitas, 64*(2), 90-97.

Chen, A., Brown, R., Archibald, N., Aliotta, S., and Fox, P.D. (2000). *Best practices in coordinated care.* Princeton, NJ: Mathematica Policy Research. Available: http://www.mathematica-mpr.com/pdfs/bestsum.pdf [March 31, 2011].

Christensen, C., Bohmer, R., and Kenagy, J. (2000). Will disruptive innovations cure health care? *Harvard Business Review, 78*(5), 102-112.

Clemson, L., Cumming, R.G., and Roland, M. (1996). Case-control study of hazards in the home and risk of falls and hip fractures. *Age and Ageing, 25*(2), 97.

Commission on Affordable Housing and Health Facility Needs for Seniors in the 21st Century. (2002). *A quiet crisis in America: A report to Congress by the Commission on Affordable Housing and Health Facility Needs for Seniors in the 21st Century.* Washington, DC: Author.

Counsell, S.R., Callahan, C.M., Clark, D.O., et al. (2007). Geriatric care management for low-income seniors—a randomized controlled trial. *Journal of the American Medical Association, 298*(22), 2623-2633.

Dartmouth Atlas of Health Care. (2008). *Executive summary.* Available: http://www.dartmouthatlas.org [July 2010].

Davis, K. (2007). Paying for care episodes and care coordination. *New England Journal of Medicine, 356,* 1166-1168.

Donald, I.P. (2009). Housing and health care for older people. *Age and Ageing, 38*(4), 364-367.

Doty, P., Mahoney, K.J., and Sciegaj, M. (2010). New state strategies to meet long-term care needs. *Health Affairs, 29*(1), 49-56.

Edes, T. (2010). *Financial savings of home-based primary care for frail veterans with chronic disabling disease.* Paper session, May 13, presented at the annual meeting of the American Geriatrics Society, Washington, DC. Abstract available: http://onlinelibrary.wiley.com/doi/10.1111/j.1532-5415.2010.02850.x/pdf [April 2011].

Enguidanos, S., Pynoos, J., Siciliano, M., Diepenbrock, L., and Alexman, S. (2010). Integrating community services within a NORC: The Park La Brea experience. *Cityscape: A Journal of Policy Development and Research, 12*(2), 29.

Ewing, R., Schieber, R.A., and Zegeer, C.V. (2003). Urban sprawl as a risk factor in motor vehicle occupant and pedestrian fatalities. *American Journal of Public Health, 93*(9), 1541-1545.

Fänge, A., and Iwarsson, S. (2003). Accessibility and usability in housing: Construct validity and implications for research and practice. *Disability and Rehabilitation, 25*(23), 1316-1325.

Fisher, Jr., A.H., Tzamaras, G.P., and Scherer, J.E. (2004). American Podiatric Medical Association best walking city competition, 2003. *Journal of the American Podiatric Medical Association, 94*(2), 211-215.

Frank, L., Engelke, P.O., and Schmid, T.L. (2003). *Health and community: The impact of the built environment on physical activity.* Washington, DC: Island Press.

Frank, L.D., Schmid, T.L., Sallis, J.F., Chapman, J., and Saelen, B.E. (2005). Linking objectively measured physical activity with objectively measured urban form: Findings from SMARTRAQ. *American Journal of Preventive Medicine, 28*(2 Suppl. 2), 117-125.

Freedman, V.A. (2011). Disability, functioning, and aging. In R. Binstock and L. George (Eds.), *Handbook of aging and the social sciences* (7th ed.). Ann Arbor, MI: Institute for Social Research.

Frumkin, H. (2003). Healthy places: Exploring the evidence. *American Journal of Public Health, 93*(9), 1451-1456.

Gershon, R., Pogorzelska, M., Qureshi, K., et al. (2008). Home health care patients and safety hazards in the home: Preliminary findings. In Agency for Healthcare Research and Quality, *Advances in patient safety: New directions and alternative approaches* (vol. 1, pp. 407-422). Rockville, MD: Agency for Healthcare Research and Quality. Available: http://www.ncbi.nlm.nih.gov/books/NBK43619/ [April 2011].

Gill, T.M., Williams, C.S., Robison, J.T., and Tinetti, M.E. (1999). A population-based study of environmental hazards in the homes of older persons. *American Journal of Public Health, 89*(4), 553-556.

Gitlin, L.N. (2003). Conducting research on home environments: Lessons learned and new directions. *The Gerontologist, 43*(5), 628-637.

Gitlin, L.N. (2007). The impact of housing on quality of life: Does the home environment matter now and into the future? In H.-W. Wahl and C. Tesch-Romer (Eds.), _New dynamics in old age: Individual, environmental, and societal perspectives._ Amityville, NY: Baywood.

Gitlin, L.N., and Corcoran, M. (2000). Making homes safer: Environmental adaptations for people with dementia. _Alzheimer's Care Today, 1_(1), 50-58.

Gitlin, L.N., Hauck, W., Dennis, M., and Winter, L. (2005). Maintenance of effects of the home environmental skill-building program for family caregivers and individuals with Alzheimer's disease and related disorders. _Journals of Gerontology Series A: Biological and Medical Sciences, 60_(3), 368.

Gitlin, L.N., Winter, L., Burke, J., Cherrett, N., Dennis, M.P., and Hauck, W.W. (2008). Tailored activities to manage neuropsychiatric behaviors in persons with dementia and reduce caregiver burden: A randomized pilot study. _The American Journal of Geriatric Psychiatry, 16_(3), 229.

Gitlin, L.N., Hauck, W., Dennis, M.P., Winter, L., Hodgson, N., and Schinfeld, S. (2009). Long-term effect on mortality of a home intervention that reduces functional difficulties in older adults: Results from a randomized trial. _Journal of the American Geriatrics Society, 57_(3), 476-481.

Gitlin, L.N., Jacobs, M., and Vause-Earland, T. (2010). Translation of a dementia caregiver intervention for delivery in homecare as a reimbursable medicare service: Outcomes and lessons learned. _Gerontologist, 50_(6), 847-854.

Gitlin, L.N., Winter, L., and Dennis, M.P. (2010). Assistive devices to help manage behavioral symptoms of dementia: What do caregivers use and find helpful? (special issue in honor of Dr. Fozzard). _Gerontechnology, 9_(3), 408-414.

Gitlin, L.N., Winter, L., Dennis, M.P., Hodgson, N., and Hauck, W.W. (2010). Targeting and managing behavioral symptoms in individuals with dementia: A randomized trial of a nonpharmacologic intervention. _Journal of the American Geriatrics Society, 58_(8), 1465-1474.

Golant, S. (2006). Supportive housing for frail, low-income older adults: Identifying need and allocating resources. _Generations, 29_(4), 37-43.

Golant, S.M. (2007). Low-income elderly homeowners in very old dwellings: The need for public policy debate. _Journal of Aging & Social Policy, 20_(1), 1-28.

Hebert, L.E., Scherr, P.A., Bienias, J.L., Bennett, D.A., and Evans, D.A. (2003). Alzheimer's disease in the U.S. population: Prevalence estimates using the 2000 census. _Archives of Neurology, 60_, 1119-1122.

Institute of Medicine. (2008). _Retooling for an aging America: Building the health care workforce._ Committee on the Future Health Care Workforce for Older Americans. Board on Health Care Services. Washington, DC: The National Academies Press.

International Code Council and American National Standards Institute. (2004). _ICC/ANSI A117.1: Accessible and usable buildings and facilities._ Available: http://www.phfa.org/forms/architects/a117_1_2003.pdf [April 2011].

Iwarsson, S. (2005). A long-term perspective on person-environment fit and ADL dependence among older Swedish adults. _Gerontologist, 45_(3), 327-336.

Kagawa-Singer, M. (2001). Negotiating cross-cultural issues at the end of life. _Journal of the American Medical Association, 286_, 2993-3001.

Kai, M.C., Anderson, M., and Lau, E.M.C. (2003). Exercise interventions: Defusing the world's osteoporosis time bomb. _Bulletin of the World Health Organization, 81_, 827-830.

Kulkarni, J., Wright, S., Toole, C., Morris, J., and Hirons, R. (1996). Falls in patients with lower limb amputations: Prevalence and contributing factors. _Physiotherapy, 82_(2), 130-136.

Kunkle, F. (2010). Virginia launching portable housing for aging relatives. _The Washington Post_, B01.

LaPlante, M.P., Hendershot, G.E., and Moss, A.J. (1992). *Assistive technology devices and home accessibility features: Prevalence, payment, need, and trends.* Advance Data, No. 217. Hyattsville, MD: U.S. Department of Health and Human Services. Available: http://www.eric.ed.gov/PDFS/ED351814.pdf [April 2011].

Lau, D.T., Scandrett, K.G., Jarzebowski, M., Holman, K., and Emanuel, L. (2007). Health-related safety: A framework to address barriers to aging in place. *Gerontologist, 47*(6), 830-837.

Lawler, K., and Berger, C. (2009). Lifelong communities: Re-imagining the Atlanta region from the ground up. *Generations, 33*(2), 76-78.

Li, W., Keegan, T., Sternfeld, B., Sidney, S., Quesenberry, C.P., Jr., and Kelsey, J.L. (2006). Outdoor falls among middle-aged and older adults: A neglected public health problem. *American Journal of Public Health, 96*(7), 1192.

Maisel, J., Smith, E., and Steinfeld, E. (2008). *Increasing home access: Designing for visitability.* Washington, DC: American Association of Retired Persons. Available: http://assets.aarp.org/rgcenter/il/2008_14_access.pdf [March 31, 2011].

Matthews, J.T., Beach, S.R., Downs, J., de Bruin, W.B., Mecca, L.P., and Schulz, R. (2010). Preferences and concerns for quality of life technology among older adults and persons with disabilities: National survey results. *Technology and Disability, 22*(1-2), 5-15.

National Advisory Board. (2009). *Declaration for independence.* Available: http://www.redorbit.com/news/health/1682745/national_advisory_board_issues_declaration_for_independence_a_calltoaction_in/index.html [March 31, 2011].

National Institute on Aging. (2001). *Exercises: A guide from National Institute on Aging.* Washington, DC: U.S. Department of Health and Human Services. Available: http://www.nia.nih.gov/NR/rdonlyres/25C76114-D120-4960-946A-3F576B528BBD/0/ExerciseGuideComplete.pdf [April 2011].

Newman, S.J., and Mezrich, M.N. (1997). Implications of the 1988 Fair Housing Act for the frail elderly. In S. Lanspery and J. Hyde (Eds.), *Staying put: Adapting the places instead of the people* (pp. 237-252). Amityville, NY: Baywood.

Nishita, C., Liebig, P., Pynoos, J., Perelman, L., and Spegal, K. (2007). Promoting basic accessibility in the home: Analyzing patterns in the diffusion of visitability legislation. *Journal of Disability Policy Studies, 18*(1), 2.

Norburn, J.E., Bernard, S.L., Konrad, T.R., et al. (1995). Self-care and assistance from others in coping with functional status limitations among national sample of older adults. *Journal of Gerontology Social Sciences, 50B*, S101-S109.

Nugent, C.D., Finlay, D.D., Fiorini, P., Tsumaki, Y., and Prassler, E. (2008). Editorial home automation as a means of independent living. *IEEE Automation Science and Engineering, 5*(1), 1-9.

Oberlink, M., and Stafford, P. (2009). The Indiana advantage initiative: Measuring community elder-friendliness and planning for the future. *Generations, 33*(2), 91-94.

Olsen, R.V., Ehrenkrantz, E., and Hutchings, B. (1993). *Homes that help: Advice from caregivers for creating a supportive home.* Newark, NJ: New Jersey Institute of Technology.

Piersol, C.V., and Ehrlich, P.L. (2009). *Occupational therapy in home health care.* Austin, TX: PRO-ED.

Pinquart, M., and Sörensen, S. (2006). Helping caregivers of persons with dementia: Which interventions work and how large are the effects? *International Psychogeriatrics, 18*, 577-595.

Pynoos, J. (1993). Towards a national policy on home modification. *Technology and Disability, 2*(4), 1-8.

Pynoos, J., and Nishita, C. (2003). The cost and financing of home modifications in the United States. *Journal of Disability Policy Studies, 14*, 68-73.

Pynoos, J., Cohen, E., Davis, L., and Bernhardt, S. (1987). Home modifications: Improvements that extend independence. In V. Regnier and J. Pynoos (Eds.), *Housing the aged: Design directives and policy considerations* (pp. 277-303). New York: Elsevier.

Pynoos, J., Angelleli, J., Tabbarah, M., and Demiere, M. (1998). Improving the delivery of home modifications. *Technology and Disability,* 8(1/2), 3-14.

Pynoos, J., Liebig, P., Overton, J., and Calvert, E. (1997). The delivery of home modification and repair services. In S. Lanspery and J. Hyde (Eds.), *Staying put: Adapting the places instead of the people* (pp. 173-192). Amityville, NY: Baywood.

Pynoos, J., Rose, D., Rubenstein, L., Choi, I.H., and Sabata, D. (2006). Evidence-based interventions in fall prevention. *Home Health Care Services Quarterly,* 25(1), 55-73.

Pynoos, J., Nishita, C., Cicero, C., and Caraviello, R. (2008). Aging in place, housing, and the law. *Elder Law Journal, 16,* 77-107.

Pynoos, J., Steinman, B.A., and Nguyen, A.Q. (2010). Environmental assessment and modification as fall-prevention strategies for older adults. *Clinics in Geriatric Medicine, 26*(4), 633-644.

Roper, P., Green, F., Tziotis, M., and Veith, G. (2003). Revision of Austroads safety barriers guidelines. In *Proceedings-Conference of the Australian Road Research Board* (vol. 21, pp. 2107-2119). Melbourne, Australia: ARRB Transport Research.

Rubinstein, R.L. (1990). The home environments of older people: A description of the psychosocial processes linking person to place. *Journal of Gerontology, 44,* S45-S53.

Saelens, B.E., Sallis, J.F., and Frank, L.D. (2003). Environmental correlates of walking and cycling: Findings from the transportation, urban design, and planning literatures. *Annals of Allergy Asthma & Immunology, 25*(2), 80-91.

Sallis, J.F., and Owen, N. (1999). *Physical activity and behavioral medicine.* Thousand Oaks, CA: Sage.

Sanford, J. (2010). The physical environment and home healthcare. In National Research Council, *The role of human factors in home health care: Workshop summary* (pp. 201-246). S. Olson, Rapporteur. Committee on the Role of Human Factors in Home Health Care. Committee on Human-Systems Integration, Division of Behavioral and Social Sciences and Education. Washington, DC: The National Academies Press.

Schaie, K.W., Wahl, H.-W., Mollenkopf, H., and Oswald, F. (2003). *Aging independently: Living arrangements and mobility.* New York: Springer.

Siebert, S. (2009). The clinic called home. In C.V. Piersol and P.L. Ehrlich (Eds.), *Occupational therapy in home health care.* Austin, TX: PRO-ED.

Social Security and Medicare Board of Trustees. (2009). *A summary of the 2009 annual reports.* Available: http://www.ssa.gov/OACT/TRSUM/index.html [March 31, 2011].

Sörensen, S., Pinquart, M., Habil, D., and Duberstein, P. (2002). How effective are interventions with caregivers? An updated meta-analysis. *Gerontologist, 42,* 356-372.

Stark, S. (2008). Removing environmental barriers in the homes of older adults with disabilities improves occupational performance. In W.W. Dunn (Ed.), *Bringing evidence into everyday practice: Practical strategies for healthcare professionals* (pp. 267). Thorofare, NJ: SLACK.

Steinfeld, E., and Shea, S. (2001). Fair housing: Toward universal design in multifamily housing. In W.F.E. Preiser and E. Ostroff (Eds.), *Universal design handbook* (Chapter 35). New York: McGraw-Hill.

Story, M. F. (2001). Principles of universal design. In W.F.E. Preiser and E. Ostroff (Eds.), *Universal design handbook* (Chapter 10). New York: McGraw-Hill.

Stuck, A.E., Egger, M., Hammer, A., Minder, C.E., and Beck, J.C. (2002). Home visits to prevent nursing home admission and functional decline in elderly people: Systematic review and meta-regression analysis. *Journal of the American Medical Association, 287,* 1022-1028.

Suminski, R.R., Poston, W.S.C., Petosa, R.L., Stevens, E., and Kazenmoyer, L.M. (2005). Features of the neighborhood environment and walking by U.S. adults. *American Journal of Preventive Medicine, 28*(2), 149-155.

U.S. Census Bureau. (2010). *American fact finder: Urban and rural.* Available: http://factfinder.census.gov [March 31, 2011].

U.S. Department of Housing and Urban Development. (2009). *Leading our nation to healthier homes: The healthy homes strategic plan.* Washington, DC: Author.

U.S. Department of Veterans Affairs. (2010). *VA pamphlet 26-69-1: Questions on specially adapted housing and special housing adaptations (online version).* Washington DC: Author. Available: http://www.questmobilitysolutions.com/resources/veterans/part2_va_pamphlet_26_jrd_edits_doc_rev_11052009.pdf [April 2011].

van Haastregt, J.C.M., Diederiks, J.P.M., van Rossum, E., deWitte, L.P., and Crebolder, H.F.J.M. (2000). Effects of preventive home visits to elderly people living in the community: A systematic review. *British Medical Journal, 320,* 754-758.

Vincent, G., and Velkoff, V. (2010). *The next four decades, the older population in the United States: 2010 to 2050.* Available: http://www.aoa.gov/AoARoot/Aging_Statistics/future_growth/DOCS/p25-1138.pdf [July 12, 2010].

Vladeck, F. (2004). *A good place to grow old: New York's model for NORC supportive service programs, a special report from the United Hospital Fund.* New York: United Hospital Fund.

Wahl, H.W., Fänge, A., Oswald, F., Gitlin, L., and Iwarsson, S. (2009). The home environment and disability-related outcomes in aging individuals: What is the empirical evidence? *Gerontologist, 49*(3), 355-367.

World Health Organization. (2002). *Active aging: A policy framework.* Geneva, Switzerland: Author.

Wrosch, C., Schulz, R., and Heckhausen, J. (2002). Health stresses and depressive symptomatology in the elderly: The importance of health engagement control strategies. *Health Psychology, 21,* 340-348.

Wu, S.Y., and Green, A. (2000). *Projection of chronic illness prevalence and cost inflation.* Santa Monica, CA: RAND Health.

Young, L.C., and Pace, R.J. (2001). Fair housing: Toward universal design in multifamily housing. In W.F.E. Preiser and E. Ostroff (Eds.), *Universal design handbook* (Chapter 34). New York: McGraw-Hill.

7

Conclusions and Recommendations

Health care is moving into the home increasingly often and involving a mixture of people, a variety of tasks, and a broad diversity of devices and technologies; it is also occurring in a range of residential environments. The factors driving this migration include the rising costs of providing health care; the growing numbers of older adults; the increasing prevalence of chronic disease; improved survival rates of various diseases, injuries, and other conditions (including those of fragile newborns); large numbers of veterans returning from war with serious injuries; and a wide range of technological innovations. The health care that results varies considerably in its safety, effectiveness, and efficiency, as well as its quality and cost.

The committee was charged with examining this major trend in health care delivery and resulting challenges from only one of many perspectives: the study of human factors. From the outset it was clear that the dramatic and evolving change in health care practice and policies presents a broad array of opportunities and problems. Consequently the committee endeavored to maintain focus specifically on how using the human factors approach can provide solutions that support maximizing the safety and quality of health care delivered in the home while empowering both care recipients and caregivers in the effort.

The conclusions and recommendations presented below reflect the most critical steps that the committee thinks should be taken to improve the state of health care in the home, based on the literature reviewed in this report examined through a human factors lens. They are organized into four areas: (1) health care technologies, including medical devices and health information technologies involved in health care in the home; (2)

caregivers and care recipients; (3) residential environments for health care; and (4) knowledge gaps that require additional research and development. Although many issues related to home health care could not be addressed, applications of human factors principles, knowledge, and research methods in these areas could make home health care safer and more effective and also contribute to reducing costs. The committee chose not to prioritize the recommendations, as they focus on various aspects of health care in the home and are of comparable importance to the different constituencies affected.

HEALTH CARE TECHNOLOGIES

Health care technologies include medical devices that are used in the home as well as information technologies related to home-based health care. The four recommendations in this area concern (1) regulating technologies for health care consumers, (2) developing guidance on the structure and usability of health information technologies, (3) developing guidance and standards for medical device labeling, and (4) improving adverse event reporting systems for medical devices. The adoption of these recommendations would improve the usability and effectiveness of technology systems and devices, support users in understanding and learning to use them, and improve feedback to government and industry that could be used to further improve technology for home care.

Regulation

Ensuring the safety of emerging technologies is a challenge, in part because it is not always clear which federal agency has regulatory authority and what regulations must be met. Currently, the U.S. Food and Drug Administration (FDA) has responsibility for devices, and the Office of the National Coordinator for Health Information Technology (ONC) has similar authority with respect to health information technology. However, the dividing line between medical devices and health information technology is blurring, and many new systems and applications are being developed that are a combination of the two, although regulatory oversight has remained divided. Because regulatory responsibility for them is unclear, these products may fall into the gap.

The committee did not find a preponderance of evidence that knowledge is lacking for the design of safe and effective devices and technologies for use in the home. Rather than discovering an inadequate evidence base, we were troubled by the insufficient attention directed at the development of devices that account, necessarily and properly, for users who are inadequately trained or not trained at all. Yet these new users often must

rely on equipment without ready knowledge about limitations, maintenance requirements, and problems with adaptation to their particular home
settings.

The increased prominence of the use of technology in the health care
arena poses predictable challenges for many lay users, especially people
with low health literacy, cognitive impairment, or limited technology experience. For example, remote health care management may be more effective when it is supported by technology, and various electronic health
care ("e-health") applications have been developed for this purpose. With
the spectrum of caregivers ranging from individuals caring for themselves
or other family members to highly experienced professional caregivers,
computer-based care management systems could offer varying levels of
guidance, reminding, and alerting, depending on the sophistication of the
operator and the criticality of the message. However, if these technologies
or applications are difficult to understand or use, they may be ignored or
misused, with potentially deleterious effects on care recipient health and
safety. Applying existing accessibility and usability guidelines and employing user-centered design and validation methods in the development of
health technology products designed for use in the home would help ensure
that they are safe and effective for their targeted user populations. In this
effort, it is important to recognize how the line between medical devices
and health information technologies has become blurred while regulatory oversight has remained distinct, and it is not always clear into which
domain a product falls.

> *Recommendation 1.* **The U.S. Food and Drug Administration and the
> Office of the National Coordinator for Health Information Technology
> should collaborate to regulate, certify, and monitor health care applica-
> tions and systems that integrate medical devices and health information
> technologies. As part of the certification process, the agencies should
> require evidence that manufacturers have followed existing accessibil-
> ity and usability guidelines and have applied user-centered design and
> validation methods during development of the product.**

Guidance and Standards

Developers of information technologies related to home-based health
care, as yet, have inadequate or incomplete guidance regarding product
content, structure, accessibility, and usability to inform innovation or evolution of personal health records or of care recipient access to information
in electronic health records.

The ONC, in the initial announcement of its health information technology certification program, stated that requirements would be forthcom-

ing with respect both to personal health records and to care recipient access to information in electronic health records (e.g., patient portals). Despite the importance of these requirements, there is still no guidance on the content of information that should be provided to patients or minimum standards for accessibility, functionality, and usability of that information in electronic or nonelectronic formats.

Consequently, some portals have been constructed based on the continuity of care record. However, recent research has shown that records and portals based on this model are neither understandable nor interpretable by laypersons, even by those with a college education. The lack of guidance in this area makes it difficult for developers of personal health records and patient portals to design systems that fully address the needs of consumers.

Recommendation 2. **The Office of the National Coordinator for Health Information Technology, in collaboration with the National Institute of Standards and Technology and the Agency for Healthcare Research and Quality, should establish design guidelines and standards, based on existing accessibility and usability guidelines, for content, accessibility, functionality, and usability of consumer health information technologies related to home-based health care.**

The committee found a serious lack of adequate standards and guidance for the labeling of medical devices. Furthermore, we found that the approval processes of the FDA for changing these materials are burdensome and inflexible.

Just as many medical devices currently in use by laypersons in the home were originally designed and approved for use only by professionals in formal health care facilities, the instructions for use and training materials were not designed for lay users, either. The committee recognizes that lack of instructional materials for lay users adds to the level of risk involved when devices are used by populations for whom they were not intended.

Ironically, the FDA's current premarket review and approval processes inadvertently discourage manufacturers from selectively revising or developing supplemental instructional and training materials, when they become aware that instructional and training materials need to be developed or revised for lay users of devices already approved and marketed. Changing the instructions for use (which were approved with the device) requires manufacturers to submit the device along with revised instructions to the FDA for another 510(k) premarket notification review. Since manufacturers can find these reviews complicated, time-consuming, and expensive, this requirement serves as a disincentive to appropriate revisions of instructional or training materials.

Furthermore, little guidance is currently available on design of user training methods and materials for medical devices. Even the recently released human factors standard on medical device design (Association for the Advancement of Medical Instrumentation, 2009), while reasonably comprehensive, does not cover the topic of training or training materials. Both FDA guidance and existing standards that do specifically address the design of labeling and ensuing instructions for use fail to account for up-to-date findings from research on instructional systems design. In addition, despite recognition that requirements for user training, training materials, and instructions for use are different for lay and professional users of medical equipment, these differences are not reflected in current standards.

Recommendation 3. The U.S. Food and Drug Administration (FDA) should promote development (by standards development organizations, such as the International Electrotechnical Commission, the International Organization for Standardization, the American National Standards Institute, and the Association for the Advancement of Medical Instrumentation) of new standards based on the most recent human factors research for the labeling of and ensuing instructional materials for medical devices designed for home use by lay users. The FDA should also tailor and streamline its approval processes to facilitate and encourage regular improvements of these materials by manufacturers.

Adverse Event Reporting Systems

The committee notes that the FDA's adverse event reporting systems, used to report problems with medical devices, are not user-friendly, especially for lay users, who generally are not aware of the systems, unaware that they can use them to report problems, and uneducated about how to do so. In order to promote safe use of medical devices in the home and rectify design problems that put care recipients at risk, it is necessary that the FDA conduct more effective postmarket surveillance of medical devices to complement its premarket approval process. The most important elements of their primarily passive surveillance system are the current adverse event reporting mechanisms, including Maude and MedSun. Entry of incident data by health care providers and consumers is not straightforward, and the system does not elicit data that could be useful to designers as they develop updated versions of products or new ones that are similar to existing devices. The reporting systems and their importance need to be widely promoted to a broad range of users, especially lay users.

Recommendation 4. The U.S. Food and Drug Administration should improve its adverse event reporting systems to be easier to use, to collect data that are more useful for identifying the root causes of events related to interactions with the device operator, and to develop and promote a more convenient way for lay users as well as professionals to report problems with medical devices.

CAREGIVERS IN THE HOME

Health care is provided in the home by formal caregivers (health care professionals), informal caregivers (family and friends), and individuals who self-administer care; each type of caregiver faces unique issues. Properly preparing individuals to provide care at home depends on targeting efforts appropriately to the background, experience, and knowledge of the caregivers. To date, however, home health care services suffer from being organized primarily around regulations and payments designed for inpatient or outpatient acute care settings. Little attention has been given to how different the roles are for formal caregivers when delivering services in the home or to the specific types of training necessary for appropriate, high-quality practice in this environment.

Health care administration in the home commonly involves interaction among formal caregivers and informal caregivers who share daily responsibility for a person receiving care. But few formal caregivers are given adequate training on how to work with informal caregivers and involve them effectively in health decision making, use of medical or adaptive technologies, or best practices to be used for evaluating and supporting the needs of caregivers.

It is also important to recognize that the majority of long-term care provided to older adults and individuals with disabilities relies on family members, friends, or the individual alone. Many informal caregivers take on these responsibilities without necessary education or support. These individuals may be poorly prepared and emotionally overwhelmed and, as a result, experience stress and burden that can lead to their own morbidity. The committee is aware that informational and training materials and tested programs already exist to assist informal caregivers in understanding the many details of providing health care in the home and to ease their burden and enhance the quality of life of both caregiver and care recipient. However, tested materials and education, support, and skill enhancement programs have not been adequately disseminated or integrated into standard care practices.

Recommendation 5. **Relevant professional practice and advocacy groups should develop appropriate certification, credentialing, and/or training standards that will prepare formal caregivers to provide care in the home, develop appropriate informational and training materials** for informal caregivers, and provide guidance for all caregivers to work effectively with other people involved.

RESIDENTIAL ENVIRONMENTS FOR HEALTH CARE

Health care is administered in a variety of nonclinical environments, but the most common one, particularly for individuals who need the greatest level and intensity of health care services, is the home. The two recommendations in this area encourage (1) modifications to existing housing and (2) accessible and universal design of new housing. The implementation of these recommendations would be a good start on an effort to improve the safety and ease of practicing health care in the home. It could improve the health and safety of many care recipients and their caregivers and could facilitate adherence to good health maintenance and treatment practices. Ideally, improvements to housing design would take place in the context of communities that provide transportation, social networking and exercise opportunities, and access to health care and other services.

Safety and Modification of Existing Housing

The committee found poor appreciation of the importance of modifying homes to remove health hazards and barriers to self-management and health care practice and, furthermore, that financial support from federal assistance agencies for home modifications is very limited. The general connection between housing characteristics and health is well established. For example, improving housing conditions to enhance basic sanitation has long been part of a public health response to acute illness. But the characteristics of the home can present significant barriers to autonomy or self-care management and present risk factors for poor health, injury, compromised well-being, and greater dependence on others. Conversely, physical characteristics of homes can enhance resident safety and ability to participate in daily self-care and to utilize effectively health care technologies that are designed to enhance health and well-being.

Home modifications based on professional home assessments can increase functioning, contribute to reducing accidents such as falls, assist caregivers, and enable chronically ill persons and people with disabilities to stay in the community. Such changes are also associated with facilitating hospital discharges, decreasing readmissions, reducing hazards in the home, and improving care coordination. Familiar modifications include installation of such items as grab bars, handrails, stair lifts, increased lighting, and health monitoring equipment as well as reduction of such hazards as broken fixtures and others caused by insufficient home maintenance.

Deciding on which home modifications have highest priority in a given setting depends on an appropriate assessment of circumstances and the environment. A number of home assessment instruments and programs have been validated and proven to be effective to meet this need. But even if needed modifications are properly identified and prioritized, inadequate funding, gaps in services, and lack of coordination between the health and housing service sectors have resulted in a poorly integrated system that is difficult to access. Even when accessed, progress in making home modifications available has been hampered by this lack of coordination and inadequate reimbursement or financial mechanisms, especially for those who cannot afford them.

> *Recommendation 6.* **Federal agencies, including the U.S. Department of Health and Human Services and the Centers for Medicare & Medicaid Services, along with the U.S. Department of Housing and Urban Development and the U.S. Department of Energy, should collaborate to facilitate adequate and appropriate access to health- and safety-related home modifications, especially for those who cannot afford them. The goal should be to enable persons whose homes contain obstacles, hazards, or features that pose a home safety concern, limit self-care management, or hinder the delivery of needed services to obtain home assessments, home modifications, and training in their use.**

Accessibility and Universal Design of New Housing

Almost all existing housing in the United States presents problems for conducting health-related activities because physical features limit independent functioning, impede caregiving, and contribute to such accidents as falls. In spite of the fact that a large and growing number of persons, including children, adults, veterans, and older adults, have disabilities and chronic conditions, new housing continues to be built that does not account for their needs (current or future). Although existing homes can be modified to some extent to address some of the limitations, a proactive, preventive, and effective approach would be to plan to address potential problems in the design phase of new and renovated housing, before construction.

Some housing is already required to be built with basic accessibility features that facilitate practice of health care in the home as a result of the Fair Housing Act Amendments of 1998. And 17 states and 30 cities have passed what are called "visitability" codes, which currently apply to 30,000 homes. Some localities offer tax credits, such as Pittsburgh through an ordinance, to encourage installing visitability features in new and renovated housing. The policy in Pittsburgh was impetus for the Pennsylvania Residential VisitAbility Design Tax Credit Act signed into law on October 28, 2006, which offers property owners a tax credit for new construction and rehabilitation. The Act paves the way for municipalities to provide tax credits to citizens by requiring that such governing bodies administer the tax credit (Self-Determination Housing Project of Pennsylvania, Inc., n.d.).

Visitability, rather than full accessibility, is characterized by such limited features as an accessible entry into the home, appropriately wide doorways and one accessible bathroom. Both the International Code Council, which focuses on building codes, and the American National Standards Institute, which establishes technical standards, including ones associated with accessibility, have endorsed voluntary accessibility standards. These standards facilitate more jurisdictions to pass such visitability codes and encourage legislative consistency throughout the country. To date, however, the federal government has not taken leadership to promote compliance with such standards in housing construction, even for housing for which it provides financial support.

Universal design, a broader and more comprehensive approach than visitability, is intended to suit the needs of persons of all ages, sizes, and abilities, including individuals with a wide range of health conditions and activity limitations. Steps toward universal design in renovation could include such features as anti-scald faucet valve devices, nonslip flooring, lever handles on doors, and a bedroom on the main floor. Such features can help persons and their caregivers carry out everyday tasks and reduce the incidence of serious and costly accidents (e.g., falls, burns). In the long run, implementing universal design in more homes will result in housing that suits the long-term needs of more residents, provides more housing choices for persons with chronic conditions and disabilities, and causes less forced relocation of residents to more costly settings, such as nursing homes.

Issues related to housing accessibility have been acknowledged at the federal level. For example, visitability and universal design are in accord with the objectives of the Safety of Seniors Act (Public Law No. 110-202, passed in 2008). In addition, implementation of the *Olmstead* decision (in which the U.S. Supreme Court ruled that the Americans with Disabilities Act may require states to provide community-based services rather than institutional placements for individuals with disabilities) requires affordable and accessible housing in the community.

Visitability, accessibility, and universal design of housing all are important to support the practice of health care in the home, but they are not broadly implemented and incentives for doing so are few.

Recommendation 7. **Federal agencies, such as the U.S. Department of Housing and Urban Development, the U.S. Department of Veterans Affairs, and the Federal Housing Administration, should take a lead role, along with states and local municipalities, to develop strategies that promote and facilitate increased housing visitability, accessibil-**

ity, and universal design in all segments of the market. This might include tax and other financial incentives, local zoning ordinances, model building codes, new products and designs, and related policies that are developed as appropriate with standards-setting organizations (e.g., the International Code Council, the International Electrotechnical Commission, the International Organization for Standardization, and the American National Standards Institute).

RESEARCH AND DEVELOPMENT

In our review of the research literature, the committee learned that there is ample foundational knowledge to apply a human factors lens to home health care, particularly as improvements are considered to make health care safe and effective in the home. However, much of what is known is not being translated effectively into practice, neither in design of equipment and information technology or in the effective targeting and provision of services to all those in need. Consequently, the four recommendations that follow support research and development to address knowledge and communication gaps and facilitate provision of high-quality health care in the home. Specifically, the committee recommends (1) research to enhance coordination among all the people who play a role in health care practice in the home, (2) development of a database of medical devices in order to facilitate device prescription, (3) improved surveys of the people involved in health care in the home and their residential environments, and (4) development of tools for assessing the tasks associated with home-based health care.

Health Care Teamwork and Coordination

Frail elders, adults with disabilities, disabled veterans, and children with special health care needs all require coordination of the care services that they receive in the home. Home-based health care often involves a large number of elements, including multiple care providers, support services, agencies, and complex and dynamic benefit regulations, which are rarely coordinated. However, coordinating those elements has a positive effect on care recipient outcomes and costs of care. When successful, care coordination connects caregivers, improves communication among caregivers and care recipients and ensures that receivers of care obtain appropriate services and resources.

To ensure safe, effective, and efficient care, everyone involved must collaborate as a team with shared objectives. Well-trained primary health care teams that execute customized plans of care are a key element of coordinated care; teamwork and communication among all actors are also essential to successful care coordination and the delivery of high-quality care. Key factors that influence the smooth functioning of a team include a shared understanding of goals, common information (such as a shared medication list), knowledge of available resources, and allocation and coordination of tasks conducted by each team member.

Barriers to coordination include insufficient resources available to (a) help people who need health care at home to identify and establish connections to appropriate sources of care, (b) facilitate communication and coordination among caregivers involved in home-based health care, and (c) facilitate communication among the people receiving and the people providing health care in the home.

The application of systems analysis techniques, such as task analysis, can help identify problems in care coordination systems and identify potential intervention strategies. Human factors research in the areas of communication, cognitive aiding and decision support, high-fidelity simulation training techniques, and the integration of telehealth technologies could also inform improvements in care coordination.

Recommendation 8. **The Agency for Healthcare Research and Quality should support human factors–based research on the identified barriers to coordination of health care services delivered in the home and support user-centered development and evaluation of programs that may overcome these barriers.**

Medical Device Database

It is the responsibility of physicians to prescribe medical devices, but in many cases little information is readily available to guide them in determining the best match between the devices available and a particular care recipient. No resource exists for medical devices, in contrast to the analogous situation in the area of assistive and rehabilitation technologies, for which annotated databases (such as AbleData) are available to assist the provider in determining the most appropriate one of several candidate devices for a given care recipient. Although specialists are apt to receive information about devices specific to the area of their practice, this is much less likely in the case of family and general practitioners, who often are responsible for selecting, recommending, or prescribing the most appropriate device for use at home.

Recommendation 9. **The U.S. Food and Drug Administration, in collaboration with device manufacturers, should establish a medical device database for physicians and other providers, including pharmacists, to use when selecting appropriate devices to prescribe or recommend** for people receiving or self-administering health care in the home. Using task analysis and other human factors approaches to populate the medical device database will ensure that it contains information on characteristics of the devices and implications for appropriate care recipient and device operator populations.

Characterizing Caregivers, Care Recipients, and Home Environments

As delivery of health care in the home becomes more common, more coherent strategies and effective policies are needed to support the workforce of individuals who provide this care. Developing these will require a comprehensive understanding of the number and attributes of individuals engaged in health care in the home as well as the context in which care is delivered. Data and data analysis are lacking to accomplish this objective.

National data regarding the numbers of individuals engaged in health care delivery in the home—that is, both formal and informal caregivers—are sparse, and the estimates that do exist vary widely. Although the Bureau of Labor Statistics publishes estimates of the number of workers employed in the home setting for some health care classifications, they do not include all relevant health care workers. For example, data on workers employed directly by care recipients and their families are notably absent. Likewise, national estimates of the number of informal caregivers are obtained from surveys that use different methodological approaches and return significantly different results.

Although numerous national surveys have been designed to answer a broad range of questions regarding health care delivery in the home, with rare exceptions such surveys reflect the relatively limited perspective of the sponsoring agency. For example,

- The Medicare Current Beneficiary Survey (administered by the Centers for Medicare & Medicaid Services) and the Health and Retirement Survey (administered by the National Institute on Aging) are primarily geared toward understanding the health, health services use, and/or economic well-being of older adults and provide no information regarding working-age adults or children or information about home or neighborhood environments.
- The Behavioral Risk Factors Surveillance Survey (administered by the Centers for Disease Control and Prevention, CDC), the National Health Interview Survey (administered by the CDC), and the National Children's Study (administered by the U.S. Department of Health and Human Services and the U.S. Environmental Protection Agency) all collect information on health characteristics, with limited or no information about the housing context.

- The American Housing Survey (administered by the U.S. Department of Housing and Urban Development) collects detailed information regarding housing, but it does not include questions regarding the health status of residents and does not collect adequate information about home modifications and features on an ongoing basis.

Consequently, although multiple federal agencies collect data on the sociodemographic and health characteristics of populations and on the nation's housing stock, none of these surveys collects data necessary to link the home, its residents, and the presence of any caregivers, thus limiting understanding of health care delivered in the home. Furthermore, information is altogether lacking about health and functioning of populations linked to the physical, social, and cultural environments in which they live. Finally, in regard to individuals providing care, information is lacking regarding their education, training, competencies, and credentialing, as well as appropriate knowledge about their working conditions in the home.

Better coordination across government agencies that sponsor such surveys and more attention to information about health care that occurs in the home could greatly improve the utility of survey findings for understanding the prevalence and nature of health care delivery in the home.

Recommendation 10. **Federal health agencies should coordinate data collection efforts to capture comprehensive information on elements relevant to health care in the home, either in a single survey or through effective use of common elements across surveys. The surveys should collect data on the sociodemographic and health characteristics of individuals receiving care in the home, the sociodemographic attributes of formal and informal caregivers and the nature of the caregiving they provide, and the attributes of the residential settings in which the care recipients live.**

Tools for Assessing Home Health Care Tasks and Operators

Persons caring for themselves or others at home as well as formal caregivers vary considerably in their skills, abilities, attitudes, experience, and other characteristics, such as age, culture/ethnicity, and health literacy. In turn, designers of health-related devices and technology systems used in the home are often naïve about the diversity of the user population. They need high-quality information and guidance to better understand user capabilities relative to the task demands of the health-related device or technology that they are developing.

In this environment, valid and reliable tools are needed to match users with tasks and technologies. At this time, health care providers lack the tools needed to assess whether particular individuals would be able to perform specific health care tasks at home, and medical device and system designers lack information on the demands associated with health-related tasks performed at home and the human capabilities needed to perform them successfully.

Whether used to assess the characteristics of formal or informal caregivers or persons engaged in self-care, task analysis can be used to develop point-of-care tools for use by consumers and caregivers alike in locations where such tasks are encouraged or prescribed. The tools could facilitate identification of potential mismatches between the characteristics, abilities, experiences, and attitudes that an individual brings to a task and the demands associated with the task. Used in ambulatory care settings, at hospital discharge or other transitions of care, and in the home by caregivers or individuals and family members themselves, these tools could enable assessment of prospective task performer's capabilities in relation to the demands of the task. The tools might range in complexity from brief screening checklists for clinicians to comprehensive assessment batteries that permit nuanced study and tracking of home-based health care tasks by administrators and researchers. The results are likely to help identify types of needed interventions and support aids that would enhance the abilities of individuals to perform health care tasks in home settings safely, effectively, and efficiently.

Recommendation 11. **The Agency for Healthcare Research and Quality should collaborate, as necessary, with the National Institute for Disability and Rehabilitation Research, the National Institutes of Health, the U.S. Department of Veterans Affairs, the National Science Foundation, the U.S. Department of Defense, and the Centers for Medicare & Medicaid Services to support development of assessment tools customized for home-based health care, designed to analyze the demands of tasks associated with home-based health care, the operator capabilities required to carry them out, and the relevant capabilities of specific individuals.**

REFERENCES

Association for the Advancement of Medical Instrumentation. (2009). *ANSI/AAMI HE75:2009: Human factors engineering: Design of medical devices.* Available: http://www.aami.org/publications/standards/HE75_Ch16_Access_Board.pdf [April 2011].
Self-Determination Housing Project of Pennsylvania, Inc. (n.d.) *Promoting visibility in Pennsylvania.* Available: http://www.sdhp.org/promoting_visitability_in_pennsy.htm [March 30, 2011].

Appendix

Biographical Sketches of Committee Members and Staff

David H. Wegman (*Chair*) is professor emeritus in the Department of Work Environment at the University of Massachusetts Lowell and adjunct professor at the Harvard School of Public Health. He was founding chair of the Department of Work Environment as well as founding dean of the School of Health and Environment. His epidemiological research includes study of acute and chronic occupational respiratory disease, occupational cancer risk, and occupational musculoskeletal disorders, with special interests in study of subjective outcomes as early indicators of health effects and in surveillance of occupational conditions and risks. He is a national associate of the National Research Council and chaired the Committee on the Review of NIOSH Research Programs and the Committee on External Evaluation of NIDRR and Its Grantees. He chaired the Mine Safety and Health Administration's Advisory Committee on the Elimination of Pneumoconiosis Among Coal Mine Workers and previously served on the Boards of Scientific Counselors for NIOSH and for the National Toxicology Program as well as on the Science Advisory Board of the U.S. Environmental Protection Agency. In 2006, he was appointed chair of the International Evaluation Group for an analysis of Occupational Health Research in Sweden. He is coeditor of *Occupational and Environment Health: Recognition and Prevention of Disease and Injury*. He has a B.A. from Swarthmore College and M.D. and M.Sc. degrees from Harvard University.

Sara Czaja is a professor of psychiatry and behavioral sciences at the University of Miami Miller School of Medicine and the Department of Industrial Engineering at the University of Miami. She is also director of the Center on Research and Education for Aging and Technology Enhancement (CREATE) and scientific director of the Center on Aging at the Miller School of Medicine. The focus of CREATE is on making technology and technology applications more useful and usable to older adult populations. She served as the principal investigator at the Miami site of the REACH program, a multisite project that evaluated the efficacy of a multicomponent psychosocial intervention in terms of enhancing the quality of life and reducing burden and stress for family caregivers of Alzheimer's patients. Her primary research interests are aging and cognition, human-computer interaction, family caregiving, training, and intervention research. She is a fellow of the American Psychological Association, the Human Factors and Ergonomics Society, and the Gerontological Society of America. At the National Research Council, she was cochair of the Panel on Human Factors Research Issues for an Aging Population and participated in the Workshop on Technology for Adaptive Aging. She is also a member of the Board on Human-Systems Integration. She has an M.S. (1976) in industrial engineering and a Ph.D. (1980) in industrial engineering/human factors, both from the State University of New York at Buffalo.

K. Eric DeJonge is director of geriatrics at the Washington Hospital Center in Washington, DC, where he is responsible for overall operations of the Medical House Call Program and the Geriatrics Division. In 1999, in partnership with George Taler, he cofounded the Medical House Call Program to promote the health and dignity of frail elders in their own homes. He was named the National House Call Physician of the Year in 2003 by the American Academy of Home Care Physicians and is engaged in efforts to promote innovative health policy reform for Medicare and Medicaid. He received an M.D. from Yale School of Medicine in 1991, completed residency in primary care internal medicine at the Johns Hopkins Bayview Medical Center in 1994, and is an assistant professor of medicine at Johns Hopkins University. He completed fellowships in health policy at Georgetown University and in geriatric medicine at Johns Hopkins. He is board certified in internal medicine and geriatrics.

Molly Follette Story (*former Study Director*) was senior program officer of the Committee on Human-Systems Integration at the National Research Council. She is co-editor of *Medical Instrumentation: Accessibility and Usability Considerations* and co-author of *Principles of Universal Design* and *The Universal Design File: Designing for People of All Ages and Abilities*. She holds six utility patents and has served as a human factors consultant to many companies in the medical device and consumer products industries. She is a member of the Human Factors and Ergonomics Society, the Association for the Advancement of Medical Instrumentation (AAMI), and the Rehabilitation Engineering and Assistive Technology Society of North America; she was also a member of AAMI's Human Factors Engineering Committee, which developed the recommended practice, HE75: 2009, Human Factors Engineering–Design of Medical Devices. She has a B.S.E. in civil engineering from Princeton University, an M.S. in product design engineering from Stanford University, and an M.S. and a Ph.D. from the School of Public Health at University of California, Berkeley.

Daryle Jean Gardner-Bonneau is the principal of Bonneau and Associates, a human factors consultancy in Portage, Michigan, and is also an adjunct associate professor at Western Michigan University. She has been working in the human factors field for over 25 years, first as an academician and then in industry and consulting. During the past 15 years, her work has concentrated on the design and evaluation of products, services, and systems, specifically with respect to their usability by older adults and people with special needs. She is also heavily involved in both national and international standards work focusing on this topic, chairs the U.S. TAG to ISO TC159–Ergonomics, and serves as a member of the Human Engineering Committee of the Association for the Advancement of Medical Instrumentation. She has been the editor of *Ergonomics in Design* (1992-1995) and *The International Journal of Speech Technology* (2000-2006) and has served on the editorial board of *Human Factors* as well as the advisory boards to the Rehabilitation Engineering Research Centers on Accessible Medical Instrumentation and Tele-rehabilitation. She has also served on peer review panels for translational research on aging and medical simulation at the National Institutes of Health. Most recently, she completed human factors work on a project on remote telemonitoring and education of patients with chronic obstructive pulmonary disease and heart failure. She has a Ph.D. in human performance from Ohio State University (1983).

Michael Christopher Gibbons is an associate director of the Johns Hopkins Urban Health Institute and an Assistant Professor of Medicine, Public Health and Health Sciences Informatics at Johns Hopkins. His research focuses on technology and health care disparities. He is an adviser and expert consultant to several state and federal agencies and policy makers in the areas of health information technology, e-health, minority health, and health care disparities. His current research focuses on the impact of consumer health informatics applications on health care disparities and on the role of information technologies in providing patient-centered care. He is also working with the Robert Wood Johnson Foundation on the future design of personal health records. He is the author of four books, including *eHealth Solutions for Healthcare Disparities*, and his research is leading the development of the emerging field of "populomics." He has been named a health disparities scholar by the National Center for Minority Health and Health Disparities at the National Institutes of Health. He received a medical degree from the University of Alabama, then completed residency training in preventive medicine, a molecular oncology research fellowship, and an M.P.H. degree focusing on health promotion among urban and disadvantaged populations, all from Johns Hopkins University.

Laura N. Gitlin, an applied research sociologist, is currently a professor in the School of Nursing, Johns Hopkins University. During the deliberations of the committee for this report she was a professor in the Department of Occupational Therapy and founding director of the Jefferson Center for Applied Research on Aging and Health and Jefferson Elder Care (an evidence-based service and training division) at Thomas Jefferson University. She conducts programs of funded research related to developing and testing innovative home and community-based interventions to address dementia care, quality of life, functional decline, depression, and chronic disease and its management. Her intervention research focuses primarily on home environmental and behavioral approaches to helping older people and their family members to age in place and adapt to age-related challenges. She is also currently involved in numerous translational research initiatives. Jefferson Elder Care seeks to translate proven interventions into real-world settings, train health and human service providers in proven programs, and deliver these evidence-based programs directly to consumers. Her publications include an introduction to research emphasizing both qualitative and quantitative methodologies used widely to train health professionals in research and a book describing the Home Environmental Skill-building Program, a proven occupational therapy home-based intervention for dementia caregivers.

Mary Ellen O'Connell is deputy director for the Board on Behavioral, Cognitive, and Sensory Sciences and the Board on Human-Systems Integration. She has served as study director for five consensus studies at the National Research Council: on prevention of mental disorders and substance abuse, international education and foreign languages, ethical considerations for research on housing-related health hazards involving children, reducing underage drinking, and assessing and improving children's health. She also served as study director for the Committee on Standards of Evidence and the Quality of Behavioral and Social Science Research, a division-wide strategic planning effort; developed standalone workshops on welfare reform and children and gun violence; and facilitated meetings of the national coordinating committee of the Key National Indicators Initiative. Previously, she spent 8 years in the Office of the Assistant Secretary for Planning and Evaluation, U.S. Department of Health and Human Services (HHS), most recently as director of state and local initiatives. Prior to HHS, she worked at the U.S. Department of Housing and Urban Development on homeless policy and program design issues and for the Commonwealth of Massachusetts as the director of field services. She has a B.A. (with distinction) from Cornell University and an M.S. in the management of human services from the Heller School for Social Policy and Management at Brandeis University.

Misha Pavel is currently a program director at the National Science Foundation in charge of a program called Smart Health and Wellbeing. Prior to this appointment, he was a professor and head of the Division on Biomedical Engineering, with a joint appointment in the Department of Medical Informatics and Clinical Epidemiology, at Oregon Health and Science University. At the same time, he was the director of the Point of Care Laboratory, which focuses on unobtrusive monitoring and neurobehavioral assessment and modeling. Prior to his academic career, he was a member of the technical staff at Bell Laboratories, where his research included network analysis and modeling. Prior to his academic career, he was a member of the technical staff at Bell Laboratories, where his research included network analysis and modeling. His current research is at the intersection of computational modeling of complex behaviors of biological systems, engineering, and cognitive science with a focus on information fusion, pattern recognition, augmented cognition, and the development of multimodal and perceptual human-computer interfaces. He developed a number of quantitative and computational models of perceptual and cognitive processes, eye movement control, and a theoretical framework for knowledge representation; the resulting models have been applied in a variety of areas, ranging from computer-assisted instruction systems, to enhanced vision systems for aviation, to augmented cognition systems. He has a Ph.D. in experimental psychology from New York University, an M.S. in electrical engineering from Stanford University, and a B.S. in electrical engineering from the Polytechnic Institute of Brooklyn.

P. Hunter Peckham is professor of biomedical engineering and orthopedics at Case Western Reserve University. He also serves as director for the Functional Electrical Stimulation Center at the Louis Stokes Veterans Affairs Medical Center and director of orthopedic research for the Rehabilitation Engineering Center at MetroHealth Medical Center. He is a member of the National Academy of Engineering and serves on the Committee on Spinal Cord Injury: Strategies in a Search for a Cure. He is an expert in the areas of neural prostheses and the use of electrical stimulation of nerves to restore function in cases of central nervous system paralysis and holds multiple patents related to his work. Dr. Peckham is the recipient of numerous honors and awards for his innovative research, including the Paul B. Magnuson Award and the U.S. Food and Drug Administration Commissioner's Special Citation. In 2000, he was elected Engineer of the Year by Design News. In 1996-1997, he chaired the National Institutes of Health National Advisory Board to the National Center for Medical Rehabilitation Research. He received his Ph.D. from Case Western Reserve University.

Jon Pynoos is the UPS Foundation professor of gerontology, policy and planning at the Andrus Gerontology Center of the University of Southern California (USC) where he teaches in the Davis School of Gerontology. He is also director of the National Resource Center on Supportive Housing and Home Modification and codirector of the Fall Prevention Center of Excellence. He has spent his career researching, writing, and advising the government and nonprofit sectors concerning how to improve housing and long-term care for the elderly. He has conducted a large number of applied research projects based on surveys and case studies of housing and aging in place. He is the coauthor of *Linking Housing and Services for Older Adults: Obstacles, Options, and Opportunities*; *Housing the Aged: Design Directives and Policy Considerations*; and *Housing Frail Elders: International Policies, Perspectives and Prospects*. He was a delegate to the last three White House Conferences on Aging, serves on the public policy committee of the American Society on Aging, and was vice president of the Gerontological Society of America. He is a founding member of the National Home Modification Action Coalition. Before moving to USC in 1979, he was director of an area agency on aging/home care corporation in Massachusetts that provided a range of services to keep older persons out of institutional settings and in their own homes and communities. He has won numerous awards for his work including Guggenheim and Fulbright Fellowships. He has undergraduate, master's, and Ph.D. degrees from Harvard University.

Robert M. Schumacher is managing director and co-owner of User Centric, Inc., one of the world's largest user research companies. He is a member of the adjunct faculty at Northwestern University's Feinberg School of Medicine, where he is also associated with the Program on Usability Enhancement in Health Information Technology. He has been actively involved designing and evaluating usability criteria for electronic health record systems and is currently engaged in a grant with the National Institute of Standards and Technology (NIST) on the development of a usability evaluation program; he is active in the Healthcare Information and Management Systems Society's Usability Taskforce as well as other professional societies. He has authored several user interface standards and guidelines documents, including the Ameritech Graphical User Interface Standards and Design Guidelines, which are still influential in both their form and content. Most recently, he coauthored the NIST *Guide to the Processes Approach for Improving the Usability of Electronic Health Records*. He has a Ph.D. in cognitive and experimental psychology from the University of Illinois at Urbana-Champaign.

Judith Tabolt Matthews is the associate director of the Gerontology Program at the University Center for Social and Urban Research and faculty in the School of Nursing at the University of Pittsburgh. Her career in community health nursing practice, education, and research has particularly focused on application and evaluation of existing and emerging technologies that may enhance independent living and self-management of chronic disorders among older adults and persons with disabilities. Her recent research has included usability and field testing of prototype robotic devices capable of offering navigational guidance to persons with wayfinding difficulty or real-time instruction and feedback during performance of therapeutic exercise at home. She serves on the faculty of the Quality of Life Technology Engineering Research Center, a collaboration involving Carnegie Mellon University and the University of Pittsburgh, with projects focused on exploring potential users' concerns and preferences regarding intelligent systems capable of providing context-aware and responsive physical and cognitive support for routine activities. Her teaching responsibilities have included courses in community health nursing, chronic disorders, applied statistics, and ethics, as well as a project-based, robotic applications course taught with faculty from the Robotics Institute at Carnegie Mellon University. She has a B.S. in nursing from the Pennsylvania State University, an M.S. in community health nursing, with an emphasis in gerontology, from Boston University, and both a Ph.D. in nursing and an M.P.H. in epidemiology from the University of Pittsburgh.

Susan Van Hemel was a senior program officer in the Division of Behavioral and Social Sciences at the National Research Council (NRC) for more than 10 years before retiring in May 2010. She managed the first phase of this study on the role of human factors in home health care, which culminated in the workshop summary report. Her previous projects at the NRC include studies of early childhood assessment, staffing standards for aviation safety inspectors at the Federal Aviation Administration, organizational modeling research for the U.S. Air Force, and Social Security disability determination for individuals with visual and hearing impairments and workshops on technology for adaptive aging and on decision making in older adults. Before coming to the NRC, she managed and performed work on commercial driver fatigue and commercial driver license vision requirements and numerous other studies on topics related to human performance and training. She is a member of the Human Factors and Ergonomics Society and its technical groups on health care and aging. She has a Ph.D. in experimental psychology from the Johns Hopkins University.

Mary Weick Brady is a senior advisor in the Office of Surveillance and Biometrics/Center for Devices and Radiological Health in the U.S. Food and Drug Administration (FDA). Ms. Brady began her career at the Mayo Clinic working as a hematology nurse. She then moved to Ecuador, where she worked as a public health nurse in the Peace Corps for 2½ years. She came to the Washington DC area to work as a clinical supervisor in a long-term care and hospice facility while pursuing her master's degree. Ms. Brady worked part-time for the Visiting Nurse Association of Northern Virginia as a home care nurse for 7 years while she was working full time for the FDA as a registered nurse monitoring and analyzing adverse events associated with medical devices. She went on to supervise the team that analyzed the adverse events and eventually became a deputy division director in the division that interpreted the medical device reporting regulation and handled the contract for data entry of these reports. She currently serves as a U.S. representative to the International Standards Organization collateral draft standard on home medical equipment and is an FDA representative on the Global Harmonization Task Force that is working to harmonize regulatory bodies throughout the world. She began the Center for Devices and Radiological Health's Home Care Committee in 2001 to monitor the safe migration of medical devices going into the home and continues to chair this group. The committee is pursuing a national labeling repository for all medical devices, home use labeling guidance, educational materials, and research studies in the area of home health. Ms. Brady graduated with a bachelor's degree in nursing from Augustana College in Sioux Falls, South Dakota, in 1981. She earned her master's degree in nursing administration and a graduate certificate in international health in 1989 from George Mason University in Fairfax, Virginia.

Jennifer L. Wolff is an associate professor in the Department of Health Policy and Management at the Johns Hopkins University Bloomberg School of Public Health with a joint appointment in the Johns Hopkins School of Medicine, Division of Geriatric Medicine and Gerontology. Trained in gerontology and health services research, Dr. Wolff studies chronic and long-term care delivery of services to frail and multimorbid older adults. Her current research seeks to describe and understand factors that precipitate the presence of older adults' family members in health care delivery processes and the implications for quality of health care and patient outcomes, as a means to identifying and intervening on provider practice and health system infrastructure to better prepare patients' families for the roles that they assume. Dr. Wolff has received a career development award from the National Institute of Mental Health. She holds a Ph.D. in health services research and an M.H.S. in health finance and management from the Johns Hopkins University Bloomberg School of Public Health and a B.A. in economics from Bucknell University.